Nepad

Nepad

Toward Africa's Development or Another False Start?

Ian Taylor

LYNNE
RIENNER
PUBLISHERS

BOULDER
LONDON

Published in the United States of America in 2005 by
Lynne Rienner Publishers, Inc.
1800 30th Street, Boulder, Colorado 80301
www.rienner.com

and in the United Kingdom by
Lynne Rienner Publishers, Inc.
3 Henrietta Street, Covent Garden, London WC2E 8LU

Library of Congress Cataloging-in-Publication Data
Taylor, Ian, 1969–
   Nepad : toward Africa's development or another false start? /
Ian Taylor.
      p.   cm.
   Includes bibliographical references and index.
   ISBN 1-58826-351-7 (hardcover : alk. paper)
   1. New Partnership for Africa's Development.   2. Africa—Economic
policy.   3. Africa—Foreign economic relations.   I. Title.
   HC800.T39 2005
   338.96—dc22

                                                    2005005660

British Cataloguing in Publication Data
A Cataloguing in Publication record for this book
is available from the British Library.

Printed and bound in the United States of America

The paper used in this publication meets the requirements
of the American National Standard for Permanence of
Paper for Printed Library Materials Z39.48-1992.

   5   4   3   2   1

To my forefather,
Alexander McKenzie Sutherland (1846–1904),
who left Scotland and settled in Africa in 1877

And to my daughter,
Blythe Isobel Sutherland Taylor,
born in Botswana in 2004

Contents

Acknowledgments

This book was conceived when I attended a conference in Accra, Ghana, in April 2002, entitled "Africa and the Development Challenges of the New Millennium" and organized by the Council for the Development of Social Science Research in Africa (CODESRIA). My experience at the conference prompted me to conduct research on Nepad and write the book. I would like to thank Adebayo Olukoshi for inviting me to the conference and for being supportive of my work.

I have accumulated a number of debts during the course of this project. For helping me to clarify some of my ideas, I wish first to thank Roger Tangri, my colleague at the University of Botswana (UB), who read the chapters as they were written and provided extensive comments. Paul Williams of the University of Birmingham also read a number of the chapters and provided his usual trenchant and insightful observations. Jane Parpart of Dalhousie University and Gladys Mokhawa (UB) were particularly helpful in clarifying my thoughts for Chapter 6. I would also like to acknowledge the useful discussions I have had with Daniel Bach, Morten Bøås, Patrick Bond, Christopher Clapham, Scarlett Cornelissen, Kenneth Good, John Makumbe, Pamela Mbabazi, Henning Melber, Godisang Mookodi, Xenia Ngwenya, Oleosi Ntshebe, Francis Nyamnjoh, Mzukisi Qobo, David Sebudubudu, Timothy Shaw, Fredrik Söderbaum, and Janis van der Westhuizen. All have influenced and challenged me in different ways. I would also like to thank the anonymous reviewers of the manuscript, who made valuable comments and suggestions.

Many of the ideas in this book were first tested with my students, initially at the University of Stellenbosch and later at the University of Botswana, Dalhousie University, and the University of St. Andrews. I thank them for their feedback and insights. The civil servants I spoke with in Botswana, Mauritius, and South Africa, who, with frankness and candor, provided me with much useful information, also deserve my gratitude. Though I cannot name them, they know who they are.

I am indebted to Lynne Rienner, who phoned me in Gaborone one night to encourage me to write this book. Such enthusiasm really spurred me on. Lisa Tulchin at Lynne Rienner Publishers has also been a great help.

Finally I would like to express thanks to my wife, Joanne, who has helped me throughout this study and has always been supportive. Her encouragement and love are always appreciated.

Nepad

1

Putting Nepad in Its Place

The New Partnership for Africa's Development, or Nepad, the latest African recovery plan, has been enthusiastically pushed by a select number of countries in Africa, as well as by the G8, as a means to stimulate what has been termed the "African Renaissance" (see www.uneca.org/nepad/nepad.pdf). Nepad was launched in Abuja, Nigeria, in October 2001, when its strategic framework document was finalized and an organizational management structure to advance the recovery program was established. Its strategic framework arose from the mandate granted to five African heads of state (Algeria, Egypt, Nigeria, Senegal, South Africa) by the then Organization of African Unity (OAU) to work out a development program to spearhead Africa's renewal.

Nepad has succeeded in placing the question of Africa's development onto the international table and has managed to obtain a fairly high profile and awareness, particularly in Western capitals. The proponents of Nepad claim that it is a political and economic program aimed at promoting democracy, stability, good governance, human rights, and economic development on the continent. So what does this really mean, and what are Nepad's chances of success? Evaluating this question is the fundamental aim of this book.

To accomplish this goal, I critically analyze Nepad in light of its expressed commitments, omissions, history, and performance. In doing so, on one level I seek simply to contrast rhetoric with reality. Thus, I reject the type of analysis that asserts that Nepad represents "a new generation of enlightened African leaders [who have] now decided to stake Africa's claim to the twentieth century" (Hope, 2002: 387). Any coherent study of Nepad cannot take at face value the pronouncements made on its behalf—rather, we need to seriously examine and unpack such statements if we are to arrive at a meaningful evaluation. Furthermore, in scrutinizing the Nepad strategic framework document, we need to investigate the overall philosophy behind it and the messages that emanate from its promoters, as well as their actions. Where does Nepad see Africa with regard to economic policy? What routes can/should the continent take, according to its framework document, if Africa is to escape its developmental impasse? And are its authors serious in their commitments to such a project? These are the questions that are explored in this book. But before we can begin to try and answer them, we need to think over the nature of the postcolonial African state and the characteristics of governance on the continent. This is necessary in light of the essentially elitist nature of Nepad and the fact that the recovery plan is grounded in the deeds and conduct of existing African leaders and on the premise that "good governance" is a prerequisite for Africa's renewal and something that, under Nepad, continental leaders will now introduce and support. Understanding the broader modalities of rule in Africa is a requirement for analyzing the potential of Nepad to deliver progressive development on the continent. Without this context, analysis of Nepad cannot move beyond commenting on speeches and documents by Africa's leaders, rather than a concrete exploration of what Nepad is really about.

The Postcolonial State in Africa

In talking about something as broad as "the African state," generalizations are necessary, and the applicability of such an overview to each individual African country is contingent. Having said that, it cannot be denied that many postcolonial African countries, bounded by formal frontiers and with an international presence at various international institutions such as the United Nations, function quite differently from conventional understandings of what a formal Western state is and should do. This is, of course, not surprising, and in order for Africanists to understand the politics of the state on the continent, the concept of neopatrimonialism has largely become the standard tool of analysis (LeVine, 1980; Jackson and Rosberg, 1982; Medard, 1982; Callaghy, 1984 and 1987; Sandbrook, 1985; Crook, 1989; Bayart, 1993; Bratton and Van de Walle, 1994 and 1997; Chabal, 1994; Tangri, 1999; Chabal and Daloz, 1999). Nevertheless, very few studies of Nepad have recognized this feature of politics on the continent (cf. Chabal, 2002), resulting in a failure to situate Nepad in its proper context, as well as a naiveté in evaluating its potential to bring about change in Africa.

In a traditional Weberian patrimonial system, all ruling relationships are personal relationships and the difference between the private and public sphere is nonexistent (Weber, 1974). Under a neopatrimonial system the separation of the public from the private is recognized (even if in practice only on paper) and is certainly publicly displayed through outward manifestations of the rational-bureaucratic state—a flag, borders, a government and bureaucracy, and so on. However, in practical terms the private and public spheres are habitually not detached and the outward manifestations of statehood are often facades hiding the real workings of the system. In many African countries, particularly those marked by enclave economies (see below), the official state bureaucracies inherited from the colonial period, however weak and ineffective, have become dysfunctional and severely constrained in their official, stated, duties. Postcolonial African leaders have rather relied on effected control and patronage through capturing power over the economy, rather than through the state in the form of a functioning administration. In a good number of states postindependence, this swiftly degenerated into outright personal dictatorships (Decalo, 1989). Although clientelism and patronage are *not* unique to Africa (see Lemarchand and Eisenstadt, 1980; Clapham, 1982; Fatton, 2002), the type of intensive neopatrimonialism, if not "pathological patrimonialism" (Ergas, 1987a) that we can observe across large swathes of the continent is indeed noteworthy.

In the postcolonial period, where inherited bureaucracies are still in existence, because access to resources depends upon being inside the state apparatus, patrons reward supporters with sinecures in the government and nationalized industries. The inherited bureaucracies have "sooner or later [been] transformed into far larger patrimonial-type administrations in which staff [are] less agents of state policy (civil servants) than proprietors, distributors and even major consumers of the authority and resources of the government" (Jackson and Rosberg, 1994: 300). Handing out bureaucratic posts has become an important way in which leaders can secure support. For instance, in Zambia the number of super-scale posts in the civil service (top echelon positions and de facto gatekeepers to state resources) rose from 184 in 1967, to 865 in 1971, to 1,116 in 1974 (i.e., a 600 percent increase in twelve years) (Turok, 1979: 74). In other words, the outward manifestation of the state—the institutions, bureaucracies, and so forth—enjoyed an exponential increase immediately after independence, largely to service patron-client impulses. Structural adjustment programs (SAPs) have not radically altered this scenario.

Clientelism is central to neopatrimonialism, with widespread networks of clients receiving services and resources in return for support. This is well understood and even expected in many African countries; the party contesting a Nigerian election under the rubric "I Chop, You Chop Party" is a manifestation of this well-known game and reflects the mutual benefits that neopatrimonialism confers to both patron (the Big Man) and client. Indeed, the exercise of personalized exchange, clientelism, and corruption is internalized and constitutes "essential operating codes for politics" in Africa (Bratton and van de Walle, 1997: 63). This is "accepted as normal behaviour, condemned only in so far as it benefits someone else rather than one-self" (Clapham, 1985: 49).

Resources extracted from the state or the economy in this clientelism are deployed as the means to maintain support and legitimacy, with the concomitant effect that the control of the state is equivalent to the control of resources, which in turn is crucial for retaining one's power. Control of the state serves the twin purposes of lubricating patronage networks *and* satisfies the selfish desire of elites to enrich themselves, in many cases in a quite spectacular fashion. That is what lies at the heart of the profound reluctance by African presidents to hand over power voluntarily and why many African regimes end messily, often in coups (Decalo, 1990). In most cases the democratic option is either absent or is not respected by the loser—the stakes simply are too high as once one is out of the loop vis-à-vis access to state resources, the continuation of one's status as a Big Man and the ability to enrich oneself becomes virtually impossible. Politics in Africa thus tends to be a zero-sum game. At the beginning of the twenty-first century, 39 percent of Africa's rulers have been in power for over ten years, and 28 percent have been presidents for fifteen years or more. A resilient 19 percent have sat on the throne of power for twenty years or more and two have been heads of state for over thirty years—one of whom sits on Nepad's Heads of State Implementation Committee (HSIC).

Neopatrimonialism has survived the waves of democratization that swept through the continent as the Cold War ended (Bratton and Van de Walle, 1997), with very few exceptions (Santiso and Loada, 2003). As Omolo (2002: 219–220) has noted regarding the democratic transition in Kenya:

> In Kenya "big man" politics has outlasted the change from the one party to the multi-party system. Aside from the implementation of laws allow-ing for multiparty politics, there has not occurred a fundamental structural change in the country's politics. Moreover, the enduring political values of a single party order are reinforced by a preponderance of political play-ers from the *ancien regime*. In the typical fashion of patrimonialism, poli-tics remains a cottage industry with significant economic gains for the favoured: it offers exclusive access to public sector jobs seen as sinecures for prebends and economic rents for the privileged elite. The lucky few can become incredibly rich in a short span of time. Inevitably though, the process has led to a pervasive atrophy of state institutions and an increase in poverty for the average citizen.

National development and a broad-based productive economy are far less a concern (in fact, might stimulate opposition) to elites within such systems than the continuation of the gainful utilization of resources for the individ-ual advantage of the ruler and his clientelistic networks. At the same time, the bureaucracy has developed its own set of interests (personal survival) and logic as prebendary organizations that further distort their role away from the ideal-type rational-bureaucratic model inherent in the Western representation of developmental agencies and more toward a loose set of skeleton institutions lacking in most capacities other than to act as predators upon the population or gatekeepers to resources. Such an environment has had the effect of creating a whole swathe of politically connected persons who are dependent upon largesse from state elites and who act as a support constituency, whilst mediating between those at the top and the masses below. In such circumstances, the state has become ever more predatory—particularly in states with extractive economies.

The Extractive State and Enclave Production

Leonard and Straus (2003) provide a convincing account as to why neopatrimonial states are particularly destructive and why the international system sustains this behavior. Such an analysis has important ramifications for Nepad and needs to be discussed. Essentially, according to the aforementioned authors, colonialism inserted Africa into the world economy, in the main, as enclave economies dependent upon one or two commodities and minerals. An enclave economy is an economy that exports extractive products that are concentrated in relatively small geographic areas. The mines of Shaba province in the Democratic Republic of Congo, the rubber plantations of Liberia, and the copper mines of Zambia being good examples. What this means is that revenue generation is physically confined to small locales, with the prime markets for the products being external (international). This makes "the general economic health of areas outside the enclave quite secondary, if not irrelevant. In enclave economies, then, elites gain little from any deep, growing, economic prosperity of the masses of the population" (Leonard and Straus, 2003: 13).

Individuals who have gained access to rents from such enclaves may benefit handsomely, but the system fundamentally fails to promote economic growth and development and in actual fact, across the continent, has rapidly sabotaged the high aspirations of independence (Yates, 1996). As Clapham has asserted, "the use of power over other people for the purpose essentially of private gain is corrupt, not merely because it fails to correspond to formal rules of essentially Western origin, or to meet the demands of 'good governance' laid down by external aid donors, but because of its impact on the lives of the people most harshly affected by it" (Clapham, 1996a: 251–252).

The idea that resources should rather be channeled toward the nebulous concept of "national development," as demanded by Nepad, is generally not on the agenda of many elites in Africa as wealth generation and survival does not depend on productive development, but is dependent upon control over select areas of the country (i.e., where the mines and plantations are) or by the manipulation of the market for personal gain. Unfortunately for Africa, elite survival (i.e., access to rents to distribute to patronage networks and thus retain key support) can be based on the capture of relatively limited geographic areas. That is all (to varying degrees) that is required to lubricate the machinery of patronage. In other words, investment in infrastructure and the advancement of policies that bring in revenue for the elites but that also benefit broad swathes of the population (general agricultural policies that encompass large sections of the community) is not required: "enclave economies do not need functioning states or infrastructure to generate revenues for elites" (Leonard and Straus, 2003: 16).

States that have managed to relatively avoid such depredations are those where the elites do not simply rely on enclave production for their revenues. Senegal, with its embedded export crop production that encompasses large segments of the population is one example (though caution should be sounded on this—see Boone, 1992). Botswana, with an elite rooted in cattle ownership and beef exports (which needs infrastructure and investment), is another, albeit one that also possesses features of an enclave economy (Samatar, 1999; Taylor, 2004). Neither country is free of patronage politics, but neither are simply based on efforts to create and sustain rent-seeking opportunities for the elites. South Africa, with its diversified and relatively mature capitalist economy, is another example. But, these examples aside, broadly speaking, the net effect at the political level across Africa of the nature of personal rule has been to erode any sense of broad public accountability (Hyden, 2000). All of this is sustained and distorted by the nature of the enclave economies that dominate Africa and their relationships with the global economy. This then is the reality of contemporary Africa, helping to produce the "shattered illusion of the integral state" (Young, 1994). The repercussions of this scenario, as well as the implications of neopatrimonialism, for Nepad will be explored throughout the book. Indeed, a central aim of this volume is to investigate whether or not political and economic conditions on the continent are conducive to implementing and advancing a program such as Nepad, based as it is on liberal governance principles and certain assumptions about the functioning of governments and economies.

Nepad as a Program of Renewal

If this is the political and economic context within which Nepad must function, what are its broad prescriptions? According to official Nepad sources (the website, www.nepad.org/en.html, as well as numerous other Nepad-related documents), the project is based on the following principles:

- good governance as a basic requirement for peace, security, and sustainable political and socioeconomic development
- African ownership and leadership, as well as broad and deep participation by all sectors of society
- anchoring the development of Africa on its resources and the resourcefulness of its people
- partnership between and among African peoples
- acceleration of regional and continental integration
- building the competitiveness of African countries and the continent
- forging a new international partnership that changes the unequal relationship between Africa and the developed world
- ensuring that all partnerships with Nepad are linked to the Millennium Development Goals and other agreed development goals and targets

Following this, Nepad is divided into seven main projects. Each arm of Nepad has an assortment of constituent parts and objectives, which must be integrated. The seven initiatives are:

1. *Peace, security, democracy, and political governance.* This initiative is made up of two sections. The peace and security section refers to peacekeeping, reconciliation/peacemaking, and early warning systems. The democracy and good governance section relates to the critical area of governance standards and the idea that Africa should and will police itself. It is this section, with its attendant African Peer Review Mechanism (APRM) that has excited a great deal of outside attention. The goal of the APRM, as promoted, is getting African leaders to subject their governments to ongoing examination and review by other Africans in areas such as democracy and political governance, and economic and corporate management.

2. *Economic and corporate governance.* This initiative seeks to bring about positive growth (in the sense advanced by orthodox neoliberalism) and stable fiscal and macroeconomic management. This implies the regulatory prescriptions related to investor-friendly environments—the rule of law and efficient banking and insurance systems.

3. *Bridging the infrastructure gap.* This initiative includes general issues pertaining to infrastructure on the continent—transport routes, ports, water, electricity, sanitation, health and education facilities, and so on. Information and communications technology (ICT) is considered part of this initiative as a means to "catch up" with the rest of the world.

4. *Human resources development.* This section is a very general holis-

tic section that includes (to varying degrees) all manner of development-related issues and agendas such as gender, health, education, agriculture, poverty reduction, and the like. As noted in Chapter 6, HIV/AIDS only receives cursory reference, as does gender. Indeed, HIV/AIDS is included as part of a very general endeavor to combat other diseases such as tuberculosis and malaria.

5. *Capital flows.* This section covers investment promotion, debt reduction, enlarged aid flows and general reform of the aid industry.

6. *Market access.* This initiative's focal point on trade issues as part of the development process also asserts the need to diversify production, particularly with regard to agriculture, while promoting an increase in manufacturing.

7. *Environment.* This section makes general comments regarding environmental issues. However, as Herbert (2003: 98) argues, "there is little in the text to make clear how such 'Nepad' environmental initiatives would be distinct from the environmental initiatives already going in Africa or analysis of why these initiatives are broadly ineffective" (Herbert, 2003).

Having mentioned the above seven "priorities," it should be pointed out that "some confusion has been added subsequently, with Nepad documents defining the plan as consisting of *four* initiatives—Peace, Security, Democracy and Political Governance; Economic and Corporate Governance; Capital Flows; Market Access—and six 'Sectoral Priorities': Bridging the Infrastructure Gap, Human Resources Development, Agriculture, Environment, Culture, and Science and Technology Platforms" (Nepad, 2001a). The problem is that these priorities are not defined, nor have they been prioritized. It appears that the authors assume that all six sectoral areas will advance at the same time and with sufficient funding to allow the six to progressively develop alongside one another.

Furthermore, the latest official documents now assert that there are *three* Nepad priorities: "establishing the conditions for sustainable development," "policy reforms and increased investment," and "mobilizing resources" (www.nepad.org/en.html). That the priorities and sectoral initiatives have changed over time not only means that its advocates can (perhaps justifiably) argue that it is a work in progress, but on the negative side, suggests that the original launching of the recovery plan was a somewhat rushed affair in order to exploit what was perceived as a strategic opening for its reception. This theme will be expanded upon, but at this point it should be noted that despite the heavy amount of promotion Nepad has enjoyed and the touting of the framework document at almost all meeting points between Africa and its "partners," the actual renaissance program seems to be in a perpetual state of evolution—perhaps a good thing but something that makes pinning down the documents quite complex. As an unnamed foreign diplomat in Pretoria noted, "Nepad is like, I don't know what you call it in English . . . it's like foam" (quoted in *Business Day,* Johannesburg, December 6, 2002).

It is true, however, that Nepad's founding documents seem quite clear on their immediate desired outcomes. According to its own sources, Nepad aims to ensure the following:

- that Africa becomes more effective in conflict prevention and the establishment of enduring peace on the continent
- that Africa adopts and implements principles of democracy and good political economic and corporate governance, and the protection of human rights becomes further entrenched in every African country
- that Africa develops and implements effective poverty eradication programs and accelerates the pace of achieving set African development goals, particularly human development
- that Africa achieves increased levels of domestic savings, as well as investments, both domestic and foreign
- that increased levels of overseas development assistance (ODA) to the continent are achieved and its effective utilization maximized
- that Africa achieves desired capacity for policy development, coordination, and negotiation in the international arena, to ensure its beneficial engagement in the global economy, especially on trade and market access issues
- that regional integration is further accelerated and higher levels of sustainable economic growth in Africa are achieved
- that genuine partnerships are established between Africa and the developed countries based on mutual respect and accountability (www.nepad.org/en.html)

Overall, through examining the various priorities and initiatives, it appears that Nepad in general fits in with the growing "post-Washington consensus" that what is required for African regeneration is a competent—if not developmental—state that has the ability and political will to confront graft and in doing so, set free the potential human resources and capabilities of Africa. At the same time, Nepad openly links development, security, governance, and democracy together. In this, the framework document is admirable and can be said to indisputably echo the hopes and ambitions of most Africans. In this sense (and this has been noted by numerous observers) Nepad *does* reflect a nascent pan-Africanism that has been part of Africa's identity and hopes for decades. Having said that, it would be an exaggeration to claim, as the Executive Secretary of the United Nations Economic Commission for Africa (UNECA) does, that Nepad is "the most important advance in development thinking for Africa in the past forty years" (Amoako, 2003: 1).

The idea of partnership with the developed world is central to Nepad. Indeed, a renegotiated relationship with the global community—both through fairer trade and through what is seen as a "partnership" with the West—is repeatedly cast as being necessary, particularly if the continent is to access the resources that Nepad argues is needed to kick start and then sustain the continent's recovery. One of the most eye-catching aspects of Nepad is its stated position that if Africa is to begin to emerge from poverty, the continent requires a GDP growth rate of 7 percent per annum and that, given Africa's present low saving and investment ratio, the continent would need $64 billion of resource inflows *every* year, about 13 percent of Africa's gross national income per year. As Paragraph 147 of the Nepad framework document asserts (emphasis added):

> Africa needs to fill an annual resource gap of 12 per cent of its GDP, or $64 billion. This will require increased domestic savings, as well as improvements in the public revenue collection systems. However, *the bulk of the needed resources will have to be obtained from outside the continent.*

As a summary of what Nepad is, it can be said that it amounts to basically a deal: African leaders will hold each other accountable and will practice good governance and, in return, the West will commit itself to aiding Africa's renaissance and development. In short, it is a reaction to and stems from an environment in which the West has seemingly disengaged from the continent now that the bi-polar world has ended and from a globalizing world that appears to be leaving Africa behind. This all takes place within the broader context where it appears that "not only has the international leverage of African leaders been drastically diminished in the globalizing post–Cold War world, they now sail in the largely uncharted waters of eroding norms of sovereignty, dwindling Western concern with Africa's poverty, a vacuum of ideological visions and the growing power of external non-state actors such as multinational corporations, nongovernmental organizations, crime syndicates and CNN" (Gerhart, 2001: 195).

Though we should be most cautious in advancing the idea that Africa is marginalized from the rest of the world (Taylor and Williams, 2004), Nepad operates from the essential premise that the industrialized nations, many of them former colonialists, have dodged their historical responsibility towards Africa. Problematically, this grants outsiders the role of "rescuing" the continent from its perceived malaise, with internal actors (very much restricted to local elites) playing a supporting role at best. Noting this, critics have cast Nepad as an elaborate attempt to guarantee the continuation of resources to Africa in order to maintain the personal rulerships on the continent, rather than any genuine project to reconfigure Africa's place in the world (Chabal, 2002: 462).

At the same time, Nepad has cast itself in the role of reversing the largely negative perceptions of the continent that currently prevail and that dominate, to varying degrees, the media in the West. As Thabo Mbeki has noted, "One of the most important challenges is to address the negative perceptions amongst investors who see Africa as a high-risk area . . . In many instances, the investors get a wrong message from those who do not want Africa to succeed" (Mbeki, 2002a: 153). That is why a Nepad report claimed that one of the priorities "in the short to medium term" was to "showcase projects and investment opportunities in Africa," implying that the rest of the world is unaware of—or erroneously informed of—the situation in the continent (Nepad Secretariat, 2003b: 14). While promoting Africa is an admirable enterprise, it does however spring from a questionable understanding of Africa's image in the rest of the world:

> At best the image-problem theory asserts that Africa is no worse than anywhere else, which is essentially an admission that it is not yet a compelling business destination and needs investment decisions to be made on the basis of charity rather than financial advantage. Further, this theory shows a [distorted] way of thinking, which assumes that conspiratorial states really can control the decisions taken by private industry and that industry makes decisions based on racial agendas rather than profit. Clearly some firms are largely nationalist, but these are not the class of firms that partake in global investment. [The idea] that such multinationals are part of a cabal is to defy common sense and the reality of trillions of dollars of multinational investment around the globe (Herbert, 2003: 132).

Indeed, the impression that there is some sort of cabal or group of conspirators "who do not want Africa to succeed" is based on particular assumptions vis-à-vis global politics. As Chapter 5 demonstrates, this sort of thinking has informed Mbeki's thinking on the Zimbabwe issue and, as I will suggest, has undermined an important aspect of Nepad's credibility—its stance on democracy and good governance.

Implementation of the Partnership

According to its promoters, "The highest authority of the Nepad implementation process is the Heads of State and Government Summit of the African Union, formerly known as the OAU" (www.nepad.org/en.html). This is both a good and a bad thing. It is good because Nepad gains pan-African legitimacy from the continent's highest intergovernmental body. Without such a support, the status and direction of Nepad would be problematic. Yet, in gaining such legitimacy, Nepad opens itself up to potentially crippling handicaps, most notably the possibility of having to pander to the politics of the lowest common denominator in trying to ensure pan-African solidarity and unity. Indeed, from the start and despite denials to the contrary, Nepad's promoters have been eager to keep the project out of the grip of the African Union (AU). In the main this is because the project's initiators were "very keen that it should not become subject to the slow and cumbersome procedures of [AU] decision-making. They were wary of the dangers of it being derailed by the interference of small, ill-governed countries wanting to ensure that their voices were heard and their rulers paid off" (De Waal, 2002: 467). This contrasts somewhat with the statement in Nepad's Paragraph 45 that "democracy is spreading, backed by the African Union, which has shown a new resolve to deal with conflicts and censure deviation from the norm."

Be that as it may, the official implementation structure of Nepad is contained in the Heads of State Implementation Committee. This committee is made up of three states per region of the AU, as mandated by the OAU Summit in Lusaka in July 2001. The HSIC is supposed to meet every four months and is made up of 15 countries: Central Africa's Cameroon, Gabon, and São Tomé and Principe; Eastern Africa's Ethiopia, Mauritius, and Rwanda; Northern Africa's Algeria, Egypt, and Tunisia; Southern Africa's Botswana, Mozambique, and South Africa; and Western Africa's Mali, Nigeria, and Senegal. According to Cilliers, the main functions of the HSIC are to identify strategic issues that need to be researched, planned, and managed at the continental level; set up mechanisms for reviewing progress in the achievement of mutually agreed targets and compliance with agreed standards; review progress in the implementation of past decisions; and taking appropriate steps to address problems and delays (2002: 2).

The HSIC must report to the AU Summit on an annual basis, but in the interim directs a Steering Committee that meets once a month and is made up of the five founding states of Nepad (Algeria, Egypt, Nigeria, Senegal, and South Africa). To drive the achievement of its goals, Nepad has set up five work teams made up of these five key states. These are in charge of the following: "Peace and Security," headed by South Africa, with the AU; "Economic and Corporate Governance," headed by the UNECA; "Infrastructure," led by Senegal in partnership with the African Development Bank (ADB); "Agriculture and Market Access," under the remit of the AU; and "Financial and Banking Standards," headed by the ADB in partnership with Nigeria. A Secretariat is based in Pretoria under the head of Wiseman Nkuhlu (a South African). This secretariat was established to oversee projects and program development as well as supervise the construction of business plans for the priority areas. It should be noted that the secretariat is staffed by only 47 persons, and that this was made possible only because a Nepad business group in South Africa seconded corporate staff to it.

The above program and its institutional makeup appears quite reasonable, its critical understaffing aside. Yet, analysis of Nepad cannot leave its promises alone nor take at face value these commitments—however level-headed they might appear. Among other salient questions regarding the plan, which will be developed in this book, one has to question not only the commitment of many of the heads of state driving the HSIC to advance Africa's recovery, but also the structural limitations placed upon such leaders. These two themes stake out the mission of this book.

In essence, this book is an attempt to construct an interpretation of Nepad's potentiality, based on critically examining aspects of the plan beyond the rhetoric and pronouncements. In short, it looks at Africa and Nepad within their political, economic, and global contexts. Chapter 2 examines the recovery plans advanced over the past decades, interrogating their contents and situating them within their historical framework. In doing so, the past genesis of Nepad is traced and explained. Chapter 3 examines the fate of Nepad's African Peer Review Mechanism, which has been advanced as the central selling point of the whole program, certainly to the G8. Chapter 3 also examines the pedigrees and track records of some of Nepad's promoters, asking a central question as to whether or not their expressed support for the program's strictures on good governance and democracy can be taken seriously. Chapter 4 then provides an overview of Nepad's economic prescriptions, looking at how the program approaches the question of Africa's place in the global economy and whether its proposals are meaningful given the African context. Chapter 5 proceeds to hold Nepad accountable for its rhetoric by examining responses by key Nepad elites to the situation in Zimbabwe. As a theme of the book is to contrast rhetoric with action, the chapter critically examines what difference, if any, Nepad has made to the state of affairs in the southern African state and, perhaps more importantly, whether or not membership in Nepad has influenced the behavior of significant Nepad promoters such as Mbeki and Obasanjo. Chapter 6 then examines how and in what ways gender is addressed within the program and the way in which HIV/AIDS is treated by the recovery program. It is contended that these aspects of Africa's current malaise, particularly gender oppression and the ongoing advance of the AIDS pandemic, are missing dimensions within the plan. Finally, the book ends with an overview of Nepad, given the evidence provided in the body of the volume. An alternative partnership with Africa is suggested, one less open to the vagaries of elite politics and one more centered on the ordinary African citizen. Given that Africa's elites are granted a—if not *the*—pivotal role in the continent's regeneration, I believe that making the case for this alternative stance is the only way the continent will move forward.

2

From the Lagos Plan
to the New Partnership

N epad has not, obviously, sprung from a vacuum, and indeed there are a host of predecessors to the partnership that allows observers to place this latest African renewal program within its broader historical and intellectual context. Indeed, it is deemed vital for any coherent understanding of Nepad's prescriptions that its strategic framework document is placed within its proper historical circumstances, both vis-à-vis previous African recovery projects and the broader global political economy. That is the purpose underpinning this chapter. Any evaluation of this wider milieu must recognize that since the early 1980s a philosophical approach to economics and development, one that is broadly in alignment with the orthodox strictures of liberalization, privatization, and the "free market," has progressively become dominant and that this has gradually but profoundly influenced pan-African strategies for development, ending in Nepad. In short, the values and norms associated with liberal prescriptions have become the starting point from which African elite dialogue with their Western counterparts bases its broad foundations, even if such a foundation is contested by many and reluctantly engaged in (or not) by most (Van de Walle, 2001). That understandings of Africa's developmental options based on liberalization is grafted onto highly dysfunctional political and economic systems is rarely commented upon by the promoters of such "solutions."

At the same time, alternative visions for Africa have largely lost credence, particularly outside of Africa but also from within. This, after all, is implicit in Nepad. Yet though Nepad has abandoned the stance popular in the 1970s of seeking to blame all of Africa's predicament on the colonial legacy, the baby has been thrown out with the bathwater—there is now little appreciation of the manner by which the continent has been inserted into the global economy and, in particular, how and why this has stimulated and perpetuated neopatrimonial systems of governance (see Chapter 4).

This chapter aims to demonstrate that the discourse that runs through the Nepad framework document, which generally seeks to ameliorate the worst effects of globalization, is a long-running trend in the broader discussion over Africa's developmental path and one that has over time shifted the terms of the debate away from the dependency-tinged, state-centric model implied in the Lagos Plan of Action (LPA) (see below). In this sense, Nepad, which can be seen as essentially accepting the broader principles of liberalization and an "open" global economy in which Africa must seek to integrate as much as possible, is a radical departure from what was formerly the lodestar of Africa's developmental visions. How and in what ways "responsible" African elites can take advantage of globalization is now (rhetorically at least) the key strategy of Nepad.

The Nepad project itself acknowledges that previous plans have largely failed. Paragraph 42 of the strategic framework document states that:

> The New Partnership for Africa's Development recognizes that there have been attempts in the past to set out continent-wide development programs. For a variety of reasons, both internal and external, including questionable leadership and ownership by Africans themselves, these have been less than successful. However, there is today a new set of circumstances, which lend themselves to integrated practical implementation.

But, in stating this, the document shows little appreciation or understanding of the true nature of postcolonial politics on the continent. Indeed as Chabal (2002: 448) points out, Paragraph 42 raises two important questions: "The first is whether African leaders, and those who advise them, are willing to study the 'variety of reasons' that have hitherto prevented development. The second is whether there really is today a new 'set of circumstances' when it comes to the exercise of power on the continent." As Chabal then notes, "Unless the lessons of the past are learnt, there is very little reason to believe that the nature of politics in Africa will change simply because of the (admittedly) admirable ambition displayed by Nepad" (Chabal, 2002). But we are jumping ahead of ourselves.

The Best Laid Plans

Although debate regarding Africa's development emerged before, during, and immediately after the decolonization process (most symbolically launched at the Bandung Conference of 1955), it was really in the 1970s that questions pertaining to how and where Africa would "fit" into the wider international political economy became prominent. Most resolutions adopted by African leaders through the OAU in the early years of independence had been aimed at the notion that the economic integration of Africa was a prerequisite for real independence and development. This was the main theme of the declarations from Algiers (1968), Addis Ababa (1970 and 1973), Kinshasa (1976), and Libreville (1977). But from the late 1970s onward, Africa became progressively inundated with various plans, frameworks, agendas, and declarations all aimed (to varying degrees) at promoting development and, later, democracy. The main programs are listed below:

- Lagos Plan of Action (LPA) and the Final Act of Lagos (1980). Claimed to promote autocentric development and greater cooperation within Africa.
- The African Charter on Human and People's Rights (Nairobi 1981) and the Grand Bay Declaration and Plan of Action on Human Rights. Spearheaded by African civil society but adopted by the OAU to encourage human rights on the continent.
- Africa's Priority Program for Economic Recovery (1985).
- OAU Declaration on the Political and Socio-Economic Situation in Africa and the Fundamental Changes Taking Place in the World (1990). Claimed to emphasize Africa's determination to determine its own destiny.
- The Charter on Popular Participation adopted in 1990. Claimed to place ordinary Africans at the "center of development."
- The Kampala Document (1991). Stipulated that peace, security, and stability are inseparable conditions and the basis for development and cooperation in Africa.
- The Abuja Treaty establishing the African Economic Community— 1991.
- The Mechanism for Conflict Prevention, Management, and Resolution (1993). African leaders pledged themselves to promote peace and stability in Africa.
- Cairo Agenda for Action (1995). Claimed to "relaunch" Africa's political, economic, and social development.
- African Common Position on Africa's External Debt Crisis (1997). Sought to find a common strategy for tackling Africa's debt crisis.
- The Algiers Decision on Unconstitutional Changes of Government (1999) and the Lomé Declaration on the framework for an OAU Response to Unconstitutional Changes (2000).
- The 2000 Solemn Declaration on the Conference on Security, Stability, Development, and Cooperation. Claimed to establish principles for the sponsorship of democracy and "good governance" in Africa.
- The Constitutive Act of the African Union. Adopted in 2000 at the Lomé Summit (Togo), entered into force in 2001.
- The Omega Plan. Prepared in 2001 by Abdoulaye Wade, president

of Senegal and premised on four central pillars, dealing with the building of infrastructures, notably information and communication technology (ICT), education and human resource development, health, and agriculture.

- The New Africa Initiative of 2001, promoted by Mbeki, Obasanjo, and Bouteflika and the precursor to Nepad.
- The New Partnership for Africa's Development (Nepad). Adopted as a program of the AU at the Lusaka Summit (2001).

In short, Africa has never been short of plans and programs. However, what arguably has united such declarations has been the fact that the vast majority have been elitist programs drawn up with very little popular consultation. Even a widespread knowledge of their existence on the continent has often been lacking.

Early postcolonial economic proposals were generally motivated by the desire (at least rhetorically) to surmount what were regarded as problems emanating from the legacy bequeathed by colonialism. Thus stress was laid on accelerated projects to develop infrastructure and education while import-substitution, encouraged at the time by development agencies and international financial institutions (IFIs), was meant to stimulate industrialization (Anyang'Nyong'o and Coughlin, 1991). This strategy fell apart before the twin problems of the collapse in the price of primary commodities and the debilitating effect of malgovernance eroded the resources and capacity of a great many African states to pursue such policies. On the "purely" economic front, the collapse of the value of primary commodities on the global market meant that import substitution policies became more and more untenable as the public fiscus increasingly accrued ruinous external debt, increasing a debilitating dependence on exogenous actors. And as the capacity of the state declined, alongside the collapse of what infrastructure that existed that might have facilitated exports, combined with destructive domestic policies that disadvantaged agricultural producers, Africa lost out more and more to other competitors for the supply of commodities to the global economy.

Having said that, it would be wrong to ascribe responsibility for the continent's decline to solely exogenous factors, such as the collapse of commodity prices or the oil crisis. Proponents of such a position have perhaps forgotten that:

By April 1970, Liberia and Somalia had already received seven stand-by agreement loans from the IMF to help them address balance of payments and budgetary crises; Burundi had received five such loans; Ghana, Mali, and Rwanda four loans; Sierra Leone and Sudan three; Congo/Zaire had completed its first IMF supervised devaluation. The granting of multiple stand-by agreements in less than a decade of independence suggests an almost immediate deterioration in management (Van de Walle, 2001: 121).

By the late 1970s, African development had begun to manifestly stall on a continental level and solutions and explanations for the emerging crisis of development were required and necessary. Certainly by the mid-1970s much of Africa was no longer experiencing the golden days of the immediate postindependence period. During the 1960s for instance, African agriculture performed relatively adequately and only 17 out of 45 sub-Saharan states suffered negative annual growth rates in their per capita food production. However, by 1976 the number of countries experiencing negative rates was 29 (Onimode, 1988). The continent's average annual growth also declined precipitously. Between 1965 and 1973 the 45 countries of black sub-Saharan Africa enjoyed an average annual growth rate of 2.9 percent (although if one excludes Nigeria then that growth rate was only 1.2 percent). However, between 1973 and 1980 (i.e., the time when the Lagos Plan was being formulated), Africa's annual growth rate had declined to a minimal 0.1 percent or, if we take Nigeria out of the equation, a disastrous -0.7 percent (World Bank, 1989: 221). Simultaneously, Africa's foreign debts were increasing exponentially. Thus, in 1970 Kenya had an external public and private debt of $406 million but by 1980 this had become $2.675 billion. Other countries had equally depressing debt burdens: Zaire went from $311 million in 1970 to $4.294 billion by 1980; Zambia from $653 million to $2.274 billion; Ghana from $497 million to $1.138 billion. Even a tiny country such as Gambia, which in 1970 only had a total debt of $5 million had, a decade later, one of $106 million (World Bank, 1989: 256).

Crucially, reflections on how and why this disastrous situation had arisen came at the tail end of the push for a New International Economic Order (NIEO). This "NIEO moment" in itself was influenced by dependency theory (e.g., Cardoso and Faletto, 1979; Frank, 1967, 1975; Wallerstein, 1974, 1979), which broadly argued that the South's relationship to the North was historically contingent and that its status of impoverishment and dependence was rooted in the process by which it had been integrated into the capitalist world economy during the colonial period, a theme that drew its intellectual heritage from Lenin. Although originally drawn up by Latin Americanists, scholars working on Africa soon applied the theory to the continent, arguing that Africa had been integrated into the world economy at a subordinate position in the emerging global division of labor (see Rodney, 1972). Much of the intellectual oeuvre within Africanist academia at the time broadly supported the dependency position (see Gutkind and Wallerstein, 1976).

This perceived dependent position played itself out in the way Africa came to supply the North with mainly primary products, seen to be problematic as the instability of markets for primary commodities acted as a sword of Damocles over Africa's future development. The concomitant importing of processed goods from the metropole presented equally difficult problems, with a continual run on foreign exchange reserves. In light of dependency theory's assertion that the relationship between the North and the South was one of a core and periphery in which the best the latter could hope for was dragging itself up to the nebulous concept of the "semi-periphery," rethinking global relations was deemed necessary.

The call for a NIEO therefore was a reaction to problems leaders in the developing world felt they were being subjected to due to the workings of the global capitalist system, rather than because of any policies or practices they may have been pursuing. The NIEO as applied to Africa was supposed to address the various issues surrounding the ongoing global trade and investment regimes that were felt to hinder the continent's development. Promoting an ideological mix of global Keynesianism heavily influenced by dependency theory, the NIEO called for a restructuring of the perceived external and structural constraints on development (Singer, 1984: 14–17). One of the most forceful African advocates at the time of both the NIEO and the broadly *dependencia* position was Adebayo Adedeji, then Director-General of the UN Economic Commission for Africa (UNECA). Adedeji was to become a leading figure behind the push for both the Monrovia meeting and the later Lagos Plan of Action (see Adedeji, 1989).

The Lagos Plan of Action

African leaders meeting in Monrovia, Liberia, in July 1979, advanced the idea that the continent's development could not be contingent on simply waiting for benefits to accrue from the types of special relationships crafted with Europe through the Yaoundé and Lomé agreements, nor could Africa progress without actively tackling the legacy of underdevelopment left by its insertion into the global capitalist economy by colonization. Autocentricity and the continued demand for a NIEO were intrinsically wrapped up in this thrust (Mathews, 1989: 52–57). The Monrovia meeting determined that a number of strategic tasks were necessary in order for Africa to develop (implicitly understood along Western ideas of what it was to be "modern" and "developed") and overcome the impasse that the continent was experiencing by the mid-1970s. Among other resolutions, Monrovia pronounced that the creation of national and regional bodies was necessary to pursue autocentricity and that Africa had to develop self-reliance in food production while engaging in development-oriented planning. The lofty aim at the time was to create modern and developed economies by the year 2000—or at least discernibly developing (if economic growth rates are measured). Borrowing from the Europeans, it was decided a Common Market needed to be in place by 2025, something that Clapham (1996a: 116) has noted was "entirely unrealistic," given the then political and economic situation. The Monrovia Declaration closed with the decision to direct the OAU's secretary general and the executive secretary of the UNECA to formulate a program to stimulate such development.

This process continued in July 1980 with the Second Extraordinary Session of the Heads of States and Governments, which was held in Nigeria and produced the much-vaunted Lagos Plan of Action and the Final Act (OAU, 1980). Essentially, the Lagos Plan of Action was a clarification of the broad philosophy that Monrovia had indicated and was a document that sought to arrive at strategies that might promote growth on a continent that was disengaged and less influenced by the vagaries of the global market (Onwuka et al., 1985). An emphasis on inter-African trade and investment through regional cooperation was central to the LPA, despite, or perhaps because, "by 1980—when the LPA was adopted—almost all the economic co-operation schemes optimistically launched in the 1960s—the halcyon days of African integration—had become largely moribund" (Asante, 1985: 82). The reduction in external debt, import-substitution policies, and a general goal of autocentric development further underpinned the Lagos Plan.

Perhaps unsurprisingly given both the dependency approach that provided the framework for its analysis and (and this is perhaps the most important) the fact that it was African elites themselves conducting the exercise, the LPA's conclusions were "a classic dependency interpretation of the African condition. It exonerated African leaders and blamed the historical injustices suffered by the continent and the continued dependence on external forces for the crisis" (Owusu, 2003; 1657). Certainly, the LPA went out of its way to absolve the postcolonial elites of any responsibility for Africa's predicament. It quite explicitly stated that "despite all efforts made by its leaders, [the continent] remains the least developed" (OAU, 1980: 7). In other words, the LPA failed to generally consider the broad issues of malgovernance and accountability but rather focused on the external as the source of all of Africa's woes, a situation that had frustrated "all efforts." In general, "the tendency of the Lagos Plan was to list the problems that African countries were facing, suggest [solutions] without even a vague hint of how these could be financed, and then recommend the creation of numerous international institutions to help African countries" (Herbst, 1993: 139).

That the LPA failed is incontrovertible. Based on faulty assumptions about Africa's economic condition, and ignoring systematic malgovernance, its prescriptions were described as "economically illiterate" by Clapham (1996a: 176). Primarily, the LPA strategy was based on a continuation of import substitution and hinged on three conditions that Africa simply did not possess. The assumptions made by the LPA were that:

> The actual surplus extracted from the agricultural sector is, in fact, invested in the industrial sector, where it will be converted into additional manufacturing capacity . . . Second, peasants must continue to produce—indeed expand production—despite conditions that clearly work against them. Third, certain (heavy) industries need specialized manpower and relatively large markets to be efficient and viable. None of these conditions were really met in Africa (Ergas, 1987b: 309).

Indeed, "why these measures should be taken and what priority should be given to them [were] never stated because the Lagos Plan [did] not suggest how the agrarian crisis the African states [were] facing originated" (Herbst, 1993: 139). To do so, it is suggested, would have involved apportioning degrees of blame, which would have inevitably led to African leaders having to take their fair share, something which was scrupulously avoided and dodged by the plan and its architects.

The Era of Structural Adjustment

A year later, in 1981, the World Bank responded to the LPA with its own analysis. Entitled *Accelerated Development in Sub-Saharan Africa: An Agenda for Action* (also known as the "Berg Report" after its main author, Professor Elliot Berg), the bank came out strongly against most of the LPA's positions, in particular the notion that the state should be the main engine of growth and the absolution by the LPA of the malevolent role played by African elites in their continent's demise (World Bank, 1981). Meddling by the state in the supposed free running of the market was particularly criticized and was seen as a main reason for Africa's declining growth record, coupled with malgovernance (Arrighi, 2002: 5–35). The perceived over-ambitious targets of the LPA, such as a pancontinental Common Market á la the European Community, were also critiqued. But "such analyses challenged the evidently self-serving perceptions of African elites and their sympathisers [captured in the LPA] and aroused the hostility of institutions such as the United Nations Economic Commission for Africa" (Clapham, 1996b: 811).

In essence, the Berg Report was a rebuttal of the dependency-tinged, NIEO-informed LPA and the opening salvo in a decade-long campaign to shape developmental discourse in Africa along lines favored by the key global economic players (Browne and Cummings, 1985). In this regard it should be noted that the Monrovia Declaration and the LPA were launched on the eve of the election to government of conservative neoliberals in

Britain and the United States, and the Plan of Action in particular advanced a vision at sharp variance with the gathering thrust of global capitalism and the views of key elites in the developed world. Indeed, separate from the failure of African elites to really do anything about Africa's declining situation, the demise of the Plan's vision played itself out as an integral part of the reassertion of Western-centered hegemony—"America's quest for supremacy [over] the Third World" as Augelli and Murphy (1988) have put it. This was coupled with the steady demise, though not outright extinction—as the initial position of the ANC in the early 1990s in South Africa demonstrated (Taylor, 2001)—of a protesting voice in Africa's relations with the developed world.

Although various adjustment packages had been implemented in Africa before the 1980s, the Berg Report was to usher in a new era in African politics and development, the era of structural adjustment programs (SAPs). Just as the LPA had skated over the behavior of African elites, the Berg Report remained relatively uncritical of donor activities. The report advanced a dual strategy for the continent: privatization and liberalization. Reform packages that were rolled out in the 1980s by all the main creditors and donors contained these two basic elements as essential conditions of disbursements. A structural adjustment package, granted in 1981 to Côte d'Ivoire and soon to become the first of what would eventually become 26 SAPs to that country, captures the basic ingredients:

> The reforms envisaged by the program are designed to improve the level of public savings and the efficiency in the use of public resources; restructure the agricultural planning system and associated development institutions so that an expanded, well-designed investment program yielding high returns can be mounted in the sector; reflect the costs of providing public services to the sector; assure that rational prices and world market conditions would guide decisions to invest and produce; restructure public enterprise, management, financing and accountability to ensure efficient market oriented operations; restructure incentives, to promote efficient export-oriented industrial investments (World Bank, 1981).

These elements staked out both an economic and political project and came at a historical juncture when financial indebtedness and economic mismanagement were acting to drastically undermine the continent's development trajectory. At the same time, leaders within Africa began to realize that agreeing to the ongoing restructuring process as promoted through SAPs, even if their commitment was only rhetorical, was necessary for political survival (Van de Walle, 2001).

The means to overcome Africa's crisis was identified (even if unconsciously) as a return to two old theoretical approaches: neo-classical economics, and modernization theory (Mengisteab and Logan, 1995). Within SAPs was an implicit echoing of the modernizers' argument that the "fun-

damentals" had to be in place to assure economic development. Not bring-
ing such fundamentals in place was blamed for the lack of success of SAPs
in many African countries (Harvey, 1996). Indeed, the failure to implement
SAPs has been held to be a contributing factor in explaining Africa's continued demise even after SAPs were introduced (Van de Walle, 2001).
There was a considerable disparity between rhetorical and practical commitment to economic and political reform. In fact, new loans disbursed by
the IFIs as part of a SAP were often seen simply as new sources of largesse
to distribute to supporters and clients, with minimal intention to fulfill
signed commitments. Yet, the pretense that both donor and recipient were
engaged in serious reform was often played out for public consumption. As
Van de Walle (2001: 224) noted:

> Meetings between the government and its creditors, UN summits, and the
> annual meetings of the IFI were replete with communiqués and announce-
> ments "commending" African governments for the "hard work" they had
> demonstrated. Governments complained about the austerity that was
> demanded of them and complained of the sociopolitical difficulties
> involved with implementing reform programs. The impression was given
> that adjustment was a kind of favor that governments were extending to
> the West, at tremendous cost.

However, the supposed "one-size-fits-all" approach that characterized
many of the SAPs generated a counterreaction in the form of the Africa's
Priority Program for Economic Recovery 1986–1990 (APPER). Later
transformed and repackaged as the United Nations Program of Action for
Africa's Economic Recovery and Development (UN-PAAERD), the aim of
both initiatives was ostensibly to attempt to work with SAPs through projects that might allow African states to connect with the global market
through "shared commitments" and joint efforts (OAU, 1986). Essentially,
the debt issue and the scant levels of domestic investment were seen as
major stumbling blocks to any successful implementation of the SAPs
(rather than elite resistance and obstruction) and thus, foreshadowing
Nepad's prescriptions some twenty years later, an injection of capital was
deemed necessary if the continent was to be developmentally kick started
and if the SAP-affected countries were to be cushioned from the more negative effects of the programs. Thus assisting African states to put into practice policy reforms in line with the SAPs was deemed essential to the whole
recovery project.

The impact of SAPs on Africa and African elites' positions, particularly as glasnost and perestroika made Africa's strategic position less and less
clear, resurfaced in July 1989 with the UNECA's African Alternative
Framework to Structural Adjustment Programs for Socio-Economic
Recovery and Transformation (AAF-SAP) (OAU, 1989). The framework

sprang from studies by Adebayo Adedeji and other African economists, frustrated at the perceived sidelining—by both African elites and their industrialized partners—of their LPA.[1] The AAF-SAP started out from the concept that "Up to this day, this blueprint [the LPA] contains a valid analysis and the right prescriptions for African countries to transform their economies" (OAU, 1989: 3). Thus the AAF-SAP maintained that huge capital investment in Africa was necessary to spur economic growth while questioning the insistence by donors that Africa should increase its exports as a means of escaping the crisis of development. AAF-SAP asserted that a change in consumption patterns to favor locally or regionally produced goods over imported products was required, while internationally the framework demanded that donors should support programs designed and implemented by African governments themselves and aimed at tackling specific national problems, rather than seeking to impose the perceived blanket programs associated with SAPs. In other words, the AAF-SAP in effect demanded increased flows of aid but with little control by the donors on how this was to be spent, arguing that African leadership was best placed to decide how to spend such resources.

Yet, the assertion that there should be some sudden change in consumption patterns, without addressing the fundamental problem of rapacious elites (who were the main source of such distortions) was bound to fail, as was the idea that capital resources should be simply handed over to African leaders to spend as they saw fit. Certainly, "the claim that no changes were required in the management of African states themselves was unsustainable" (Clapham, 1996a: 176). In fact, the AAF-SAP "was especially critical of reliance on foreign experts and managers in national economic decision making in Africa. Indeed, it seemed to blame the presence of foreigners more than . . . external factors as the debt burden for Africa's crisis" (Herbst, 1993: 141). This suggests that the AAF-SAP was perhaps little more than a nationalist counterreaction against SAPs.

Indeed, the AAF-SAP's understanding of the African crisis was limited in scope, "dangerously simplistic" as Herbst (1993: 143) puts it, and largely restricting itself to commenting that "the crisis that struck Africa in the 1980s had many causes. The drought resulted in one of the worst famines Africa experienced in the twentieth century. The fall in the prices of Africa's major commodities made foreign exchange become very scarce and very expensive" (OAU, 1989: 12). Thus, just as the LPA did, African leaders effectively absolved themselves from any responsibility, finding in the weather, foreign experts, and external factors such as falls in commodity prices, alibis for the continent's demise. Problematically, the AAF-SAP "seem[ed] not at all concerned about the performance of African states even though over the last two decades, all evidence suggest[ed] that this performance ha[d] been abysmal" (Herbst, 1993: 145).

The AAF-SAP of 1989 was however adopted by the UN General Assembly, which voted in favor of it. A resolution invited the General Assembly to consider the framework as a basis for "constructive dialogue" and "fruitful consultation." This, despite the observation that it was "a warmed-over version of the Lagos Plan of Action with vague and contradictory, largely statist, policy proposals that could not be implemented under the best of conditions, all of which [were] linked to renewed demands for substantially increased external resource flows and debt relief" (Callaghy, 1991: 55). However, like almost all previous plans in Africa, the AAF-SAP never got off the ground, primarily due to the lack of commitment by both those African leaders who had signed the framework (thus echoing the fate of the LPA) and also the IFIs and Western governments. For instance, Zimbabwe adopted an IMF-tailored SAP within a year of African finance ministers rushing to pledge support for the AAF-SAP and supposedly rejecting SAPs!

Interestingly, just as the Lagos Plan had been followed by the Berg Report, the AAF-SAP was rapidly followed by a new World Bank document in 1989, *Sub Saharan Africa: From Crisis to Sustainable Growth.* This report argued that sound incentives and a decent infrastructure were required to construct an enabling environment for African growth to develop. The report also, however, argued that "African governments and foreign financiers (commercial banks and export credit agencies as well as donor agencies) must share responsibility [for the continent's crisis]. Foreign financiers and suppliers promoted capital exports with attractive credits, and poor coordination among donors caused duplication and waste" (World Bank, 1989: 27). The report additionally touched on malgovernance as a major cause of Africa's impasse, asserting that "foreign aid has greatly expanded the opportunities for malfeasance exacerbated by the venality of many foreign contractors and suppliers" (World Bank, 1989: 27). But, somewhat signaling a shift from its previous hard-nosed stance towards the role of the state, the report asserted that human resource development was required (a role that the state could perform) and that a social safety net was also needed. An acceptance of the normative principles of neo-liberalism, while advocating amelioration of their effects on vulnerable groups, and while sharing the blame on endogenous and exogenous factors, now emerged as defining principles—something that has been maintained to date and informs Nepad's own prescriptions to varying degrees.

Such broad tendencies were not simply confined to the discussion around Africa's specific problems, but also played themselves out at a wider level where the debate on what constituted development was more and more influenced by the collapse of the socialist bloc, the emerging New World Order, and the overarching prescriptions of neoliberalism.

Indeed, with the Cold War now over and the "triumph" of the alleged "Western way of life" (i.e., liberal economics and politics) apparently in ascendance, civic organizations on the continent began to argue that Africa needed to face up to the governance problem; dictatorships and corruption could no longer be ignored with reference to the fight against communism (or equally, the fight against capitalism). Thus, the UNECA convened the Arusha conference on Popular Participation for Democracy in Africa, subsequently issuing *The African Charter for Popular Participation for Development* (1990). The conference (in contrast to the later genesis of Nepad) was a collaborative endeavor between African NGOs, African governments, and UN agencies and sprang from the call by NGOs that emanated from the 1988 mid-term review of the UN-PAAERD. Indeed, given Nepad's later lack of consultation with civil society it is curious that nothing was learned from the Arusha conference, where over five hundred participants from a diverse array of NGOs, grassroots organizations, and associations were in attendance.[2] Perhaps because it was heavily influenced by ordinary African people, the Arusha conference asserted that Africa's problems sprang from a "political context of socioeconomic development [that] has been characterized, in many instances, by an over-centralization of power and impediments to the effective participation of the overwhelming majority of the people in social, political and economic development" (African Charter for Popular Participation in Development and Transformation, 1990).

At the same time the African Charter demanded that African governments respect "freedom of association, especially political association" and the "presence of democratic institutions," it called for the "rule of law and social and economic justice" and "political accountability of leadership at all levels." In other words, contrary to Nepad promoters' claims to its uniqueness and path-breaking vision, the African Charter was demanding much the same elements for African renewal as Nepad, but over ten years earlier and with a particular emphasis on elite accountability. Ordinary Africans, through their grassroots involvement in the African Charter, had placed, for the first time, the notion that democracy and accountability was central and that the blame for Africa's demise could be sourced to a large degree (but not, obviously, exclusively) from within Africa—or rather, from within the palaces of African presidents. In this context, the UN moved to bring into being its *New Agenda for Development of Africa* (UN-NADAF, 1991).

Like so many other previous agendas and plans, the UN-NADAF was produced mainly because, unfortunately, a previous program (in this case, the UN-PAAERD) had not reached its objectives or been implemented in any meaningful way. The UN-NADAF asserted that a basic precondition for economic development was political and social stability. No longer was there a pretense that governance had nothing to do with poor economic performance or that Africa's woes were all exogenous, as the much-vaunted LPA had tried to assert. Essentially, the rapid evaporation of the optimism associated with the end of the Cold War and its supposed implications for an Africa now free of East-West rivalry meant that a new analysis of Africa's predicament was deemed necessary, building on the African Charter. But again, the UN-NADAF included ingredients that were to reemerge with Nepad. For instance, the Norwegian Minister of Development Cooperation (Nordheim-Larsen, 1995) saw in the UN-NADAF a message asserting that:

> A foundation for economic development can only be found in societies where the political stability is based on the democratic participation of the population, respect for human rights and an equitable distribution of income. The international community has a clear responsibility to help foster such a development and channel development assistance to where it is conducive for good governance.

This last element is now replicated in the notion of Nepad's peer review and the $64 billion in new investment and assistance to "good" African polities. At the same time, market access for African economies, in particular the ability to export to the developed world, was identified as crucial, and measures to enable this should be implemented as a matter of urgency within the framework of the World Trade Organization (WTO). In this understanding, the UN-NADAF saw the WTO as having strengthened a rules-based trading system and that furthering liberalization opened up opportunities for sustainable development and growth if African countries seized the occasion *and* if they reformed themselves.

With this apparent breakthrough in the involvement of civil society, the Africa Leadership Forum, a pan-continental organization led by Chief Olusegun Obasanjo of Nigeria, in discussion and partnership with the Organization for Economic Cooperation and Development (OECD), Economic Commission for Africa (ECA), and the OAU, organized a number of meetings that ended with what became known as the Kampala Forum of May 1991. This conference, attended by some 500 participants from Africa, adopted a proposal (known as the Kampala Document) to establish a Conference on Security, Stability, Development and Cooperation in Africa (CSSDCA).

The background to the CSSDCA was that in the early 1990s, a gathering of African statesmen, academics, and civil leaders from throughout the continent had met to put together a comprehensive plan to make the continent become less dependent on the rest of the world and prepare it to compete in the global economy. Those who gathered to write what would come to be known as the Kampala Document envisioned an organization that would succeed where the OAU had proven ineffectual. This CSSDCA was aimed at providing a forum for the debate on democratization, security issues, and sustainable development (Deng and Zartman, 2001). Its aim was to set up a normative framework that would make up and lay out yardsticks states might be able to measure themselves against. In theory, the CSSDCA represented a site where the advancement of certain shared values might progress. Importantly, and echoing the later evolution of Nepad, mechanisms to make certain that decisions adopted by adherents were actually implemented was part of the project. The Report of the First Ministerial Meeting of the CSSDCA (held in Abuja in May 2000) was endorsed by the OAU/African Economic Community (AEC) Summit in Lomé, 2000.

The Liberal Democratic Panacea: Some Reflections

Problematically, the democracy advanced as an accompaniment to the SAPs has, as it turned out, referred to a system by which those elites that promise "reform" and "liberalization" are largely entrenched and where popular involvement in decisionmaking is limited to periodic leadership choices via carefully managed elections, organized by contending elites (Robinson, 1996). In other words, the formulaic type of democracy that is practiced has served somewhat to soothe social and political pressures created by SAPs, but amounts to little more than "low intensity democracy" (Gills et al., 1993). By its very nature, such democracy dissipates much of the energies of the marginalized into parliamentary procedures that in themselves are acted out by political factions whose power and prestige, not to mention access to resources and patronage, rapidly have become dependant on participation in parliamentary politics, however "really" democratic such exercises have turned out to be. Indeed, the promotion of such democracy has been "instrumental in some cases (e.g., Zambia) in disempowering the poor by introducing the multiparty mantra as a new political panacea, while it [has] entrenched a new, rather exclusive elite in reality" (Liebenberg, 1998: 5). As one analysis put it:

> The assertion that the majority of African governments are now democratic is premised on contentious notions of democracy with external origins. Apart from this, the assertion has no empirical basis. It is true that multiparty elections are now common in Africa, but this truth does not describe a fundamental development. The change is strategic, not substantive. Multiparty elections have not led to new power relations in Africa. Just look at Zambia and Malawi since the fall of Kenneth Kaunda and the late Kamazu Banda (Moyo, 1998: 11).

In such formulations, the call to end corruption and mismanagement and the push for democratic accountability has become linked to a rather narrow understanding of democracy. Thus while many African states have undergone "democratization," such projects have largely been short lived and/or contained what can only be regarded as a democratic façade. One need only think of the type of transitions that have occurred in states such as Malawi, Mozambique, and Zambia to acknowledge that there has been scant concrete progress for the average person.

Indeed, the very logic of personal rule and neopatrimonial politics on the continent has meant that even though there have been "democratic transitions," there has been only a limited change in the political structures in most of Africa. Because political power grants one access to resources (customs revenues, foreign aid, possibly taxation, and often, parastatals), elections on the continent are about much more than simply the chance to be the head of state but are almost life-and-death struggles for the ability to maintain oneself as a Big Man. Political slogans for "democracy" and an end to corruption are useful mobilizing devices and may even be believed by many ordinary people, but having captured political power, the new incumbent's clients will invariably anticipate and demand material benefits for their support:

> Out of self-interest many actors may support demands for democracy precisely because access to the state and to its resources will then become easier. Once democracy has been achieved, however, their behavior is not conducive to its consolidation. The characteristics of the patrimonial system reassert themselves (Callaghy, 1986: 45).

As Chabal and Daloz note (1999), neither the voters nor the political competitors appear to be intrinsically opposed to such patronage systems. Rather, the aim is to be on the winning side and even if the profits from such a system are unevenly circulated, those inside the loop who gain from such arrangements do not complain—it is only when they slip out of the charmed circle that grievances and criticism against corruption generally emerge. Structural, rather than simply agential, explanations as to the persistence of patrimonial regimes are thus necessary. The "democratic transitions" of the late 1980s, rather than entrenching democracy on the continent, have instead amplified the pressure on political actors to disperse patronage. Elections are an opportunity for the Big Man to show that he is more munificent, more of a father figure, than his opponent and once elected, he must award his supporters. As Kourouma wryly notes in his remarkable fictitious treatment of an African president:

> [The president] must appear to be the wealthiest man in the land. There is no future, no influence to be had in independent Africa for he who wields

supreme executive power if he does not parade the fact that he is the richest and most generous man in his country. A true, great African leader gives gifts, ceaselessly, every day (2003: 221).

But, even after political changes, the entrenchment of democratic values remains relatively shallow and compromised, even if such transitions have allowed a greater space for different voices to be heard these days, compared to the one-party era of the 1960s and 1970s.

As the growing consensus on what was wrong with Africa—namely a lack of democracy and excessive state interference in the economy—emerged, confrontation with the developed world over the evils of a dependency generated by the global capitalist system gave way to "dialogue." This actuality was confirmed with the formulation of the African Economic Community (AEC) in 1991. The AEC was established at an OAU Summit in June 1991, but only came into force in May 1994 after the requisite numbers signed up for ratification. Its main aim was to establish a pan-continental economic community by 2025, predicated on the by-now standard fare of "the gradual removal, among Member States, of obstacles to the free movement of persons, goods, services and capital" (Treaty Establishing the African Economic Community, 1991).

So far, like many other African plans and declarations, the Abuja Treaty has failed to meet its stated objectives. Even taking 1994 and not 1991 as its starting point, the treaty has thus far failed in meeting its First Stage (1994–1999), which was to be the strengthening of existing regional economic communities within a period not exceeding five years. It is unlikely, judging on the evidence so far, that its Second Stage (1999–2007), of stabilizing tariff barriers and non-tariff barriers, customs duties, and internal taxes within a period not exceeding eight years, will be met. Time will tell whether all its other stages will follow the same fate. The specific objectives of the AEC are:

- to promote economic, social, and cultural development and the integration of African economies in order to increase economic self-reliance and promote an endogenous and self-sustained development
- to establish, on a continental scale, a framework for the development, mobilization, and utilization of the human and material resources of Africa in order to achieve a self-reliant development
- to promote cooperation in all fields of human endeavor in order to raise the standard of living of African peoples, and maintain and enhance economic stability, foster close and peaceful relations among Member States, and contribute to the progress, development, and the economic integration of the Continent

- to coordinate and harmonize policies among existing and future economic communities in order to foster the gradual establishment of the Community (African Economic Community, 1991)

Many of these ideals are now replicated by Nepad. Interestingly, the AEC treaty includes punishment for states not adhering to its conventions, something that Nepad promoters have, as various "test cases" demonstrated, shied away from (see Chapter 5). After all, the AEC treaty states quite clearly that "Any Member State, which persistently fails to honor its general undertakings under this Treaty or fails to abide by the decisions or regulations of the Community, may be subjected to sanctions by the Assembly" (African Economic Community, 1991). Among such general undertakings are the "recognition, promotion and protection of human and peoples' rights" and "accountability." So, the idea advanced by Nepad promoters that its peer review mechanism and the notion, sold to the G8, that censure and action against miscreants was part of the uniqueness of Nepad is once again somewhat misleading.

Toward the African Renaissance

All of the above plans, declarations, frameworks, and programs provide the broader context of what was to develop in the late 1990s—a concerted attempt by a select few African presidents to repackage and exclusively define the question of Africa's development to the wider world. It is important to provide the above detailed context to demonstrate that not only did Nepad not emerge from a vacuum, but also to show that Africa's history is replete with previous initiatives and in this light there is a danger that Nepad might simply be another one added to the list. The failure of the previous plans is largely due to the lack of capacity and resources *and* a systematic lack of political will on behalf of African leaders to seriously attempt to implement what they have agreed to. This is not to arbitrarily dismiss the very real exogenous constraints placed upon African maneuverability or overlook the debilitating effect the debt burden has placed on African budgets. Certainly, African agency has been inhibited to an unusual degree. But, it remains true, seventeen years after it was written, that:

> Slavery and colonialism . . . exacted an extremely heavy toll in sub-Saharan Africa and that the international exchange system does not always function to the benefit of [developing countries]; but African governments did have some room to maneuver, to bring about more development; they have, in the final analysis, proven to be notoriously deficient in that respect (Ergas, 1987b: 308).

It is that context that the "African Renaissance" sought to address. Certainly, the genesis of Nepad, aside from the plethora of abovementioned projects, can be sourced to Thabo Mbeki's "vision" of an African Renaissance. Since late 1996 when Mbeki started to play a more active role in the formulation of South Africa's foreign policy, the idea of a continental renewal has developed momentum within his thinking. Mbeki formally introduced the idea of a renaissance in an address to an American audience in April 1997. Also in 1997, a document entitled *The African Renaissance: A Workable Dream* was released by the Office of South Africa's then–Deputy President (Mbeki). It suggested five areas of engagement with the African continent: the encouragement of cultural exchange; the "emancipation of the African woman from patriarchy"; the mobilization of youth; the broadening, deepening, and sustenance of democracy; and the initiation of sustainable economic development (Vale and Maseko, 1998: 274). As part of this, Mbeki (1999) asserted that "political organizations and governments in all African countries should be mobilized to act in furtherance of the objectives of the African Renaissance."

Intriguingly, "whereas the Renaissance in Europe was a process that occurred independent of any program designed to deliver it, Mbeki suggested that a renaissance could and should be consciously induced in Africa" (Barrell, 2000: 3). Thus having interpreted the European Renaissance as a sort of willed project that motored Europe into modernity, rather than an amorphous process that went in many directions, Mbeki sought to place South Africa at the forefront of solving Africa's problems through his advocacy of the renaissance concept and active diplomacy. This culminated in the birth of Nepad.

In an address at the United Nations University in April 1998, Mbeki expanded on some of the core elements that formed the substance of his vision. Among these were included the need to establish and maintain systems of good governance; to introduce new economic policies which seek to create conditions that are attractive for the private sector; to reduce the participation of the state in the ownership of the economy and to build modern economies; to establish regional economic arrangements to lessen the disadvantages created by small markets; introduce policies that would ensure access to good education, adequate health care, decent houses, clean water, and modern sanitation (Mbeki, 1999). In spite of the impassioned rhetoric, the essential features of the African Renaissance and how to encourage its development remained vague: "high on sentiment, low on substance" (Vale and Maseko, 1998: 277). Furthermore, in light of the various plans previously advanced on the continent, they were not particularly original:

> They amounted to little more than a list of objectives of the kind that any democrat might formulate if he was intent on good governance and sound

> economic management in order to achieve a better quality of life for his
> compatriots in an African context. By presenting them as the sufficient
> conditions for a renaissance in Africa, Mbeki was doing little more than
> giving a set of fairly ordinary policy objectives the lustre of a grand cause
> (Barrell, 2000).

While their advocacy by the president of the most developed country in
Africa was of note, Mbeki's pronouncements constituted little more than an
endorsement of the existing prescriptions vis-à-vis development, albeit presented in Africanist terms. Indeed, much of Mbeki's pronouncements were
couched as contemporary commonsense and broadly fitting with Mbeki's
own domestic economic program (Taylor, 2001). In fact, it was admitted
that Mbeki's version of the African renaissance acceded to orthodox
notions of what constitutes "best practice" and "good" economic policy.
One leading South African government official for instance conceded that
the "attempt on our part to attract investments [and] the tendency . . . for us
to start behaving (without being derogatory) like beauty queens on a cat-
walk, with a judge based in Europe or in the Americas who will say 'yes,
beautiful' and therefore we will invest or we will provide aid" is real
(Netshitenzhe, 1999). In return for such restructuring, Mbeki and other
leaders—as Nepad was to later demonstrate—expected a quid pro quo from
international society, in particular, a concerted international effort to provide debt relief for Africa; the introduction of measures to encourage larger
flows of capital into the continent; reasonable trade policies, to provide for
market access to African products; and an assurance that Africa can eventually occupy "her due place within the councils of the world" (Mbeki, 1999).

Mbeki's definition of the African Renaissance was thus based upon the
expressed desire to promote the liberalization of markets, free trade and liberal democratic institutions across the continent. In this sense, the latest
version(s) of Africa's recovery plans have settled quite comfortably into a
post–Cold War era where the hegemony of the market has been reasserted.
Mbeki's prescriptions reflect the orthodox view in both contemporary
development discourse and international relations. Indeed, according to
Cheru (1997:239), they reflect the arguments made by "the World Bank and
other donors who would like to see South Africa take the leading role to
facilitate collective economic liberalization across the region by improving
conditions for a more active role by private agents." However, the strategic
juncture that elevated Mbeki et al.'s plans above previous declarations was
the evolving state of affairs at the international level.

The Strategic Juncture

The debacle at the WTO meeting in Seattle in December 1999 meant that a
new realization by the world's elites dawned after concerns over the direc-

tion that globalization was taking threatened to overturn the global trading regime as defined by the WTO (Melber, 2004). Indeed, South Africa's Minister of Trade and Industry, Alec Erwin, argued that after Seattle, Pretoria "had been able to convey to them [the USA] that if they wanted a deal with the WTO, they would have to see certain things from the perspective of developing nations" (*Financial Mail,* Johannesburg, June 9, 2000). Essentially Erwin was arguing that if the United States, and by extension other Western developed countries, wished to pursue further liberalization within the WTO, then the concerns and interests of the (elites of the) developing world would have to be accommodated. Seattle had demonstrated quite clearly that the WTO process could be quite effectively—and very publicly—stopped in its tracks. The later meltdown at Cancun in 2003 proved this to be the case, particularly when it was combined with the concerns of domestic constituencies in the West who could vote in elections. It was thus seen as strategically preferable by the West's elites to engage with reformers of Mbeki's and Obasanjo's credentials, who are relatively "moderate," rather than risk allowing a process to develop whereby all sorts of "unreasonable" demands reminiscent of the NIEO might be put on the table (Melber, 2004).

In light of this opening, South Africa exerted a great deal of energy in constructing a nascent bloc of initially developing but later specifically African countries from which a broadly orthodox but reformist agenda could be launched to reinvigorate Africa and address concerns about the global trading regime and Africa's stalled development. In Cairo in March 2000 South Africa met with Brazil, India, Nigeria, and Egypt to launch a developing nations trade bloc to challenge the G7 in the post-Seattle round of WTO negotiations. At that time it became apparent that a troika of reform-minded African leaders, namely Thabo Mbeki, Egyptian President Hosni Mubarak, and Nigerian President Olusegun Obasanjo were joining together in a variety of multilateral initiatives to push their agenda at every opportunity.

South Africa, enervated by the idea of an African Renaissance, emerged as the pivotal state in trying to forge a common strategy and approach to global trade and development. Foreign Minister Nkosazana Dlamini-Zuma claimed that South Africa and selected like-minded countries would "form a nucleus of countries in the South that can interact [with the North] on behalf of developing countries." This "is a serious priority for SA," she went on to say (*Financial Mail,* Johannesburg, February 18, 2000). Also, the profile of Mbeki was raised at international fora, particularly with his so-called Mbeki Global Initiative for Africa being touted as the foundation for the continent's renewal by Western leaders, principally to those who styled themselves as adherents of the kinder "Third Way" (Blair, Schroeder, Clinton, Chretien, etc.).

Mbeki's profile received a boost at the G-77 meeting in Havana in

April 2000 when the body adopted a resolution that agreed with his vision of a united South within global trading bodies such as the WTO. At the same meeting, it was clear that Mbeki's approach was shared by key African leaders, such as Obasanjo and Algeria's Abdelaziz Bouteflika, who reiterated the position that the developing world was being excluded from global decisionmaking mechanisms and processes, resulting in the perpetuation of inequitable relations. Indeed, the G-77 summit was cast as the starting point of a collective process that would come to reconfigure the future of the global system. Obasanjo said the G-77 was sending "a clear message to the developed countries that their reluctance to reform the international financial system is a major threat to international peace and security" (*Business Day,* Johannesburg, April 14, 2000). The G-77 agreed to form a directorate to drive this process and Mbeki was included, along with Obasanjo and Mahathir Mohamed of Malaysia (*Financial Mail,* Johannesburg, April 21, 2000).

Within Africa, the three most active presidents in the calls for renewal and reform (Bouteflika, Mbeki, and Obasanjo) requested a mandate from the OAU to draw up a new plan for the continent's development. This was granted at the OAU's Extraordinary Summit held in Sirte, Libya, during September 1999. The three leaders then engaged in a flurry of diplomacy, with the mandate for drawing up a recovery program being extended by the G-77 at the summit in Havana in April 2000. These trips, dominated by Mbeki, included flying visits to the United States, Britain, Germany, and Denmark. During the visit to Washington in late May 2000, Mbeki won the backing of President Clinton for a supposed far-reaching package of measures to address Africa's problems, including proposals on debt relief, world trade rules, the restructuring of international financial institutions, and investment promotion for Africa. The proposed plan or program of action was the first specific elaboration of Mbeki's call at the EU-Africa summit in Cairo in April 2000 for a new global system. At this time it seemed that Pretoria was emerging as the de facto acknowledged leader of Africa, a position seemingly recognized when the EU invited Mbeki as the sole "special guest" to a two-day EU summit in Feira in northern Portugal in June 2000. The EU regarded Mbeki's presence as "a mark of the warm and growing relations between the EU and South Africa," and saw it as reaffirming the commitments given at the first-ever summit between Africa and the European Union, held April 2000 in Cairo (European Union, 2000).

A month after Feira, the OAU Summit (in Togo, July 2000) mandated the three leaders (Bouteflika, Mbeki, and Obasanjo) to enter into discussion with the North on behalf of Africa in order to develop more details regarding the proposed partnership for the continent's rebirth. That same month, Mbeki and Obasanjo had addressed a summit of the G7 in Okinawa, Japan. Earlier, Mbeki had met the leaders of the Nordic countries to set out a shared vision for Africa. The Skagen Declaration of June 2000 agreed on the need to review the global economic system as well as the "global financial architecture" to ensure a significant transfer of resources and capital from North to South in the form of long-term capital flows and direct investment. Mbeki's stance that globalization should concomitantly lead to expanded access to markets and technology transfers for Africa was also accepted. Importantly, the Skagen summit found the Nordic prime ministers willing—rhetorically at least—to join Mbeki in working toward more agreeable terms of trade for Africa during the post-Seattle round of WTO talks. Overall, "the Nordic Prime Ministers agreed on the need to actively support Africa's participation in the New World Economy" (*South African Press Agency,* Johannesburg, June 8, 2000).

Following the raising of the issue of a partnership with the leaders of the G7 at their summit in Japan, work on developing the Millennium Africa Recovery Plan (MAP) began in earnest and a process of engagement on a bilateral and multilateral level was pursued. The first concept paper was drawn up by Mbeki and his advisers and was quickly accepted by the other two presidents (Bouteflika and Obasanjo) in September 2000 with a steering committee being set up to work out a comprehensive agenda. The MAP sought to be the "declaration of a firm commitment by African leaders to take ownership and responsibility for the sustainable economic development of the continent. The starting point is a critical examination of Africa's postindependence experience and an acceptance that things have to be done differently to achieve meaningful socioeconomic progress." In return for this critical introspection and a pledge for better governance, the plan demanded wealthier countries commit themselves to substantially increase aid and investment to Africa. The MAP introduced the idea of "a constructive partnership between Africa and the developed world," later the cornerstone of Nepad, and was "a pledge by African leaders based on a firm and shared conviction that they have a pressing duty to eradicate poverty and to place their countries, both individually and collectively, on a path of sustainable growth and development" (Department of Foreign Affairs, 2001). From this base, the MAP avowed that "the priority areas" of any renewal project would include:

- creating peace, security, and stability, including democratic governance, without which it will be impossible to engage in meaningful economic activity
- investing in Africa's people through a comprehensive human resource strategy
- harnessing and developing Africa's strategic and comparative advantages in the resource-based sectors to lead the development of an industrial strategy

- the diversification of Africa's production and exports
- increasing investments in the information and communication technology sector, in order to bridge the digital divide
- the development of infrastructure including transport and energy
- developing financing mechanisms (Department of Foreign Affairs, 2001)

According to the MAP, "participating African leaders would form a Compact committing themselves to the Program," and "every attempt will be made . . . to be inclusive of all countries that agree to the elements of the Compact" (Department of Foreign Affairs, 2001). Mention of a compact was of note as, at the same time that the MAP was being touted, the UNECA was promoting its Compact for African Recovery, which had been initiated by the executive secretary, K. Y. Amoako. In a speech made by Amoako, to the Eighth Session of the ECA Conference of African Ministers of Finance in November 2000, Amoako had called for a compact by which the developed world would increase aid, grant debt relief and open up markets in return for African states implementing political reforms that would ensure economic take off.

In short, the compact was based on the notion that enhanced partnerships with the developed world, mutual accountability and peer review, were central to development. This would be overseen by a "Forum of African Leaders," who would make decisions about sub-programs and review progress on the compact's implementation. The genesis of the African Peer Review Mechanism (APRM) (see Chapter 3) springs, then, from the compact, as well as from the Kampala Forum. After all, the compact stated that "the quality of governance [was] critical for poverty reduction" as "poor governance leads to [a] vicious circle of impoverishment, conflict, and capital flight" which, "in a globalizing economy [where] international capital seeks secure, rule governed, countries," would undermine development. In response to Amoako's speech, the finance ministers requested that the UNECA develop the compact for consideration by the Joint ECA Conference of Ministers of Finance and Ministers of Economic Development and Planning, planned for May 2001 in Algeria. However, the MAP and Omega Plan (see below), later merged, subsumed the compact, although taking on board elements of the UNECA's ideas.

Returning to the MAP, the whole program was predicated upon an "important prerequisite," namely "a partnership with the rest of the world, especially the developed countries, multilateral institutions and (global and national) private sector players." In this, "the focus of the MAP is not increased aid but increased investments in viable infrastructure and business opportunities" (Department of Foreign Affairs, 2001). As a result, "substantial consultations with the leaders of developed countries and multilateral institutions are also taking place" (Department of Foreign Affairs, 2001).

As part of the rhetoric, this new initiative was said to "offer a historic opportunity for the advanced countries of the world to enter into a genuine partnership with Africa, based on mutual interests and benefit, shared commitment and binding agreement, under African leadership" (Department of Foreign Affairs, 2001). This would "mark the beginning of a new phase in the partnership and cooperation between Africa and the developed world."

Mbeki made a presentation on MAP to the World Economic Forum in Davos, Switzerland, in January 2001. At this Forum, he went to greater lengths to explain the degree of consultation he and his colleagues had done:

> During the year 2000, we spent some time meeting the political leadership of the developed world—the North. Accordingly, in May we met Prime Minister Blair and President Clinton in London and Washington D.C., respectively. We also met the then Governor George W. Bush in Austin, Texas. In June, we were part of the Berlin meeting on progressive governance . . . In the same month, we visited to participate in and addressed the meeting of Nordic Prime Ministers. Again in June, we addressed the meeting of the European Council held in Portugal, which was attended by all heads of government of the EU. In July, together with Presidents Obasanjo and Bouteflika, we met heads of state and governments of G7 in Tokyo, and had the opportunity to hold bilateral discussions with the Japanese Prime Minister, Yoshiro Mori. While in Tokyo, we also met the President of the World Bank, Jim Wolfensohn. Later, in Pretoria, we also held discussions with the Managing Director of the IMF, Horst Kohler. In September, we addressed the UN Millennium Summit and had an opportunity to meet Presidents Putin of Russia, among others. Before this, we had also interacted with the UN Secretary General, Kofi Annan, who committed the UN to cooperate with us as we worked on the MAP (Mbeki, 2001).

Mbeki went out of his way to claim legitimation and support from the developed world. As he remarked, "we [i.e., Mbeki] mention all of these meetings because they enabled us to present to these political leaders the imperative of addressing especially the challenges of African development . . . [It was] very inspiring to hear the entire political leadership of the countries of the North express firm commitment to the idea of a new and concerted effort to address, among others, the challenge of African poverty and underdevelopment" (Mbeki, 2001). Yet, all of these meetings took place without any feedback to African civil society and no interaction or debate with actors outside of the narrow confines of the MAP initiators and ministerial meeting rooms. It is thus barely credible that Mbeki should later boldly state that Nepad was "the outcome of [an] independent African process to confront the particular challenges of our day" (Mbeki, 2002b) or that the Executive Secretary of the UN's Economic Commission for Africa should claim that Nepad is an agenda "with plans prepared through participatory processes, giving voice to [the] people" (Amoako, 2003: 25). Indeed, the lack of dialogue within Africa, contrasted with the activist approach to getting Western approval, provoked President Jammeh of Gambia, to remark:

> If it is an African project, why take it to the Westerners to approve it? Was it necessary to take it to the G8 Summit? That is why I am skeptical about it. . . . If the problem is an African one, what I believe is that before talking to the G8 . . . we should have brought it to Africa, and each country should have gathered its intellectuals and allowed them to debate it—as we did with the African Union project (quoted in *New African,* London, issue 410, September 2002: 18).

Although the plan was still in its embryonic stage, Thabo Mbeki announced that the advocates of the MAP would seek to enroll like-minded elites across the continent: "participating African leaders would form a compact committing them to the program and a forum of leaders who would make decisions about sub-programs and initiatives" (*Citizen,* Johannesburg, January 30, 2001).

The contents of both the MAP and Nepad (which effectively replaced it) can be seen as recycled elements from previous plans and statements that have marked out Africa's postindependence experience at regular intervals. As one commentator framed it, "there have been a number of African initiatives . . . to deal with its [the continent's] problems, and agreements and instruments have been approved, signed and even ratified, without being used effectively to deal with wars, human rights' violations, genocide, and also with prevailing under-development and poverty" (*Mmegi,* Gaborone, February 2–8, 2001). This conundrum is an obstacle facing Nepad's credibility. In other words, given the large number of initiatives, and their rapid consignment to the history books, why should Nepad be different?

Meanwhile, Senegal's President Abdoulaye Wade was touting the so-called Omega Plan as another recovery plan. The Omega Plan was first presented at the Franco-Africa Summit in Yaoundé, Cameroon, in January 2001, and was then showcased at the OAU's Extraordinary Summit in Sirte in March 2001. The MAP was "designed to present a common front when Africa deals with the developed world, [to] seek aid and investment in return for good governance, and unite African countries against social and economic problems like AIDS. On the other hand, the Omega Plan, drawn up by the Senegalese president, set goals and define[d] financial means to narrow infrastructural gaps" (*This Day,* Lagos, July 23, 2001). Only hard bargaining managed to prevent Wade's Omega Plan from sabotaging African unity before it had even begun, particularly when Wade began claiming that his plan was "a practical initiative for overcoming Africa's economic difficulties" while asserting that the MAP was "more of a manifesto" (*Daily News,* Gaborone, June 28, 2001). Of note, and highly revealing, the South African Department of Foreign Affairs admitted that "the three original MAP Presidents [only] became aware of the Omega Plan for the first time at the World Economic Forum in Davos on 30 January 2001" (Department of Foreign Affairs, 2003).

Yet, Wade's plan was highly problematic. It involved obtaining repayable treasury bonds from the developed world to finance what was essentially a pan-continental infrastructure scheme that, Wade readily admitted and advertised, would advantage Western contractors and businesses. As Wade asserted, "I will show how the West will benefit. To carry out all this infrastructure work we will need foreign and European firms, which are technically more advanced than ours and which can build roads much faster than we could do . . . two-thirds of the resources I'm talking about would go to Western companies to carry out the work" (quoted in "Interview with Abdoulaye Wade," February 8, 2001, www.allafrica.com). However, because, according to Wade, "it was inconceivable to appear divided in front of the international community [Africa] had to speak out in a single voice. Therefore, after 48 hours of long and intense discussions in Pretoria, on July 2 and 3, 2001, [it was] agreed to combine the two projects" [Omega and MAP] (Wade, 2002). This meeting, attended by the five core MAP steering committee countries (South Africa, Nigeria, Algeria, Senegal, and Egypt) and also involving the UNECA executive secretary and representatives from the OAU, developed what became known as the MAP Final Draft 3 (b).

The New Africa Initiative

The MAP Final Draft 3 (b) was presented to the OAU Summit in Lusaka, Zambia (July 9–11, 2001) as a *New African Initiative: Merger of the Millennium Partnership for the African Recovery Program and the Omega Plan* (NAI) and was adopted in the form of Declaration 1 (XXXVII) of the OAU Summit. This gave the NAI indispensable political legitimacy and—at least in principle—pan-African buy-in. At the same time, the endorsement made the plan (now known as Nepad), at least on paper, a subsidiary of the pan-continental body, though the selectivity that must necessarily go with Nepad's strictures on good governance and democracy means that Nepad will be (should be) more discerning. This is because, as various commentators have noted, any plan dependent on or subjected to the whims of the diverse membership of the African Union will likely die a very quick death. After all, the AU is a body made up of "53 sovereign states that still owe the OAU R400-million in back dues [approximately $66 million], are constrained by economies typically no bigger than a U.S. city of 60,000 and insist that virtually all decisions be by universal consent" (*Sunday Times,* Johannesburg, July 7, 2002). Progress from such a body will, undoubtedly, be excruciatingly slow. This paradox, of being officially a pan-continental initiative but one that is by its nature bound to be discriminatory if it is to be taken seriously, is a weakness that is commented on in other chapters.

After endorsement by the pan-African body, the NAI promoters went about garnering international support, beginning with the UN's Economic and Social Council (UNECOSOC) Ministerial meeting on July 16, 2001, in Switzerland, the G8 Summit in Genoa, Italy, on July 20, and the Southern African Development Community (SADC) Summit in August 2001 in Blantyre, Malawi. In a perhaps unintentional—but still damning—indictment of the G8's track record on priorities, Italian foreign minister Renato Ruggiero claimed that "the G8 is, *for the first time in its history* dealing with the questions of poverty [and] access of the commodities from the developing south to international markets" (*Business Day,* Johannesburg, July 24, 2001, emphasis added). But equally, as one commentator put it, "it was inevitable that [the NAI] would be well received by the G8 since it was spot on in terms of timing and political correctness. When you have rioters trashing Genoa in the name of kinder Third World treatment, no politician is going to say it is a bad idea" (*Mail and Guardian,* Johannesburg, July 27–August 2, 2001).

The first meeting of the Heads of State Implementation Committee (HSIC) of the NAI met in Abuja, Nigeria, on October 23, 2001. This HSIC was made up of Algeria, Botswana, Cameroon, Egypt, Gabon, Mali, Mauritius, Mozambique, Nigeria, Senegal, South Africa, Tunisia, Ethiopia, Rwanda, and São Tomé and Principe. One of its key achievements was to change the name from the NAI to the New Partnership for Africa's Development, or Nepad. The HSIC also settled upon the management structures of Nepad, in particular mandating an implementation committee to meet three times a year, reporting back to the AU's annual summit. Maintaining the momentum, the Nepad HSIC, at its March 2002 summit in Abuja, endorsed the Draft Report on Good Governance and Democracy as well as the African Peer Review Mechanism (APRM). The Democracy and Political Governance Initiative (DPGI), as it has subsequently become, was planned to be the basis for determining which states could take part in Nepad, and at what level. The DPGI ostensibly established a set of norms, values, and standards by which African leaders taking part in Nepad would hold each other accountable. The APRM on the other hand stressed the need to motivate political leaders to maintain the key commitments and obligations of Nepad.

Concluding Remarks

This then is the origin and context of Nepad. Unlike the LPA and many other plans and frameworks, Nepad—at least on paper—addresses what it sees as an issue in Africa's developmental malaise, namely the poor levels of governance and the role of African leaders, while at the same time calling for globalization to benefit Africa. But what really sets Nepad apart from similar previous endeavors is that it contains the African Peer Review Mechanism, which seeks to monitor and advise on governance issues. This is a considerable move forward for the continent, particularly as any attempt to apportion "blame"—or even suggest that malgovernance might be a problem—manages to generate considerable debate and controversy. Even today, well into Africa's fourth decade of independence, there are those who still cast Africa's problems as an exogenous problem against which African leaders battle hard to implement real reforms and development, only to be frustrated by hostile (nameless) external forces. A recent comment by Adebayo Adedeji (2002) captures this mentality:

> Every attempt that has been made by the Africans to forge their future and to craft their own indigenous development strategies and policies has been pooh-poohed by the international financial institutions (IFIs) with the support, or at least the connivance, of the donor community. While African leaders can be faulted in many ways, they have made a series of heroic effort [sic] since the early 1970s to craft their own indigenous development paradigms in the light of their own perceptions.
>
> Unfortunately, all of these were opposed, undermined and jettisoned by the Bretton Woods institutions and Africans were thus impeded from exercising the basic and fundamental right to make decisions about their future.

But is it really true that African leaders made a series of "heroic efforts" to implement Africa's development programs? The Senegalese president does not think so: "The previous projects were made to be put in drawers! There wasn't even an attempt to implement them. Not even the slightest attempt!" (Wade, 2002).

Like virtually all other previous plans and programs, with the exception of the African Charter on Human and People's Rights, Nepad is fundamentally a project initiated and drawn up by state leaders. After all, the whole rationale behind the APRM is to underline the need to maintain the necessary political will by African heads of state to adhere to the partnership's core values and obligations. This perhaps is one of the main weaknesses facing the successful implementation of Nepad—the divorce between rhetoric and action. As one commentary put it, "African Governments have largely failed to act on Africa-initiated programs and plans. They have failed to act on the decisions reached at different levels of their own continental meetings, including summit conferences" (*Food Security,* no date). As such, Nepad cannot be seen as an organic program that can count on grassroots support and, more importantly, if some (perhaps many) African leaders are a source of many of the continent's problems, can Nepad gain legitimacy by advancing these same elites as the source of the solution? This is a subject I turn to in the next chapter.

Notes

1. The choice of the word "their" is deliberate. The AAF-SAP was seen in many quarters as very much Adedeji's project and an attempt to defend and justify his LPA—consider Asante, 1991, for example.

2. I am aware of the limitations of the civil society concept and its applicability to Africa—see Bayart, 1986; Makumbe, 1998.

3

Elite Politics, the State, and Nepad Diplomacy

N epad has been sold as a bargain: African countries will set up and police standards of good government across the continent—while respecting human rights and advancing democracy—in return for increased aid flows, private investment, and a lowering of obstacles to trade by the West. As noted previously, an extra inflow of $64 billion from the developed world has been touted as the reward for following approved policies on governance and economics.

According to Mbeki, "the African Renaissance demands that we purge ourselves of the parasites and maintain a permanent vigilance against the danger of the entrenchment in African society of this rapacious stratum with its social morality according to which everything in society must be organized materially to benefit the few" (Mbeki, 1998b: 298). Indeed, Paragraph 1 of Nepad opens with the statement that "This New Partnership for Africa's Development is a pledge by African leaders, based on a common vision and a firm and shared conviction, that they have a pressing duty to eradicate poverty and to place their countries, both individually and collectively, on a path of sustainable growth and development." Paragraph 6 follows with the assertion that "What is required . . . is bold and imaginative leadership that is genuinely committed to a sustained human development effort and poverty eradication."

Bearing in mind that many countries have been independent for over forty years, and perhaps seeking to preempt the question of why it is only now that the elites seemingly recognize that they have duties to their constituents, Paragraph 42 of Nepad declares "there is today a new set of circumstances" that make Nepad and responsible leadership possible. This new set of circumstances is stated in Paragraph 44 where it is claimed that "the numbers of democratically elected leaders are on the increase. Through their actions, [such elites] have declared that the hopes of Africa's peoples for a better life can no longer rest on the magnanimity of others."

And Paragraph 45 makes the assertion that "backed by the African Union (AU), which has shown a new resolve to deal with conflicts and censure deviation from the norm" Africa's leaders have turned the corner.

A great deal of expectation has been raised about the possibilities opened up by Nepad, particularly with regard to the promise to develop a credible peer review process to advance democracy and good government in Africa.[1] Much of this, I would argue, is unrealistic—the logic and modus operandi of neopatrimonial rule and the dominance and nature of extractive economies in Africa, and their relationships with the international system, mean that Nepad's strictures on good governance and democracy cannot be implemented without eroding the very nature of the postcolonial African state and undermining the positions of incumbent elites—an unlikely possibility. Furthermore, such realities have already derailed Nepad's African Peer Review Mechanism (APRM), the cornerstone of the whole project in many observers' eyes and the key ingredient of Nepad as it was sold to ostensible G8 partners.

Essentially, what is argued is that Nepad (and studies endorsing its credibility) ignore the reality that power in African politics must be understood as the utilization of patrimonial power and not as the performance of legitimacy drawn from the sovereign will of the people. In other words, in spite of the façade of the modern state, power in most African polities progresses informally, between patron and client along lines of political reciprocity, is intensely personalized, and is not exercised on behalf of the public good. "The state itself remains the major vortex of political conflict precisely because it presides over the allocation of strategic resources and opportunities for profit making" (Othman, 1989: 114). And the extractive and often enclavist nature of many African economies serves to create a situation whereby broad-based economic activity and long-term planning for development militates against the imperatives of patrimonialism:

> An economy heavily based on the extraction of minerals . . . through multinational companies inevitably turned the state, as the agency through which domestic profits of these enterprises were channeled, into a centralised source of benefits which easily outweighed any rewards that could be achieved through genuinely private economic activity (Clapham, 1989: 107).

The irony is that the type of solutions advanced by Nepad (and dominant agents within the global political economy) would deprive rulers of the means to maintain their patronage networks. In short, to have an Africa based on the enunciated principles of Nepad would actually erode the material base upon which the neopatrimonial state is predicated. And yet Nepad seems to advance the idea that the very same African elites who benefit from the neopatrimonial state will now commit a form of class suicide. The possibility seems improbable. As Chabal and Daloz (1999: 15) point out:

> If political domination becomes embodied in the recognised juridical universe of the bureaucratic state [as Nepad's strictures on good governance demands] political elites would no longer have to justify their prominence through the fulfillment of their patrimonial duties. What this would mean however is that they would have to accept both the supremacy of institutions over individuals and the temporary nature of their political eminence.

With very few exceptions (Botswana, Mauritius, Senegal, South Africa) most of the heads of state involved in Nepad are quintessentially heads of neopatrimonial regimes and certainly do not regard their rule as "temporary" or believe that institutional law should constrain their preeminence. In other words, most African presidents behave in ways that are the antithesis of what Nepad says regarding good governance. Furthermore, a good number of them are heads of enclave economies whose very logic dictates that clientelism is more or less the norm, particularly as very few have ever bothered trying to diversify their economies. What this means is that the commitment shown to the APRM by state elites so far (note, only 24 out of 53 members of the AU have actually signed up to the review) needs to be taken with a grain of salt. The countries that have so far signed on are: Algeria, Angola, Benin, Burkina Faso, Cameroon, Congo-Brazzaville, Egypt, Ethiopia, Gabon, Ghana, Kenya, Lesotho, Mali, Malawi, Mauritius, Mozambique, Nigeria, Rwanda, Senegal, Sierra Leone, South Africa, Tanzania, Uganda, and Zambia. Of these, only two would probably pass Nepad's own strictures on clean government and democracy (Mauritius and South Africa), while perhaps four others (Ghana, Kenya, Mali, and Rwanda) might be—as this is written—given the benefit of the doubt regarding efforts toward moving forward to universal standards of governance and democracy. Others are highly dubious, not least one of the most recent signatories, Angola: "Oil producer Angola is the latest inclusion. Analysts say it will be interesting to see the evaluators report on Angola, where international agencies say as much as $4 billion in oil revenues—equivalent to 10 percent of GDP—has been lost to graft over the past five years. They have also set their eyes on Nigeria, where corruption has eroded billions of dollars in oil earnings" (*Reuters*, Kigali, March 11, 2004).

Certainly, it will be most interesting to see how the regime in Angola plans to be evaluated on its governance standards, bearing in mind it is essentially a military dictatorship where the elites are methodically looting the public coffers to the tune of billions of dollars and where patronage, cronyism, and corruption are systemic (Hodges, 2001). This is a country where:

Lack of transparency remains the norm for all key financial accounts, such as those used for oil revenues and diamond revenues and those of the National Bank of Angola and the national treasury. Parliament faithfully votes each year to approve a budget in which a substantial portion of the monies received by the Angolan state simply does not appear. The official budget is thus a document which bears no relationship to reality, and in any case it is just not implemented for the most part (Messiant, 2001: 292).

It might be advanced that Dos Santos' apparent commitment to the governance agenda of Nepad, like the Angolan budget, bears no relationship to reality and cannot, unless Dos Santos is prepared to voluntarily unravel the whole state apparatus in Angola, be taken particularly seriously. Certainly, his behavior while president of Angola make him and his regime somewhat curious signatories to the APRM and raises interesting questions not only about Angola, but also about other signatories. As Frederik van Zyl Slabbert put it, "Angola is a plundered and failing state. If Angola says it buys into Nepad, what does it mean? It means nothing" (quoted in *Sunday Times,* Johannesburg, December 28, 2003). As this book seeks to move beyond rhetoric and investigate the reality of the current situation on the continent, it is the credentials of some selected Nepad signatories that I briefly turn to in order to cast light on such contradictions.

Nepad Elites and Their Democratic Qualifications

Next to Thabo Mbeki of South Africa, the Nigerian president, Olusegun Obasanjo, has been instrumental in advancing Nepad's claims to promote democracy and good government in Africa. Yet, Obasanjo, an ex-military ruler of Nigeria (1976–1979) is president of the country in Africa that has become synonymous with corruption and malgovernance—the "open sore of the continent" as Nigeria's Nobel Prize–winning author put it (Soyinka, 1996). This is a country where "government's business is no man's business" and where there is a well-understood dictum that there is "nothing seriously wrong with stealing state funds, especially if they [are] used to benefit not only the individual but also members of his community. Those who [have] the opportunity to be in government [are] expected to use the power and resources at their disposal to advance private and communal needs" (Osaghae, 1998: 21). Clientelism and patronage are absolutely central to the whole political economy of the country (Barnes, 1986; Reno, 1993; Aluko, 2002).

According to Paragraph 71 of Nepad, "African leaders have learnt from their own experiences that peace, security, democracy, good governance, human rights and sound economic management are conditions for sustainable development." Many observers would remark that such qualities are absent in Nigeria, even under the internationally celebrated rule of Obasanjo. While Paragraph 79 states that "Africa undertakes to respect the global standards of democracy [and] fair, open, free and democratic elections periodically organized to enable the populace choose their leaders freely," a key Nepad initiator is in power in highly dubious circumstances.

Although Obasanjo's election ended fifteen years of overt military rule, the elections in 1999 were limited only to political parties recognized by the military-backed Electoral Commission and although nine parties stood in the local elections, this was reduced to three in the presidential elections. One report summed up the elections:

> As only military-backed parties were allowed to stand in the election, this makes nonsense of claims that this was a "return to democracy." There was also little pretence of democracy in the voting process itself . . . Both Obasanjo and [his opponent] are members of the tiny elite encompassing the military top brass, which has grown fabulously wealthy at the expense of the rest of the population . . . The military fears that if they don't get someone they trust, they will be held accountable for their past human rights abuses. One could add that they don't want to lose the billions they have looted and smuggled out of the country (*IRIN,* Kaduna, February 23, 1999).

Indeed, according to Ahonsi-Yakubu (2001: 94) "there was . . . a crisis of confidence regarding the real intentions of the Government and the Military towards the political dispensation. It was widely alleged for instance that the Government and Military both of which should have been non-partisan, were in fact working for the triumph of the People's Democratic Party (PDP) [i.e., Obasanjo's party]." Ahonsi-Yakubu goes on to add that "It was widely alleged that one of the generals, Olusegun Obasanjo, who was already in the presidential race, had been anointed by the military to succeed Abubakar" (2001: 94).

The whole election process, which saw Obasanjo assume power, was characterized by confusion and fraud, which has been covered in depth by the Carter Center and the National Democratic Institute for International Affairs (NDI), which sent a large-scale delegation to observe the elections. "Among those who witnessed electoral abnormalities in person was President Carter, who saw a stack of ballots neatly placed in one ballot box in precise numerical order. Several other delegates observed instances of ballot box stuffing, including visiting polling sites where [independent election] officials or party agents illegally printed multiple ballots with their own thumbs. In at least nine states, particularly in the South-South zone, NDI/Carter Center delegates observed voter turnouts that were significantly lower than the official tally. In some states, delegates estimated that less than 10 percent of registered voters cast ballots, but official turnout rates for those same states exceeded 85 percent" (Carter Center, 1999: 28–29).

Meanwhile, "many individual polling sites recorded that all 500 registered voters had cast ballots when the NDI/Carter Center delegation and other observers saw fewer than 100 people there during the day. Another significant development that the delegation reported was the altering of results. In many instances, NDI/Carter Center observers recorded low numbers of accredited voters at polling stations, sometimes less than 10 percent of those registered. During the counting and/or the collation process later in the day, however, they found that these same polling stations reported considerably higher numbers, sometimes even 100 percent of the registered voters of the process in the areas where they occurred" (Carter Center, 1999: 16).

Problematically, "With parties and candidates largely keeping quiet about issues, 'big money' politics shaped the transition, particularly in the latter voting rounds. Delegates heard about individuals bankrolling election campaigns and widespread instances of poll officials, party agents, and voters being bribed" (Carter Center, 1999: 17). "Afterward, President Carter signed a letter on behalf of the Carter Center . . . It stated, 'There was a wide disparity between the number of voters observed at the polling stations and the final results that have been reported from several states. Regrettably, therefore, it is not possible for us to make an accurate judgment about the outcome of the presidential election'" (Carter Center, 1999: 12). Bearing in mind Obasanjo sits on the Carter Center's agriculture board and has been a member of the Carter Center's International Negotiation Network, this was quite a damning indictment.

Similarly, Obasanjo's "re-election" in April 2003 was marked by vote rigging and irregularities, which election monitoring groups refused to endorse. In Obasanjo's home state the president allegedly gained 1,360,170 votes (resulting in a North Korean–style endorsement rate of 99.92 percent of the votes cast) while his opponent received only 680. Yet, the number of votes cast in the gubernatorial vote on the same day in the same state was just 747,296. This meant that 618,071 voters apparently (and inexplicably) opted only to vote in the presidential elections and could not be bothered to vote in the governors' race (*Mail and Guardian*, Johannesburg, April 23, 2003). European monitors said in an interim report that the election was "marred by serious irregularities throughout the country and fraud in at least 11 (of Nigeria's 36) states," while American monitors said they had "observed incidences of obvious premeditated electoral manipulation" (*Mail and Guardian*, Johannesburg, April 23, 2003). In response, Obasanjo, in a fashion similar to the way Zimbabwe African National Union–Patriotic Front (ZANU-PF) justified their rigged elections (see Chapter 5), appealed to an "African way of voting," asserting that "Certain communities in this country [Nigeria] make up their minds to act as one in political matters . . . they probably don't have that kind of culture in most European countries." Indeed, according to Obasanjo, those who criticized the conduct of his reelection lacked any "understanding of African culture" (*Mail and Guardian,* Johannesburg, April 23, 2003). Later, at a press conference, which foreign journalists were forbidden to attend, President Obasanjo praised the local media for its "patriotic reporting." And although the EU observer team criticized the performance of the Nigerian media, which it said "failed to provide unbiased, fair and informative coverage," Obasanjo claimed that "the performance of the Nigerian press was just simply magnificent" (*Mail and Guardian,* Johannesburg, April 23, 2003). Just as with Zimbabwe, Mbeki rushed to ignore international opinion and endorsed the election, commenting that "Nigeria has just completed a series of elections, culminating in the re-election of President Olusegun Obasanjo into his second and last term. Naturally, we have already sent our congratulations to him." Ignoring the widespread disquiet about the fraudulent way in which Obasanjo was elected, Mbeki then asserted that it "seems clear that by and large the elections were well conducted" (Mbeki, 2003a).

By contrast, one Nigerian commentator noted that "it is very sad that it is President Obasanjo, so-called champion of democracy and good governance in Africa who, when it comes to his own election, has abandoned the principles he has promoted and preached to others [with Nepad]. Committing election fraud to stay in power was least expected of a person with such 'high ideals' as President Obasanjo, but much expected of President Daniel arap Moi" (C. Onyeani, "Nigeria Tainted Again: Obasanjo Wins Big in Fraud-Filled Elections," *African Sun Times,* New York, 2003). Later, local government elections in March 2004 were "marred by low turnout, sporadic ethnic violence and allegations of fraud," with "no more than 15% of registered voters" turning up to vote at polling stations observed by the foreign media. "Analysts attribute[d] the lack of interest to disillusion in the democratic process following last year's flawed presidential, parliamentary and state elections" (*BBC News Online,* March 29, 2004). Providing an overview of how local government works in Nigeria— second only to South Africa in promoting Nepad's claims surrounding good governance and clean government—the BBC commented that:

> The contests for the council seats . . . are being fought with unusual passion because local governments have, in the past four years [i.e., under Obasanjo's presidency] become uncontrolled centers of corruption. The federal government makes a huge statutory allocation of funds to local governments every month but there is nothing to show for the disbursements. Rather than spend the money on projects with direct impact on the lives of the people in their areas, as prescribed by the constitution, most

local government chairmen and councilors are accused of only paying staff salaries and sharing the rest among themselves. Such was the level of corruption in the local governments in the past four years that many chairmen and councilors who were of little means before their election became affluent within two years. None of them has, so far, been questioned by federal or state authorities to explain either the source of their sudden wealth or what they did with council funds. The local governments are now regarded as easy means of acquiring wealth, hence the apparent determination by many candidates to win the elections tomorrow by whatever means (*BBC News Online*, March 27, 2004).

In fact, it is for failing to do anything meaningful regarding mass corruption in Nigeria that Obasanjo was threatened with impeachment. Indeed, "[Obasanjo] has declined to target the officers who plundered billions while in power, among whom the most notable is General Ibrahim Babangida, a former military ruler who has yet to explain what happened to a windfall of nearly $12 billion that came Nigeria's way when oil prices surged during the Gulf War" (*Guardian*, London, June 15, 1999). This is probably unsurprising, bearing in mind that during Obasanjo's previous tenure as president in the 1970s "the fight against corruption which had hitherto been pursued with much vigour . . . fizzled out into empty rhetorics and harmless rituals" and that "the Obasanjo regime was enmeshed in the scandal surrounding the N2.8 billion naira missing from the coffers of the Nigerian National Petroleum Corporation (NNPC)" (Nwankwo, 2002: 10–11). Other reasons for the impeachment attempt included breaching the constitution, interfering in the affairs of the National Assembly and the judiciary, and the nonimplementation of the annual budget. The massacre of hundreds of civilians by the Nigerian army in Odi, Bayelsa State, in November 1999, and in Benue State in October 2001, was also mentioned. Obasanjo survived by summoning all his party governors, many openly critical of his administration, and promising them that they would be returned unopposed by the Peoples Democratic Party if they dropped the impeachment threat. The threat was duly abandoned. Moving away from Obasanjo's dubious democratic credentials, since being in power Obasanjo has been almost a caricature of the Big Man's operation: a bloated civil service surrounds the president, who dispenses largesse and indulges in profligate spending and ostentation. Certainly, this contradicts Nepad's bold claims as Nigeria under Obasanjo has *not* followed "commitments towards meeting basic standards of good governance and democratic behavior" (Paragraph 82, Nepad), nor has the country changed in any meaningful way, except that now it is not ruled by a military strongman; it is currently run by an ex-military strongman, with the full backing of other military strongmen.[2]

Intriguingly, it is very difficult to see how Obasanjo, one of the key initiators and promoters of Nepad, fits with its strictures relating to good governance and economic probity and management. The continuing denial of basic human rights in the Niger Delta (Okonta and Douglas, 2003) in and of itself somewhat precludes Obasanjo's administration from taking part in any recovery plan ostensibly based on democracy and equality. Certainly, how Obasanjo fulfills Paragraph 88, which states that Nepad members will "enhanc[e] the quality of economic and public financial management as well as corporate governance," is difficult to observe regarding current practice under Obasanjo's administration:

> There are about 45 ministers and over 100 special advisers, senior special advisers and special assistants. Each senior minister has a 607 Peugeot car, one Land Cruiser jeep, a 504 pilot car, a 406 saloon car, a 504 station wagon, one car for madam and where the madams are many, then several cars. Sometimes, there are mistresses who are also served accordingly. One Peugeot 504 for the children, one for the special assistant, one for the press secretary and another for the personal assistant. This means a senior minister has at least 10 cars attached to him or her and some are even known to have up to 20. . . . As well, there are about 200 cars attached to the presidency in addition to 300 CVUs,[3] which by the way include 70 long chassis Mercedes limousines. The president [also] recently bought a brand new presidential jet to add to his fleet. All this in a country where 70 percent of the population live in extreme penury . . . Whenever the president has cause to travel out of this country on any of his junkets—and such causes have arisen over 100 times since May 1999—he does so in style with more than 100 people in tow. No wonder last year [2001], even though only N6.2 billion [$49 million] was approved in the 2001 budget for the president's office, by the end of the year, the presidency had guzzled N31 billion [$243 million]. Yet he insists he has not breached the constitution. Maybe the president would need to be taught what constitutes a breach of the constitution. With all these, should it surprise anyone that our president's call for debt forgiveness of the nation's $28 billion foreign debt has been rebuffed? (*Daily Trust,* Abuja, September 16, 2002).

It should also be noted that members of Obasanjo's presidential delegation receive per diems of $1,500 for every day they travel out of Nigeria (Ikhariale, 2001). A journalist, Nnamdi Onyeuma, was arrested in June 2001—on the direct orders of Obasanjo—for alleging that Obasanjo receives $1 million in allowances for each trip he undertakes overseas and that the president had, by May 30, 2001, made $58 million in allowances in two years. The decision by Obasanjo to spend $13 million on a Nigerian satellite and $600 million on the 2003 All-Africa Games continues the trend: a demonstration of Obasanjo as a Big Man, a man of substance and modernity, even while the country falls apart.[4] Meanwhile, in November 2004 the Nepad stalwart was forced to admit that his farm alone brought in $250,000 a month to the Obasanjo accounts—while the majority of the population lives on less than $1 a day (*BBC News Online,* November 24, 2004).

In fact, it was recently revealed that about 80 percent of Nigeria's oil and natural gas revenues accrues to just 1 percent of the country's population. This means that Nigeria has the second lowest per capita oil export earnings in the world, put at $212 per person in 2004. The 2004 per capita earning compares to the $589 per person earned in 1980—a decline of more than 50 percent. The same report, based on Transparency International information, estimated that over 100,000 barrels of oil per day are stolen by well-connected insiders, which works out to be worth approximately $1.46 billion a year—and "there are indications that illegal bunkering activities will continue without a firm response from [Obasanjo's] government." At the same time, Obasanjo's 2004 budget was based on an assumption of $23 per barrel for Nigerian oil, $11 per barrel below experts' oil price forecast for Nigeria (Nigeria's crude prices have actually averaged about $40 per barrel in 2004). It is anyone's guess where the surplus finances from oil sales go—certainly not into government coffers (*Vanguard,* Lagos, October 26, 2004).

In the light of the nature of Nigerian politics and the condition of the Nigerian state (Joseph, 1987; Ikpe, 2000; Maier, 2000; Nwankwo, 2002; Rotberg, 2004), Abuja cannot at this time be taken seriously as a vehicle to move the continent beyond malgovernance. In addition, given the highly questionable way Obasanjo assumed power, the democratic credentials of one of the leading Nepad promoters should also be treated with caution. Furthermore, there is minimal buy-in vis-à-vis Nepad within Nigeria itself, even within the government, further reinforcing the perception that Nepad is an elite-driven, top-down project with negligible organic links to either African society or even within participating governments: "There appears to be no high-ranking, middle-level or articulate support staff or bureaucracy to support [Nepad] work. The situation creates doubt as to whether Nepad will outlive the present [Obasanjo] government" (*Business Day,* Johannesburg, October 23, 2002).

Unfortunately, other polities and their leaders within Nepad are equally prominent examples of neopatrimonial systems of patronage, corruption, and profligacy, as well as authoritarianism and undemocratic practices. For instance, Paul Biya of Cameroon, who sits on Nepad's HSIC has "presided over one of Africa's most corrupt governments" and has been negotiating with opposition leaders as he "needs safety from potential prosecution for human rights abuses and the corruption of his administration" (*Africa Confidential,* vol. 43, no. 17, 2002). In fact, in 1998, 1999, and 2001, Transparency International classed Cameroon as the most corrupt country in the world, and it has been regularly cited as *the* textbook case for an African neopatrimonial state (Van de Walle, 1994; Mehler, 1998). Indeed, Biya's credentials are the antithesis of what Nepad is supposedly all about, with him being described as "a predator, not a provider. His CPDM

[Cameroon People's Democratic Movement] party endures the popular acronym 'Chop People Dem Moni' in pidgin, loosely paraphrased, 'They eat our money like it's their own'" (Takougang and Krieger, 1998: 9). With regard to democracy and good governance, Biya "was a reluctant participant in the democratization project . . . [but] he has been able to manipulate it and ensure his continued monopolization of power," while Biya "has utilized corruption to co-opt opposition leaders and other competitive elites in an effort to retain . . . power" (Mbaku and Takougang, 2004: 23, 21). In October 2004 Biya was "re-elected" with 70.9 percent of the vote, with observers from the Commonwealth voicing concern that "many people who wished to vote were not on the Voters' Register, so were denied the right to vote" (*Inter-Press Service*, Johannesburg, October 27, 2004). One Cameroonian commentator noted that with Biya's "re-election," "the economic crisis will worsen. Political predation will continue. The powerful will benefit from the uncontrolled deregulation of the productive sectors and commercial networks, and the little people will try to manage to survive. Led by an absentee captain . . . our country will continue its descent into hell once that October 11 [the election] charade is legitimized" (*Inter-Press Service*, Johannesburg, October 27, 2004).

Similarly, Denis Sassou-Nguesso of the Congo-Brazzaville, one of central Africa's representatives on Nepad's HSIC, is an excellent example of what Nepad is trying to move away from—*"un dictateur criminel*,*"* according to Mayima-Mbemba (2001: 1). The former Marxist dictator of Brazzaville from 1979–1992, Sassou-Nguesso returned to power (and control of the country's rich oil reserves) when he seized the government by military force from President Pascal Lissouba in the 1997 civil war. Sassou-Nguesso had previously lost to Lissouba when he was forced to hold elections (Sassou-Nguesso won only 5 percent of the votes). After building a private army in the northern part of Congo-Brazzaville, Sassou-Nguesso forcibly retook the presidency during a conflict that claimed at least 10,000 people dead.

Later, Sassou-Nguesso scored an unbelievable 89.41 percent victory in the 2001 presidential poll, on a "dubious electoral register" (*Africa Confidential*, vol. 43, no. 6, 2002). The elected president later remarked, "the way the elections were held was exemplary. I wish all African countries behaved the same way we did!" (Sassou-Nguesso, 2002: 152). Sassou-Nguesso's army was, according to reports, "responsible for extrajudicial killings, as well as summary executions, rapes, beatings, physical abuse of detainees and the civilian population, arbitrary arrest and detention, looting, and solicitation of bribes" (United States Country Reports on Human Rights Practices, quoted in *IRIN*, Nairobi, March 6, 2002). Meanwhile, "Congo's primary commodities . . . provided incentives for civil war, but later helped the victor consolidate a new neopatrimonial regime"

(Englebert and Ron, no date: 4). Currently, Sassou-Nguesso, the head of the Congo-Brazzaville's police, and other ministers and military figures in the regime, are the subject of a case under investigation in France as the result of a suit filed in 2001 regarding the fate of more than 350 Congolese exiles "missing" at the end of the civil war in 1999.

Another Nepad stalwart and member of the HSIC is Omar Bongo, president of Gabon, who has been dictator of that country since 1967, a state described by *Africa Confidential* as "one of Africa's worst managed and most corrupt oil economies," where "Gabonese have lost interest in the perennially rigged elections. Turnout at the legislative polls [in 2001] was under 20 per cent and may be lower still in the local polls" (*Africa Confidential*, vol. 43, no. 25, 2002). Bongo has had the country's constitution amended 16 times since in power—all to his own benefit—and in 2003 it was announced that the government had made changes to the constitution in order to allow Bongo to run for office as many times as he wished. A senior opposition politician, Pierre Mamboundou, criticized the amendments saying that they had been made to ensure that Bongo held onto power for life and appealed for help from the outside world (*Daily Telegraph*, London, July 17, 2003). There has been no evidence that any other African president has expressed concern to Bongo over his actions.

Furthermore, investigations continue in the United States to establish how Bongo came to deposit over $180 million in three private Citibank accounts in New York. First raised in Senate hearings in November 1999, it is now the subject of a lawsuit against Bongo in the U.S. Federal Court, and "Bongo's lawyers are trying to establish diplomatic immunity for him as a serving head of a state" (*Africa Confidential*, vol. 42, no. 16, 2001). Meanwhile, with a GNP per head of $4,000, Gabon's peoples should be among Africa's wealthiest, yet most people live in poverty and in 1999 investigators were trying to chase a "missing" $350 million from government coffers (*Africa Confidential*, vol. 40, no. 22, 1999). The recent Elf corruption case in France, "probably the biggest political and corporate sleaze scandal to hit a Western democracy since World War II," revealed that annual cash bribes totaling about $16.7 million were made to Bongo (*Vanguard*, Lagos, November 18, 2003). In light of Nepad's commitment to gender parity and women's dignity (see Chapter 6), one is unsure how Bongo fits in, bearing in mind the scandal in February 2004 whereby Bongo lured Miss Peru to Gabon in order for her to become his lover. Miss Peru was then held for nearly two weeks when she refused. It took diplomatic intervention, Interpol, and a French anti-prostitution humanitarian aid group to get the beauty queen freed from Gabon (*Sunday Times*, Johannesburg, February 8, 2004). Perhaps more importantly though, Bongo is known to have had his political opponents murdered:

In 1971 president Bongo issued a *laisser-passer* (no. 318/71) to known mercenary Bob Denard, who on the evening of September 18th assassinated opposition leader Germain M'ba and his wife in their car while they were returning home from the movies. In 1990 president Bongo had his long-time critic Joseph Rendjambé murdered in his hotel room (Yates, 1996: 122–123).

Meanwhile, Amnesty International has long alleged that torture and human rights violations are common in Gabon under Bongo (Barnes, 1992: 62).

The fact that such men sit on the HSIC of Nepad is both a major cause for concern and, perhaps, a reflection of the nature of the recovery plan. After all, "all are invited to be part of Nepad. And all will be embraced by Nepad" (Amoako, 2002). Problematically, "the initial concept of Nepad was that it was not going to be something any old dictator could join to get the benefits, but a more narrow type of reformist club. This has now gradually shifted to become more inclusive" (*Mail and Guardian, Johannesburg,* November 20, 2002). However, such generous inclusivity somewhat undermines the argument that Nepad will be different from the old Lagos Plan of Action or all the other previous declarations. It also undermines the claim that "the Heads of State who initiated the Nepad process . . . were predominantly elected by their populations" (Kanbur, 2001a). Allowing such archetypes of malgovernance and continental graft into Nepad, HSIC skims over a major question facing Africa's recovery plan: what to do about the billions of dollars stolen by the continent's elites over the past forty years or so?

Nepad and the Missing Millions

Nepad's bargain with the G8 (increased capital flows in return for good government in Africa) is based on the idea that there is a shortfall in funds required by Africa to promote development. Curiously, however, there is very little mention in the document vis-à-vis the massive outflow of capital from the continent. Nor is there much focus on encouraging and mobilizing domestic savings. Both are briefly mentioned in one short paragraph (paragraph 148). This is all the more curious since if most of the wealth taken out of Africa (often illegally) could be returned to the continent, there would be much less need to receive increased aid and investment from the West. This is not, however, a theme with any great prominence in the Nepad document. This is unfortunate as there is increasing work being done on capital flight from Africa that shows that poor macroeconomic policies, changes in political regimes, unstable policies, and the perception of risk all spurs capital flight (Ajayi and Khan, 2000), something which Nepad recognizes, if only implicitly.

In a study of thirty sub-Saharan African countries, Ndikumana and Boyce (2002) estimated that total capital flight for the period from 1970 to 1996 amounted to $187 billion (see Table 3.1). Adding imputed interest earnings, the stock of Africa's capital flight stood at $274 billion, that is, equivalent to 145 percent of the debts owed by those countries. In 2002 sub-Saharan Africa's total foreign debt was "only" (in comparison to the amount shipped out of Africa through capital flight) $204 billion (*Africa*

Table 3.1   Indicators of Capital Flight from Thirty African Countries, 1970–1996 (US$ millions)

Country	Period Covered	Real Capital Flight	Cumulative Capital Flight (including imputed interest earnings)	Net External Assets
Angola	1985–1996	17,032.5	20,405	267.8
Benin	1974–1994	–3,457.4	–6,003.8	–271.9
Burkina Faso	1970–1994	1,265.5	1,896.6	96.5
Burundi	1985–1996	818.9	980.9	108.9
Cameroon	1970–1996	13,099.4	16,906	185.6
Central African Republic	1970–1994	250.2	459	50.8
Democratic Republic of Congo	1970–1996	10,035.4	19,199.9	327.1
Congo-Brazzaville	1971–1996	459.2	1,254	49.6
Côte d'Ivoire	1970–1996	23,371	34,745.5	324.7
Ethiopia	1970–1996	5,522.8	8,017.9	133.4
Gabon	1978–1996	2,988.7	5,028.1	87
Ghana	1970–1996	407.3	289.3	4.2
Guinea	1986–1996	342.8	434.2	11
Kenya	1970–1996	815.1	2,472.6	26.8
Madagascar	1970–1996	1,649	1,577.5	39.5
Malawi	1970–1994	705.1	1,174.8	93.8
Mali	1970–1996	–1,203.6	–1,527.2	–57.5
Mauritania	1973–1995	1,130.8	1,830	167.4
Mauritius	1975–1996	–267.8	465.9	10.8
Mozambique	1982–1996	5,311.3	6,206.9	218.4
Niger	1970–1995	–3,153.1	–4,768.9	–247.7
Nigeria	1970–1996	86,761.9	129,661	367.3
Rwanda	1970–1996	2,115.9	3,513.9	249.9
Senegal	1974–1996	–7,278.1	–9,998.2	–214.9
Sierra Leone	1970–1995	1,472.8	2,277.8	257.1
Sudan	1970–1996	6,982.7	11,613.7	161.1
Togo	1974–1994	–1,382.1	–1,618.3	–155.4
Uganda	1970–1996	2,154.9	3,316.1	54.8
Zambia	1970–1991	10,623.5	13,131.2	354.9
Zimbabwe	1977–1994	8,222.3	10,882.9	149
Total		186,796.9	273,824.3	171

Source: Ndikumana and Boyce, 2002: 44.

Recovery, vol. 17, no. 2, 2003: 10). As an aside, in September 2004 it was announced that there were over 100,000 African millionaires on the continent, worth around $600 billion in total (*African Business*, London, September 2004: 8).

A story from Kenya demonstrates the consequences this graft and malgovernance have had on Africa. A recent government inquiry into the Goldenberg scandal of the 1990s revealed that the amount stolen and the illegal gains generated by the scam could have paid for universal primary education in Kenya for a decade. Goldenberg International was established by corrupt businessmen and politicians as a vehicle to access preshipment financing and state compensation for gold and jewelry exports. Recent evidence from the government investigation has shown that over $335 million were initially siphoned from the state in this way, growing to more than $1.116 billion after numerous transactions took place, involving officials at the Central Bank and very senior Moi allies. According to one report:

> Government investigators believe this to be only half the total proceeds of Goldenberg deals. When the roads and dams that were half-finished or never built, and the sugar and rice that was smuggled in and the state utilities that were bled by graft, are accounted for, anticorruption officials believe they are chasing between £3bn and £4bn of ill-gotten gains, equivalent to more than half Kenya's external debt (*Business Day*, Johannesburg, December 17, 2003).

Despite the change of government in December 2002, a number of the officials implicated in the scandal are still serving as civil servants and members of parliament and some of these have made speeches not only about Kenya's commitment to Nepad and the importance of good governance, but also the need to forgive Kenya's debts. Yet the British high commissioner in Nairobi recently commented that a list of ministers and senior civil servants in Kenya who were not corrupt would "fit on a postcard, or possibly a postage stamp," while noting that a contract worth more than $125 million had been awarded to a company "incapable of commissioning a garden shed and discovered never to have delivered anything more than drawings more or less on the back of an envelope, and hot air" (*BBC News Online*, July 14, 2004). In fact, Kenyan ministers demanding "debt cancellation" reminds one of the comments made by the Angolan minister, Maria da Luz Magalhães, deputy minister for Welfare and Social Reintegration, that Nepad is about reducing Africa's debts and that is why Angola is interested in it (*Times of Zambia*, Lusaka, December 17, 2003). This, from a minister in an administration where the IMF reckons that at least $1 billion in oil revenues disappears each year (*Christian Century*, Chicago, March 22, 2003).

Boyce and Ndikumana (2002: 3) reveal that approximately 80 cents on every $1 borrowed by African countries left Africa as capital flight within a year. Essentially, funds borrowed in the name of African governments were misappropriated by politically connected individuals and channeled overseas as their private wealth. Indeed, "the mechanisms by which national resources are channeled abroad as capital flight include embezzlement of borrowed funds, kickbacks on government contracts, trade misinvoicing, misappropriation of revenues from state-owned enterprises, and smuggling of natural resources. Countries with rich endowments of natural resources, especially when headed by corrupt regimes, have experienced large-scale capital flight (Boyce and Ndikumana, 2002). Concerning Nigeria:

> The Morgan Guaranty Trust Company estimated that Nigeria's foreign debt of $32 billion in 1986 would have been only $7 billion without capital flight. Capital flight accelerated in the 1980s as policy reversals further undermined confidence in the banking system. By 1990 the Lagos *National Concord* reported that the $32 billion Nigerians held in foreign bank accounts was equivalent to Nigeria's huge foreign debt (Ayittey, 1995).

The problem is that to address this situation across Africa would tread on the toes of very powerful elites. That is why any such impulses are tacked on at the end of Nepad as an afterthought with the comment that the developed world is asked to "set up coordinated mechanisms to combat corruption effectively, as well as commit themselves to the return of monies (proceeds) of such practices to Africa" (Paragraph 188). However, this is neither expanded upon nor is there any real reflection or discussion of how or if this is to be done.

Nepad largely fails to ask salient questions such as why is there such a high externalization of African capital and how might that be discouraged? Furthermore, who is doing this externalization—corrupt bureaucrats and businessmen connected to the elites? Footloose African capital investing abroad? Many suspect it is both but that the former have a major share in the responsibility. As one analyst remarks:

> The case for FDIs . . . can be interpreted in two ways. One: the ruling elite has no intention to cut down on their own profligacy. Two: those who are externalising funds (legitimately or illegitimately) have no intention to put controls on their activities. If these conclusions have empirical validity, then the ruling elite's case for wanting an inflow of capital becomes all the more suspect if it is in control of both the state and the major sources of export revenues, such as oil or minerals (Tandon, 2002).

And yet Nepad pins Africa's hopes on increased flows of foreign capital rather than addressing such root causes of Africa's supposed inability to raise enough capital for development. Why this is so is perhaps answered in the response of African leaders to the African Union Convention on Preventing and Combating Corruption and Related Offences. Although adopted in July 2003 at the AU summit in Maputo, as of March 2004 it had still not been ratified, even though it only needs 15 ratifications (out of the 53 members of the AU) before entering into force. Besides, the convention's procedure permits any signatory to opt out of some or all issues related to corruption. Teeth it has not. As Global Witness's report on Angola demonstrates, the international finance and banking industry (not to mention the oil companies) are more than complicit in this looting of Africa's resources and with their no-questions-asked policies facilitate graft, thereby contributing to the continent's problems (Global Witness, 2002). As one Nigerian newspaper put it,

> It is . . . a huge joke to solicit financing of projects that are supposed to alleviate poverty on the continent from those who have more than enough information about how much African leaders are still stashing away in foreign banks. Most prospective development partners from Europe and America are aware that some African leaders who come begging for financial assistance on the wings of Nepad, are indeed richer than their countries (*Daily Champion,* Lagos, December 8, 2004).

Again, for Nepad to do something about this (this time, demanding serious action from the G8) would step on some very powerful and influential toes.

The African Peer Review Mechanism

Noting all of the above—the dubious credentials of a number of Nepad stalwarts and the skipping over of deep-rooted corruption and capital flight from the continent—most focus on Nepad has been aimed in particular at the section on political governance and peer review. As a Scandinavian ambassador commented, "It was this that captured our imagination and made Nepad that much easier to sell" (*Mail and Guardian,* Johannesburg, November 8, 2002). This was because it appeared to suggest a qualitatively different approach to Africa's problems than previous plans and declarations. The HSIC in Abuja in March 2002 approved the Draft Report on Good Governance and Democracy and the African Peer Review Mechanism (see UNECA, 2002) and Nepad's promoters have forcefully argued that the APRM is a positive and demonstrable effort to encourage African states' commitment to "good governance" (Akinrinade, 2002: 3). It was in this context that Nepad staked its claim to being a different document from previous African declarations. Here, perhaps for the first time, was a promise to self-police African leaders: "the most significant initiative ever advocated for moving the African continent from crisis to renewal," as one commentary claimed (Hope, 2002: 397). The very idea behind the peer review mechanism was to connect to the rest of the world on the basis of honesty and mutual respect with recognition of the universality of democracy, human rights, and good government.

According to Nepad's promoters, there will be four stages through which the APRM will proceed. Stage one will see studies commenced to measure the progress that various African countries have made so far towards democracy and good governance (ill defined, it should be noted). During this first phase, participating states will devise a program of action, coordinated by the UNECA. This will seek to respond to the levels of political representation, institutional effectiveness and accountability, and economic management and corporate governance in each country. According to Nepad, once such studies are complete, the UNECA will publish an "Africa Governance Report" and will call together an "African Development Forum" on the theme of "Progress towards Good Governance in Africa." Critics have already noted that this seems to be yet another series of conference meetings and declarations (*Mmegi,* Gaborone, February 12, 2004).

Stage two of the APRM will see an Eminent Persons Review Team visit the country under review to carry out "consultations" with the state administration and its leaders as well as with political parties and legislators. Representatives of civil society are said to be included, although who is to be included and who excluded has not been decided or enunciated publicly. The APRM Panel of Eminent Persons comprises the following: Adebayo Adedeji representing West Africa; Bethuel Kiplagat for East Africa; Graça Machel, Southern Africa; Dorothy Njeuma, Central Africa; Marie-Angelique Savané, West Africa; and Chris Stals, Southern Africa. The credentials of these Eminent Persons will be discussed below.

Stage three will see the review team finalizing its report on the basis of its discussions in stage two and the findings of the studies undertaken during stage one. The material and findings of the review team's report will be evaluated against the pointers contained in the UNECA's Declaration on Democracy, Political, Economic and Corporate Governance. As part of this, the African Union will review the level of democracy and assess political governance through several of its own institutional divisions. Unfortunately, many of the divisions that would naturally be best placed to review governance practices, such as the Conference on Stability, Security, Development, and Cooperation in Africa, are not actually operational, nor likely to be in the near future. Nevertheless, the report will be considered with the government under evaluation and revisions made. In other words, state elites will be given the opportunity, free of civil society oversight, to revise and amend the report as they see fit. The only limits placed on their activities will, presumably, be those placed by the Eminent Persons. This follows Nepad's already well-worn path: limited, if not minimal, engagement with civil society. After all, "until April 2002, no trade union, civil society, church, women's, youth, political-party, parliamentary, or other potentially democratic or progressive forces in Africa were formally consulted by the politicians or technocrats involved in constructing Nepad" (Bond, 2003: 9).

Finally, stage four will witness the revised and final review report, which will be known as a Nepad Country Report. This will be given to the HSIC and upon its adoption the APRM is complete. The country reviewed will then be left to implement the advice put forward by the Eminent Persons. Again, nonstate actors and civil society is not included in this end process and in fact, the reports will not be made public unless the heads of state agree. Furthermore, due to the voluntary nature of the whole process, states do not actually have to implement the APRM panel's advice, and there are no mechanisms or teeth to force them to do so. According to Nepad's position, "the participating states should first do everything practicable to engage it in constructive dialogue, offering in the process technical and other appropriate assistance. If dialogue proves unavailing, the participating Heads of State and Government may wish to put the government on notice of their collective intention to proceed with appropriate measures by a given date" (Nepad Secretariat, 2002: 11). But these "appropriate measures" continue to be indeterminate and obscure and have led to a degree of cynicism over the whole APRM process. Indeed, "these vague measures neither penalize a country for an unfavorable review nor provide it with incentives to undertake the recommendations of the review or take steps to avoid an unfavorable review" (Bekoe, 2003: 5). Yet, "this mechanism will fail in its task if reviews happen only periodically and rigorous criteria—and the consequences for deviant governments—are not spelled out. It seems that African heads of state will be left to judge their own performance. The proposed peer review shows that Nepad leaders do not yet recognize accountable governance as a relationship between governments and citizens" (*Zimbabwe Independent,* Harare, May 24, 2002).

If a country does comply with the review team's recommendations, then it will, according to Nepad process, be eventually given a grade: "Nepad Compliant," "Aspiring to Nepad Compliance, but in need of assistance," "Willfully non-compliant," or "Post-conflict countries requiring special reconciliation and reconstruction" (*Business Day,* Johannesburg, November 4, 2002). According to the logic within Nepad, this is then supposed to facilitate increased aid and foreign investment into the country, depending on the grade achieved. However, as the whole process is voluntary from the start, "The toughest aspect of peer review—awarding 'pass' or 'fail' marks—is . . . neatly dodged, because only those countries likely to make the grade will volunteer to undergo the APR[M]" (De Waal, 2002: 472).

Before discussing the APRM in more detail and the way it has back-tracked from initial commitments, it should be noted that no budget has actually been set for the APRM. Indeed, the proposed plan at the moment calls for the APRM to gather its resources primarily from those states that have volunteered to participate in the review process—countries have to pay at least $100,000 to take part. While the APRM (commendably) emphasizes the need to keep foreign financial assistance low, in order to avoid charges that it is not African-owned, the financing scheme raises deep concerns that the APRM will end up underfunded and devoid of any real political independence. First, states with no real commitment to Nepad principles can cite the lack of funds as an excuse to duck out of the review process. In addition, "resources from African states can also be used to bias the peer review. A participating state may refuse to contribute its levy, as a means of protesting an unfavorable review—holding the APRM hostage" (Bekoe, 2003: 6). Certainly, given the historical failure of African states to meet their financial commitments to previous African initiatives, such as paying their membership dues in the Organization of African Unity or the African Union, serious questions need to be asked vis-à-vis the financing of the APRM and its implications. After all, when the OAU wound down, to be replaced by the AU, the outgoing OAU Secretary General Salim Ahmed Salim indicated that only four countries had paid their dues on time. This improved somewhat by the time of the transformation into the AU: of the 53 OAU members, 16 had settled their dues. This still meant, however, that the AU inherited multi-million dollar debt. And as it stands, the African Union recently reported arrears of nearly $39.9 million out of an operating budget of $43 million. "Moreover, since the funding of the APRM will come from participating countries only and not all the 54 states in Africa, the levy will be disproportionately borne" (Bekoe, 2003: 6).

The Great Retreat

As it was originally conceived (and certainly how it was sold to partners in the G8) the peer review mechanism pledged to offer a disciplinary device to secure compliance with agreed values and norms in Africa. This was cast as a way to improve the legitimacy of African states in their dealings with outside actors and bolster the possibility of improving governance in Africa as a means to secure greater political and economic stability to reverse Africa's marginalization. The very concept of peer review was portrayed as the examination and appraisal of the functioning of a state by other states (peers), by mandated institutions, or by a combination of these (UNECA, 2002). The end objective was cast as assisting the reviewed state's progress in its adoption of approved best practices and to *ensure* it fulfilled agreed-upon principles and values. The APRM itself drew upon Western experience, where an acceptance of regular and at times intrusive peer reviews have been established for a period of time, particularly with the facilitation of the Organization for Economic Cooperation and Development (OECD). But whereas the OECD review process is mainly economic, Nepad's APRM at first promised political reviews and evaluations of governance issues, including democracy.

Indeed, initially the review mechanism was sold as having muscle to rein in malefactors. Such a review process, Nepad promoters originally insisted, had to include measures to ensure compliance. According to Obasanjo, this was because "African leaders could no longer remain silent about the shortcomings or abuses of other African leaders" (quoted in *Africa Recovery*, vol. 15, no. 4, December 2001: 10). Indeed, Mbeki "repeatedly stressed the importance of establishing a credible and effective African Peer Review Mechanism to help decide which countries benefit, and to what extent, from membership of Nepad. Peer review is vital to his vision for Africa" (*Mail and Guardian,* Johannesburg, May 10, 2002). This meant, Mbeki claimed, that the Nepad peer review process should support "certain standards of behaviour, which are agreed, which are clear, *which are capable of enforcement*" (*South African Press Agency,* Cape Town, February 12, 2002, emphasis added). In addition, Mbeki had asserted that "African leaders should set up parameters for good governance to guide their activities at both the political and economic levels. In this regard, it decided that, at its next meeting, it will consider and adopt an appropriate peer review mechanism and a code of conduct" (Nepad Secretariat, 2001b). Mbeki had also previously asserted that "the New Partnership is unique in African history in that African leaders have pledged to co-operate and be accountable to one another . . . leaders must account to their counterparts at summits and interact with their development partners in industrialised countries." African leaders should, according to Mbeki, ensure that "measures for good governance are put in place through which our governments are accountable to their peoples [and] that best practices are agreed upon and put in place for economic and political governance" (Mbeki, 2002b).

However, the whole question over what peer review implied quickly embroiled Nepad in controversy and led to a somewhat ignominious retreat to a vague and voluntary process with no measures to ensure compliance. Prior to a meeting in Abuja in 2002—to decide what form peer review should take—Mbeki suddenly declared (unilaterally it might be added) that the APRM would not review the political governance of African countries (Taylor, 2002a). Mbeki announced that political governance review was the jurisdiction of the AU and thus Nepad would simply focus on economic performance. Mbeki further claimed that Nepad was simply the African Union's "socio-economic program," and asserted that "there was never ever any suggestion that we have a Nepad peer review process that would conduct the work of the Commission on Human Rights" (quoted in *Business Day,* Johannesburg, November 5, 2002). This contradicted what the promoters of Nepad had been saying the previous twelve months or so and prompted a letter from the then chairman of the G8 (Canadian Prime Minister Jean Chrétien), requesting Mbeki to explain what had happened to the governance side of the APRM, which had been a key factor in garnering G8 support for Nepad. Mbeki's reply, circulated among diplomatic circles in South Africa, was reported by local press to have been a "technocratic" obfuscation of the position of political peer review within Nepad (*Star,* Johannesburg, November 20, 2002). One G8 diplomat in South Africa was quoted as saying of Mbeki's explanatory letter that "It [was] one of the worst letters I have ever seen . . . very technocratic, and some of the explanations [were] absurd" (quoted in *Sunday Times,* Johannesburg, November 19, 2002). Mbeki retorted that critics who disapproved of the back-pedaling regarding the APRM were racists who were "self-appointed champions of democracy and human rights in Africa" and who were infused with "contemptuous prejudice" for Africans by daring to suggest that "Africa's political leaders cannot be trusted to promote and entrench democracy and human rights" (Mbeki, 2002d).

According to a senior source in the Botswana government (interviewed by the author in August 2003), Mbeki's break from the notion of political peer review was unilateral and unexpected by the other Nepad members. Diplomats involved in Mauritius' contribution to Nepad (interviewed in Port Louis in October 2003) expressed identical opinions. Governance review was eventually retained as a watered-down voluntary process, as has been detailed above. Responsibility over the political dimension of the APRM was given over to the African Union. Inevitably, given the historic failure of the AU's predecessor, this decision can only be seen as minimizing the APRM's effectiveness. Indeed, there is now a very real danger that the APRM will experience a similar fate to that of the African Commission on Human and Peoples' Rights, which, based in Banjul, has continued to be ineffective, largely due to a distinct lack of political support from many African heads of state.

More importantly, what this practically means is that the effectiveness of the peer review process is now reliant on the influence of peer pressure and public scrutiny. Both of these are hamstrung. As one of the Eminent Persons of the APRM has asserted, "the spirit of the review is not to chastise . . . the aim is to help the country to change" (quoted by *Reuters,* Kigali, March 11, 2004). But the APRM has absolutely no recourse mechanisms if the elites of a given country turn down such offers of help. Bearing in mind the oppressive nature of many African leaders and given that states volunteering to take part in the review process can not only revise the final report as they see fit but can also apparently choose not to even make it public, it is very difficult to see how civic scrutiny will play a meaningful role in the whole process.

The retreat to a purely voluntary review might be seen as a belated realization by Nepad's promoters that an intrusive review process would never be bought by the bulk of Africa's leaders. As one African diplomat (of the Ministry of Foreign Affairs and Regional Co-operation, Mauritius, interviewed in October 2003) pointed out, Mbeki quickly realized that if a credible peer review process had been endorsed, then Pretoria would have rapidly been elevated (by the donor countries) to being the de facto police-man of good governance in Africa, a duty that Mbeki—as the debacle sur-rounding his policies towards Mugabe has shown—is not willing to per-form (see Chapter 5). In addition, pan-African elite solidarity and the historic reluctance to criticize fellow presidents on the continent meant that any review mechanism that might seek to enforce best practices and/or judge others' performances was bound to falter. Furthermore, the about-face threw into focus the overselling of Nepad by its promoters and the easy acceptance by the G8 of the initial plan—note the comment by one Western diplomat in Pretoria that "Perhaps we were naïve, but we were very taken by Mbeki going where very few other leaders—and cer-tainly no Africans has dared. It was this that captured our imagination" (quoted in *Mail and Guardian,* Johannesburg, November 8, 2002). But, the type of intrusive peer review system initially sold by Mbeki in the run up to the launch of Nepad was ahead of even the sophisticated and long-standing OECD, and the European Union has not even tried to introduce such a mechanism. As a result, looking at the current situation in Africa, a political peer review system of the type originally sold by Mbeki would only have called attention to wholesale malgovernance and corruption on the continent, thus immediately sabotaging Mbeki's rhetoric that the "African Renaissance" was already underway. Yet, at the same time, a process with no sanctions or countermeasures against those countries that fail to pass muster means that the review mechanism has no teeth. The newness of Nepad or its alleged break from the past is thus limited, to say the least.

Certainly, the suspicion now is that the evaluation panel will restrict itself to rubber-stamping governance reports of countries that were confi-dent of positive evaluations by the panel in the first place. However, surely "the major indicators of a reliable peer review mechanism should include an evaluation of the type of APRM panel members (are they truth-tellers or biased?)" (Bekoe, 2003: 5). The Eminent Persons panel (appointed in May 2003) is made up of six initial members. All of these panelists are intimately linked to the elite classes of Africa and brings into question any notion of real independence and objectivity. Certainly it makes a nonsense, I would say, of Marie-Angelique Savané's assertion that "We are controversial people back at home and we cannot be manipulated" (quoted by *Reuters, Kigali*, March 11, 2004). The six are: Graça Machel (Mozambique), the wife of Nelson Mandela; Adebayo Adedeji (Nigeria), ex-head of the UN Economic Commission for Africa and ex-minister in one of Nigeria's military-run, coup-generated governments; Marie-Angelique Savané (Senegal), former head of the UN Population Fund's Africa Bureau; Bethuel Kiplagat (Kenya), ex-ambassador under Daniel arap Moi; Dorothy Njeuma, ex-minister of education in Cameroon; and Chris Stals (South Africa), ex-head of the South African Reserve Bank.[5] Cynics have noted that this lineup will no doubt satisfy those elites in Africa who were quick to assert that "Nepad should not be used as a political tool to demand human rights, democracy and other unnecessary conditions" (Namibian Agriculture Minister Helmut Angula, quoted in *The Namibian,* Windhoek, April 15, 2003). Indeed, the whole Eminent Persons panel is devoid of credibility. Take for instance Dorothy Njeuma. In September 2004 during the Cameroonian election, Njeuma told a campaign rally that, "with Biya, there is progress, stability and development . . . if we want more development, we have to show him our support." She also stated that the people should vote for Biya, "on behalf of their sons," because if they do not support Biya, "their sons may not have the opportunity to be where they are" (*Post,* Buea, September 29, 2004). Njeuma, it should be noted, is a member of the political bureau of Biya's governing party. And yet, the Eminent Persons panel is supposed to be independent, freethinking, and willing to critique recalcitrant governments. How does this square with one of its members actively campaigning for a politician who is routinely held up by observers as being one of the worst examples of corruption and neopatrimonialism?

Certainly, from the perspective of the international community, for the reviews to be considered credible, they should not diverge too much from what international opinion knows and thinks about a country already. But this is a key point: what added value will the APRM process provide to potential investors that is not already offered by the Economist Intelligence Unit, Standard and Poors credit ratings, Human Rights Watch Africa reports, Amnesty International's overviews, and, indeed, general knowledge garnered from the media and first-hand experiences? The key answer seems to be that the APRM is "Africa-owned." But this may not be positive. After all, any repetition of the Zimbabwe debacle (Chapter 5) or the situation in Rwanda where African monitors gave the presidential elections of 2003 an unrealistically favorable endorsement of the polls, in contrast with the negative opinions of Western observers, will instantly undermine the APRM's worth:

> If the reviews are not credible then it will depend on what alternative, consistent and transparent monitoring process is applied by the partner countries. To the extent that the developed countries end up paying lip service to superficial or cosmetic reviews, they will simply be helping to entrench an ineffectual political ritual. Therefore the G8 and other developed democracies . . . have to try to make sure that the "reviews" do not simply create a smokescreen behind which corrupt but influential African governments continue with their old habits, confirming the worst fears expressed by the international NGO movement (Schlemmer, 2002: 13).

After all, "The G8 supporters of Nepad insist that the African Peer Review Mechanism (APRM) is the jewel in Nepad's crown and have clearly predicated the amount and quality of their financial support on it. Nepad's political difficulties in Western circles have not been helped by how the prognosis of the APRM has become entangled with the controversies over Zimbabwe" (Graham, 2002: 3).

While defenders of the retreat from the original premise of Nepad argue that volunteering for a review will put pressure on those that do not, this is somewhat unconvincing. The argument has been advanced that an obligatory peer review process under the rubric of Nepad would have undermined the supposedly binding nature of the provisions of the African Union regarding political governance. Yet, as any historian of the AU's predecessor—the Organization of African Unity—will tell you, adhering to "good" political governance was largely neglected by that organization, sacrificed to the pan-African principle of "non-interference" in domestic affairs and, effectively, elite solidarity (Van Walraven, 1999). Why the promoters of Nepad now claim that the AU will be qualitatively different from the OAU when the very same African elites are in power and when the nature of the African state remains largely unaltered is unclear. After all, as Adeleke notes, any renewal project for the continent "cannot be meaningful if it is spearheaded and guided by the current African political leadership, those directly responsible for undermining the very foundation upon which a viable pan-African tradition could have been built" (Adeleke, 1998: 533).

Perhaps the main motive for the about-face is linked to the fear that Nepad would actually result in a split in Africa. If it was to be implemented as a compulsory and credible review process, then various clusters of "winners and losers" would emerge within the continent. The main political (and perhaps economic) beneficiaries would almost certainly be the economically stronger African territories and/or the few leaders on the continent perceived as being serious (i.e., pro-reform liberalizers with an "approved" record on human rights and democracy) by the West. Deviants from this norm and those states with tainted leaders (i.e., unacceptable to the West), would be set aside—unless of course their value as guardians of resources warranted a tactical blind eye. Yet such a scenario would strike at the heart of one of the very few things the African Union actually stands for: pan-African unity amongst its elites. Increased polarization between these elites is not what Nepad was supposed to be about, even if the logical outcome of its governance agenda would have certainly led to such a milieu. Indeed, the APRM reflects an undeniable contradiction within the whole recovery plan: on the one hand it must be as inclusive as possible, in order to obtain pan-African "buy-in" while on the other hand it has to be as exclusive as possible in order to obtain credibility with the West. Furthermore, the APRM, as it was initially sold, created what Van der Westhuizen (2003: 389) called the "dual dilemma" of Nepad:

> First, a mechanism to provide a "seal of approval" is required to assure wary foreign investors, but such a mechanism is vulnerable to being perceived by critics as an extension of "Western imperialism" . . . The second . . . is the difficulty of relating to sovereignty and non-interference, which prohibits fellow African states from interfering in one another's domestic affairs.

A retreat from such a problematic scenario was probably inevitable.

While "good governance" is but one part of any coherent program to tackle Africa's situation, the way in which Nepad has seemingly gotten bogged down (by controversy over the backtracking regarding peer review) is noteworthy. Equally noteworthy is the de facto retreat by Mbeki over his call, linked to the APRM, that the G8 hold African leaders to their expressed promises. After all, Mbeki claimed that "I've been saying to the leadership of the developed world that they need to respond positively . . . to challenge us, to say 'this is what you say but we want to see practical action from you consistent with what you are saying'" (quoted in Mbeki, 2002a: 204). Yet, when Commonwealth leaders discussed Zimbabwe and demanded that Mbeki and other African leaders demonstrate "practical action . . . consistent with what [they had been] saying" regarding democracy and human rights, Mbeki labeled them racists who were merely "inspired by notions of White supremacy" and who felt uneasy at their "repugnant position imposed by inferior Blacks" (Mbeki, 2002c).

Concluding Remarks

The fate of the African Peer Review Mechanism reflects the broader analysis presented in Chapter 1, namely that Nepad neglects how the African state is actually maintained and managed. The retreat from a credible peer review may well be a tacit acknowledgement that aggressively going after this problem simply will not wash with Africa's Big Men. The implications for Nepad were summed up by Jean-Pierre Patat, ex-assistant of Michel

Camdessus, then France's representative in the G8 for Nepad, who stated that:

> The initial spirit of the New African Initiative and Nepad . . . the spirit of exemplarity and peer review . . . is the first condition for achieving significant progress in crucial domains. Without this, Nepad would only be another development plan, focused on large-scale public works (Patat, 2002: 92).

Obviously, Africa's regeneration is not simply a question of advancing "good leadership" or "good government"; the structural impediments to African trade are equally important, and we must avoid a voluntarist approach to Africa's development and not neglect the nature of its relationship with the international system. But, it can be said that without the construction of transparent and accountable government, Nepad's ambitious economic plans, whatever their own manifest weaknesses and the wider structural impediments of the global economy (see Bond, 2002; Taylor and Nel, 2002) are profoundly compromised. Indeed, the failure to act thus far in any meaningful way regarding governance and human rights as situations have presented themselves indicates that Nepad will have a rather muted impact (see Chapter 5). After all, the leaders of Nepad did not need to wait for the APRM to be fully functional before speaking out about misrule in places such as Zimbabwe or Swaziland (Taylor, 2002a), or Malawi or the Sudan. While one is fully aware of the historical legacies that mean that pan-African elite solidarity reigns, the question that needs to be asked is how long will this solidarity trump all else? And can it ever be used to justify inaction and nod-and-wink postures towards malevolent dictators? As Robert Rotberg notes:

> African leaders are expected to demonstrate that they are "fully aware of the responsibilities and obligations to their peoples, and are genuinely prepared to engage and relate to the rest of the world on the basis of integrity and world respect." This is a tall order. Neither Presidents Mbeki nor Obasanjo have employed peer pressure to halt the growing trend toward dictatorship in today's Africa. Neither leader has publicly condemned electoral theft in Zimbabwe or attempts to breach the constitutions of Malawi, Namibia, or Zambia. Neither they nor many of their contemporaries have criticized denials of media freedom in neighboring countries, corruption, misappropriation or squandering of foreign assistance funds, or said much about the leadership causes of the famine now engulfing 13 million people in southern Africa (quoted in *Christian Science Monitor,* Boston, June 19, 2002).

The key problem is that there is a "growing need in this globalizing world to have a strong and credible Africa-wide voice, a voice that draws its legitimacy and authority from being rooted in democratic principles.

There are two directions in which this voice needs to speak—internally, to African nations, and externally, to the court of world opinion. Internally, there is a need to show the way, and to persuade and if necessary to sanction, African nations who stray from democracy and basic human rights, and this can best be done by other African nations, through an organization that is founded on these principles" (Kanbur, 2001a). However, Nepad is unlikely to match the heady expectations that greeted its launch and the APRM certainly will not. This is because to do so involves trying to enlist the support of elites who are expected to undermine their own positions and the positions of their clients and as the Rwandan journalist Shyaka Kanuwa notes, this "brings us to the question, or rather the dilemma: how can rulers who are themselves clearly the problem be part of the solution? . . . These men are not troubled by niceties such as respect for human rights, concern for their populations' material welfare or consensual decision-making. Most preside over decaying military or police states. They benefit from a hybrid of African patronage and farcical parliamentary, judicial and other institutional procedures that contrive invariably to act in the big man's interests" (quoted in *Mail and Guardian*, Johannesburg, July 12, 2002).

In addition, expecting those who benefit under the present system to go against those interests would call into question the manner by which Africa interacts with the global economy (Bond, 2002). It is naïve to expect elites, whose very modus operandi is based on privatized patronage (in Western eyes, malgovernance) and the prohibition and erosion of democracy, to begin implementing and operating by the rubric of "good governance." To do so would not only damage their own holds on power but also reduce their ability to maintain lucrative linkages with the external world. That is why I have little confidence that the commitments to democracy and good government by members of the HSIC such as Obasanjo, Bongo, Biya, or Sassou-Nguesso go beyond anything more than rhetoric, or that the involvement of the likes of Adedeji or Njeuma on the Eminent Persons panel amounts to anything. When questioned about this contradiction between rhetoric and reality, the chairman of Nepad's steering committee, Wiseman Nkuhlu, was apparently "not bothered by the criticism" as he had "a simple answer for the critics." This answer was that "all leaders" involved in Nepad "were democratically elected. So they represented ruling parties from their own countries" (quoted in Mkhondo, 2004: 19). I would beg to differ.

This skepticism regarding the democratic credentials of a good number of Nepad's signatories is shared by others, including the policymaking community. Stephen Morrison, a former United States State Department adviser and currently director of the African program at the Center for Strategic and International Studies has commented:

No one is going to stand up and say Nepad is a bad thing. But people are talking about it less and less because they don't believe it will amount to much. The U.S. administration agrees in principle with Nepad's goals. But the inaction over Zimbabwe's persistent breaches of human rights, the inclusion of some very strange people on the Nepad steering committee and Mbeki's statement that political criteria are not part of the peer review system give rise to skepticism. The interest level in Nepad wanes as its credibility drops (*Mail and Guardian*, Johannesburg, November 8, 2002).

Thus it remains that in Africa, "a very small elite (whether civilian or military) . . . generally favors self-preservation over policies and political structures truly designed to benefit the disempowered majorities of most African countries. In case after case, ruling elites continue to impede the process of sharing political and economic power more broadly" (Schraeder, 1994: 85). And as Ottaway's study on the emergence of a group of "Africa's New Leaders" demonstrates, there are a lot of false dawns and premature speculations about the motives and anticipated behavior of elites on the continent (Ottaway, 1999).

Problematically, pointing this out is seen in some quarters as something to be avoided. In October 2004 the Belgian foreign minister, exasperated by the behavior of the elites in the DRC, complained that "there is a problem with the political class in Congo and Kinshasa . . . apparently there are few people who are aware of the historic task and the challenges they are facing. I have met a lot of people and I wonder if they are the people to transform this country into a democracy and seriously manage it" (*BBC News Online*, October 22, 2004). Anyone who knows the slightest bit about the DRC would concur, yet a Congolese minister immediately remarked that the Belgian's comments bordered on "racism and nostalgia for colonialism" and that it was "Tintin in the Congo all over again" (*BBC News Online*, October 22, 2004). Yet accepting that Africa's leaders do have a role in the continent's denouement is perhaps the first step towards constructing realistic strategies for Africa's renewal (see Mwakikagile, 2004).

This implies that any monitoring of governance standards and the improvement in democratic standards on the continent cannot remain elite-driven as is inherent in the APRM process nor, from the perspective of the donor community, dependent upon the whims of the elites within government. Nor can they be detached from a critical restructuring of Africa's global economic linkages and world trade policies (see Chapter 4). Currently, one of the main positive things about Nepad is that it is an African initiative and that it has generated a certain level of debate within Africa with regard to the continent's development impasse. These facets of the project are worth building on. However, while Nepad remains so dependent upon the Big Men to advance good governance through the APRM, something that goes against the very logic of neopatrimonial rule, then its project to promote the continent's regeneration in the new millennium will likely remain stillborn.

Notes

1. I am aware of the contentious meanings associated with the terms "democracy" and "good governance." I restrict my definitions to those provided by Africans themselves in the *Constitutive Act of the African Union* of 2000 and the *Declaration on the Framework for an OAU Response to Unconstitutional Changes of Government*, also 2000.

2. Or, as the great Nigerian singer Femi Kuti puts it:

These politicians and soldiers
Dem be one and the same
No one different from the other
My people no won know
— "Sorry Sorry," from the album *Shoki Shoki*

3. CVUs are limousines and luxury vehicles from the Conference Vehicles Unit, an arm of the Nigerian state established to provide dignitaries with transport.

4. As part of the All-Africa Games, Obasanjo ordered the construction of a new 60,000-seat stadium in Abuja (even though Nigeria already has at least eight international-sized grounds across the country). The new stadium cost at least US$347 million, about the same amount that the state budgeted for recurrent spending on education in 2001 and twice the amount of the country's health budget in 2003.

5. What is interesting here is that before being recruited onto the well-paid and high profile Eminent Persons committee, Adedeji was a prominent critic of Nepad, denouncing it for ignoring his own Lagos Plan of Action and AAF-SAP. According to Adedeji, Nepad was fundamentally flawed because it sought to make Africa "march towards its future hand-in-hand with its colonial mono-cultural, low productivity and excessively dependent and open economy" [sic] (Adedeji, 2002: 6).

4

Nepad and the
Global Political Economy

This chapter provides an analysis of the economic prescriptions Nepad advances as the solution to Africa's maldevelopment, particularly with regard to the relationship between the continent and the global economy. Much of the hearing that was granted to Nepad in its run-up and at its actual launch can be traced in good measure to the fact that the message communicated regarding the operation of the global economy fitted quite comfortably within the dominant discourse of open markets and liberalization. This is a continuation of trends that have been developing since the 1980s but now seems to have a concrete endorsement by key African elites themselves. Indeed, the proposed "partnership" from Nepad initiators sits happily alongside the current notions regarding partnerships for development as proposed by various Western actors, all of which are based on essentially neoliberal prescriptions (see Ngwenya and Taylor, 2003). Yet by accepting such liberal policies, it is opportune to ask whether or not, like the political prescriptions, the Nepad elites actually follow through with their rhetoric.

The liberalization message advanced by Nepad initiators is regarded as unlikely to advance Africa's broader population, primarily—*but not only*—because the politics of patronage continues to underpin most policy decisions made in Africa and its elites will not break the patrimonial system. Certainly, empirical evidence has suggested that the message of liberalization has not set the market "free" from political interference but has rather stimulated a useful injection of political and economic resources that has the danger of perpetuating—if not entrenching—patrimonial politics on the continent. This is more so when the "governance" strictures from the lending agencies and Western governments (and now endorsed by Nepad) lag behind—and is often subsumed—by the liberalization and privatization half of the agenda (King, 2003). Indeed, the confusion and obfuscation about what governance means has meant that both external and internal elite actors have allowed the term to become synonymous with "open markets." While this grants a privileged position to international investors and their local partners, the foundations of patrimonial politics are likely to remain secure as state elites have, over the past twenty years or so, shown a remarkable adeptness in shaping and benefiting from what liberalization that is allowed to take place (Clapham, 1996b: 173–181; King, 2003). Also, it is necessary to be cautious regarding the scale of privatization that has actually occurred, as there has been an intriguing "taming of structural adjustment" (Chabal and Daloz, 1999) across the continent:

> [Africa] has privatized only about 40% of its state-owned enterprises. And much of the divestiture has been for smaller, less valuable, often moribund manufacturing, industrial, and service concerns. Of the roughly 2,300 privatizations in 1991–2000, only about 66 involved higher value, economically important firms. An additional 92 transactions were in transport, some of which might have been classified as infrastructure. But even if these are included, less than 7% of the sales have touched upper-end infrastructure firms.
>
> Activity has been concentrated in a few countries. Of the $9 billion raised from 1991 to 2001, a third was generated by a handful of privatizations in South Africa. Another third came from sales in Ghana, Nigeria, Zambia, and Côte d'Ivoire. Some 26 African countries, together, have privatized a scant $0.7 billion in assets (UNECA, 2003: 35).

In other words, African elites have been successful in not only resisting wholesale privatization but have also retained control of those parastatals and state-owned concerns that are, in the words of the UNECA, of "higher value" and "economically important." This of course all makes perfect sense if we are to understand that economic policies and decisionmaking in Africa is, in the main, based on the need to distribute resources to furnish clientelistic networks. Certainly, the interests of the ruling elites systematically diverge from the broader idea of raising the general well-being of the populace. This has been shown time and time again in what has been termed the "partial reform syndrome" where symbolic gestures, rhetorical commitments, and promises of change mask and further lubricate the diffusion of largesse and patronage (Van de Walle, 2001). But even where the state does privatize, "African states have retained significant minority equity stakes in the few infrastructure privatizations they have concluded, holding back from the market an average of one third of the shares" (Van de Walle, 2001). What is avoided however, by hook or by crook, is structural reform and policies aimed at broad-based development.

Partial reform neatly allows the elites to demonstrate their liberalizing credentials to the donor community, by permitting limited privatization, but at the same time grants the same actors access to a continued flow of resources in the form of shares and dividends that are likely to accrue from the improved efficiency of now-privatized enterprises. And the fact that a good deal of former state-owned companies are bought up by foreign concerns means that there is limited scope for the development of an independent, indigenous private sector through the privatization schemes—a sector that African governments have been traditionally suspicious of anyway and where any nascent capitalist class has had to be more politically adept than it is economically (Leys, 1996: 161–162). Partial reform has also allowed African elites to cast themselves as "responsible" partners and in doing so has stimulated increased flows of aid in order to support ongoing SAPs. Studies have shown however that though donor funding may improve access to education and health, a moral hazard emerges whereby undesirable behavior by state elites is in danger of being stimulated—however unintentionally—because elites know that their mistakes and/or inappropriate behavior such as corruption, excessive military spending, and so on (see Tangri and Mwenda, 2003) will be covered by the donors (Brautigam, 2000). Indeed, there is the general problem regarding legitimacy when foreign funding supports sectors such as education programs while freeing up the elites to spend that portion of the budget that would (or *should*) have been spent on social services on other, often unproductive, matters.

At the same time, the rationale behind the calls within Nepad to plug the supposed "resource gap" with the injection of an additional $64 billion per annum is viewed as a potential attempt by the elites to seek new externally derived resources, with the possible effect of further postponement of the pressure for a fundamental overhaul of the destructive neopatrimonial patterns of governance on the continent. Finally, the fact that the G8 countries maintain, if not continue to entrench and expand, massive subsidy programs aimed at supporting domestic producers but in effect closing off their markets to African producers, such as agricultural exporters, raises profound and serious questions as to the authenticity of the West's commitment to Africa's renewal.

Nepad and Globalization

At first glance, the high-energy diplomatic initiatives pursued by Nepad's promoters, either singly or in concert with one another, suggested a positive development for the continent. After all, rather than continuing to blame the continent's woes on the colonial legacy or on a philosophy underpinned by *dependencia,* both explanations having more and more lost their currency in the West, they engaged the developed world on its own terms. This engagement and the call for partnership were far more likely to gain a hearing in London or Washington than the rhetoric of anti-imperialism. But, there is the very real danger that unless reality (i.e., actual policy implementation) matches the lofty rhetoric, seeds for a further marginalization of the majority of Africa's peoples exist within Nepad. Certainly, liberalization may grant a highly privileged stratum of African elites the potential to benefit from globalization *and* guarantee them a continued flow of resources to be handily deployed to lubricate patronage networks. But the ordinary African may miss out in such arrangements.

According to one commentator, a key feature of Nepad is that it reflects the position of those African states "drawn together because . . . middle-income developing countries were all feeling the pinch of Northern protectionist trade policies" (F. Khan, "South Africa Criticised for 'Ploughing Its Own Path,'" *Inter-Press Services,* Johannesburg, June 1, 2000). The linkage between globalization, relatively integrated African economies, and Nepad is in fact crucial to understand and will be discussed below. But first, it is important to understand how Africa has so far fitted into the globalizing economy of the world.

The stress placed on liberalization and export-orientated growth over the past two decades or so has led to an unparalleled increase in global merchandise trade. However, although Africa has seen a rise in its trade relative to GDP (excluding South Africa and Nigeria this increased from 45.0 to 50.4 percent between 1980–1981 and 2000–2001), Africa's share in world exports has dramatically fallen, from around 6 percent in 1980 to 2 percent in 2002. Its share of world imports has similarly fallen, from about 4.6 percent in 1980 to 2.1 percent in 2002 (UNCTAD, 2003: 1). While the value of Africa's manufactures increased by around 6 percent per year, this apparently high growth rate is only half that of the type of growth rates recorded by Asia (14 percent) and Latin America (about 12 percent) and is from a comparatively low base. Besides, Africa's growth in the value of its merchandise exports is in the main the result of noteworthy expansions in labor-intensive and resource-based semi-manufactures from only a few select states, in particular Mauritius (garments) and Botswana (rough diamonds). Lesotho, Namibia, and Swaziland also enjoyed some increase in manufactured product exports, but on the whole, the broader continent has not benefited from the growth in global trade. Why this is so is in part because 17 of the 20 most important non-fuel export items from Africa are primary commodities and resource-based semi-manufactures and these products have been growing far less rapidly than manufactures, with the added peril of collapsing primary commodity prices. Indeed, if South Africa and the continent's oil producers are left out, the continent's cumulative terms of trade losses between 1970 and 1997 were equivalent to 120 percent of GDP (World Bank, 2000: 20–21).

At the same time, consumption patterns in the West and new demands related to sanitary and phytosanitary rules stemming from the WTO and/or national requirements has helped to shut out many African exporters. The timely regular delivery and packaging of products, which is vital in the gaining of global market share, as well as high levels of productivity, seems beyond most African producers. This is not particularly surprisingly given the fact that a private sector on the continent capable of exporting industrial quantities has long been frail and largely inept in trying to compete on the world stage. There is a *political* reason for this: "because a strong private sector represent[s] a threat to the ruling group, little [has been] done to promote the advance of indigenous private capital" (Tangri, 1999: 130–131). Where the ruling elites have sought to encourage African business, it has "tended to go primarily to those with political and bureaucratic connections" (Tangri, 1999: 130; see also Himbara, 1994). Such political considerations, which dampen any development of a nascent and independent—and more crucially, *efficient*—bourgeoisie in many parts of Africa, further exacerbate the continent's notoriously unreliable and degenerated transport and communication networks. These networks' problems also have, in part, a political explanation in that many African leaders have rarely sought to promote broad-based development (which includes the maintenance of infrastructure) and instead have concentrated on the control of enclave economies in rather limited geographic spaces (Leonard and Straus, 2003). The same rationale has meant that there has been a lack of energy in trying to diversify key export commodities, with all the attendant problems this has meant vis-à-vis price collapses and fluctuations.

This last point has however spurred a relative questioning by key African elites in countries with some more or less productive industries regarding access to Western markets. Because many African countries are so dependent upon commodities, the continued high level of subsidies and barriers to trade practiced by the West has stimulated a growing call for some type of reform so as to allow exports from Africa to develop. Access to Western markets is a fundamental problem for African exporters, particularly as the bulk of trade barriers (mainly subsidies) are in agriculture, which is where Africa has an arguable comparative advantage. Indeed, how African agricultural exporters can hope to compete in the West when it is estimated that Western nations pay their farmers $350 billion per year in subsidies (nearly $1 billion a day) is clearly problematic.

The example of coffee provides insight into how Africa's engagement with the global economy with regard to commodities is constrained. Coffee beans and final processed coffee are subject to tariffs of 7.3 percent and 12.1 percent respectively in the EU, 0.1 percent and 10.1 percent in the United States, and 6 percent and 18.8 percent in Japan. Similarly, with regard to cocoa, tariffs at the raw, intermediate, and final stages are 0.5 percent, 9.7 percent, and 30.6 percent respectively in the EU; 0 percent, 0.2 percent, and 15.3 percent in the United States. Japan accords tariff-free treatment to raw cocoa beans, but cocoa products exported at the intermediate stage are subject to a 7 percent tariff, while final cocoa products are levied at 21.7 percent. In other words, the West is happy to allow Africa to export raw unprocessed primary commodities yet effectively blocks processed products. The implications for African economies is that not only do they remain dependent upon raw commodities, with their well-known volatile price fluctuation threats, but also Africa misses out on the higher prices up the value chain (UNCTAD, 2003: 23).

On the subsidies front, it has been estimated that in 2002 the global price of cotton would have been more than 25 percent higher had it not been for direct subsidies and support by the United States to their own cotton producers. Oxfam has estimated that cotton subsidies by the United States and the EU in 2002 caused a loss of up to $300 million in revenue to the African continent, which is more than the total debt relief ($230 million) approved by the World Bank and the IMF under the enhanced Heavily Indebted Poor Countries (HIPC) Initiative to nine cotton-exporting HIPCs in West and Central Africa in 2002. In fact, the cost of depressed prices for Malian cotton totaled $43 million in 2001, which was the same amount of debt relief Mali got from the international financial institutions (IFIs) under the enhanced HIPC Initiative! (Oxfam, 2003).

Of course, Africa's failure to benefit from global trade would be less important if it was not for the fact that, forty years after independence, trade among sub-Saharan African countries (i.e., Africa-to-Africa trade) accounts for only 12% of the continent's exports. And of this, five countries dominate Africa-to-Africa trade—Côte d'Ivoire, Nigeria, Kenya, Zimbabwe, and Ghana. Côte d'Ivoire accounts for 25% of the exports, Nigeria 20%, Kenya 9%, Zimbabwe 9%, and Ghana 9% (UNECA, 2003: 40). Zimbabwe's status in these ranks is likely to disappear quite soon, making inter-African trade even less significant. Thus while African countries have failed to take advantage of the growth in global trade, for internal and external reasons, they have also failed to develop in any meaningful way trade within the continent itself. There is the danger that extra-African foreign direct investment (FDI) and ODA flows induce efforts toward attracting external solutions to Africa's impasse rather than developing inter-African trade networks. This is certainly less troublesome from the perspective of the Big Men.

Interestingly, as the July 2001 summit in Genoa of the G8 demonstrated, the West's elites have become apparently concerned and seem amenable to the idea that subsidies must be reduced. But, the question needs to be asked: is the seeming ready response to Nepad genuine or not? The decision in May 2002 to introduce a six-year $51.7 billion farm bill in America, which will boost crop and dairy subsidies by 67 percent, does not exactly point in that direction. Having said that, widespread political unease among African elites at the social cost of liberalization and economic restructuring, as well as growing protests against "globalization" in all its myriad forms (particularly the topic of unfair trade) by massed ranks of dissenters at every transnational meeting point did mean that for a period at the start of the new century global elites had to contend with a number of major issues. While opposition to globalization seemed to be building in the West, the protests at Seattle, Prague, Gothenburg, and Genoa did, by all appearances, rattle the composure of Western elites. The fact that respected African leaders began to express similar misgivings, particularly those from countries relatively globalized and certainly ones where FDI and greater engagement with the West took place, meant that issues surrounding the continued thrust and direction of globalization needed to be taken onboard. And appearing to listen and worry neatly fitted in with the public personas of those like Tony Blair and Bill Clinton, whose images at that time were based on the Third Way of caring capitalism and expressions of conscience. This also neatly fitted in with some of Nepad's promoters—after all, "Blair is a new-style social democrat who promotes a Third Way. Its chief proponent in Africa is Mbeki" (*Business Day,* Johannesburg, March 23, 2000). Blair's claim that his administration would pay particular attention to the continent since, "If Africa is a scar on the conscience of our world, the world has a duty to heal it," (*Daily Telegraph,* London, September 3, 2002) thus neatly dovetailed with Mbeki's vision and agenda, even if only momentarily.

Nepad's Position

The limitations for the broader African population within the globalization debate are important if we are to understand the potentiality of Nepad's agenda. Although South African commentators claimed that Thabo Mbeki was "at the helm of the most imaginative and resolute plan yet to emerge from Africa" (*Business Day,* Johannesburg, July 24, 2001), other analysts have remarked that Nepad was "not the most radical document ever but because of that, there is more chance that the G8 leaders will buy into it" (*Sunday Independent,* Johannesburg, July 22, 2001). So, various tensions over readings of the potentiality of Nepad's agenda are of intense interest. Examining such tensions reveals profound weaknesses in any optimistic assessment of Nepad with regard to implementing its economic prescriptions.

Indeed, it must be emphasized that what Nepad mainly advocates is increased access to the world market for externally oriented fractions (thus pushing the specific class interests of a very narrow—but politically important and wealthy—fraction of society), while at the same time pressing for an increase in resource flows. This will not however necessarily be the panacea to Africa's problems that Nepad authors seem to think it will, although the initiating elites do come from countries that are more globally "locked in" than most other African economies. Crucially, the key Nepad promoters are from countries whose inward FDI stock as a percentage of GDP is the highest, with South Africa at 44 percent, Nigeria 41.6 percent, and Egypt at 22.1 percent (UNCTAD, 2003: 64). It can be said that they are pushing for greater integration, but on more or less renegotiated terms, with the accompanying agenda being for increased "compensatory" flows of resources. But these are, within the current political economy of Africa, likely to be sidetracked into clientelistic networks.

As Tangri (1999) notes, well-connected elites in Africa have not only personally benefited from what privatization and liberalization they have allowed, but have also been able to develop strengthened systems of patronage that have further emboldened their positions as patrons and Big Men. As Silver and Arrighi (2000: 6–7) remark:

> Third World elites were not the passive victims of the U.S. liquidation of the development project. At least some fractions of such elites were among the strongest supporters of the new Washington Consensus through which the liquidation was accomplished. To the extent that this has been the case, Third World elites have been among the social forces that have promoted the liberalization of trade and capital movements.

Why they have done this is, I would suggest, based on a cool evaluation of how liberalization (deftly managed and limited in scope) might not only gain favor with the international community but also provide substantial resources, thus solidifying political power while at the same time granting the illusion of compliance and cooperation, further stimulating more resources in the shape of aid and other capital. Alarmingly, the donor community seems not to particularly care too much about this:

> External financing [is] in fact appropriated by national elites and their local men of straw. That appropriation [can] take place directly—this has happened, for example, with school and hospital building projects or gifts of vehicles for the police or the civil administration. But for most of the time it has taken pace indirectly—by oiling the wheels of a rentier political economy, now privatized, the ruling classes strengthen their position, with the complicity of big private companies which are often considered by aid donors as the only reliable negotiating partners. These abuses are encouraged by the lax attitude of aid donors, who do not follow up carefully on their funding, do not check the precise use made of the funds, and impose conditionality only on increasingly weak public actors (Hibou, 2004: 5).

Numerous studies have shown that liberalization has actually helped neopatrimonial regimes to endure, albeit often transformed into even more repressive forms (Harrison, 1999; Chattopadhyay, 2000; Bartlett, 2001).

The call for liberalization, in a continent traditionally noted for its nationalization and Africanization agendas, has been greatly facilitated by the discrediting of internally oriented nationalist projects and/or calls for de-linkage. With the lost decade of the 1980s marking out Africa's fortunes, debt and decay have left a legacy that has hollowed out what little ideological and material bases of the old nationalist and inward-looking programs were left. At the same time, the opportunities afforded to those state elites in Africa with the vision to "ride the globalization wave" mean that those pushing integration and/or liberalization have had their positions strengthened and are certainly the type of "partners" that Nepad is aimed at encouraging and who the West takes more seriously.

The point is that such outward-looking elites—or at least those who express liberalizing messages—are in a stronger position to demand increased flows of aid resources, often couched in terms of facilitating liberalization and/or softening the impact of difficult economic decisions. Such elites thus have more and more attempted to make use of the global capitalist system and its attendant liberalizing values in a strategy aimed at bolstering their own domestic positions. And if it all goes horribly wrong, donor pressure and/or the perils of "globalization," the "colonial legacy," and so forth, can always be deployed as useful alibis for failure.

Beyond domestic liberalization, reformist impulses that do emerge from this process emanate from a sense that the rules of the game within global trade are unfair and need modifying. Thus, "self-evidently, the trajectory chosen . . . amounts at best to attempting to join the system, to play by its rules and, having discovered that the game is set up unfairly, to adjust these rules somewhat in the Third World's favour" (Bond, 1999: 339). The strategic choice made by Nepad can therefore be seen as an attempt to challenge the West at its own game. This is not a North vs. South engagement however and is not an attempt á la the NIEO to rewrite the global rules. Rather, it is an attempt to use the West's own rules, particularly in regard to the issue of subsidies for Western agricultural products and market access. As a South African newspaper noted, "Free trade is the only issue that [Africa] can beat the G8 over the head with; [we] must do so by shaming them in front of their voters" (*Mail and Guardian,* Johannesburg, July 27–August 2, 2001).

Rhetorically at least, the initiators of Nepad regard the integration of their territories into the global economy as not only absolutely crucial but also inevitable, and as something that can be beneficial to them and their support base. Thabo Mbeki (2000) summed up this attitude when he proclaimed that "the process of globalization is an *objective* outcome of the development of the productive forces that create wealth, including their continuous improvement and expansion," while Nigeria's Obasanjo stated that "we must get used to the idea that globalization is a fact of life. It's a reality of the new age" (quoted in *Middle East Times,* Cairo, July 23, 1999, emphasis added). However, as Cerny (1999: 152) has remarked, "globalization is driven not primarily by some inexorable economic process, but rather by politics: by ideology, by the actions, interactions and decisions of state actors, their private-sector interlocutors and wider publics." Nepad then reflects a particular stance on what opportunities globalization is perceived to offer and is not, as Mbeki or Obasanjo aver, neutral or politically impartial. But accepting this, it is of note that only a very few states in Africa seem to be benefiting from globalization thus far.

The Anointed Few

As has been noted, it is no coincidence that the initiators of Nepad are those elites who come from states at the forefront in advancing liberalization and/or attract the most FDI on the continent, although this point is less salient than at first glance. Of course, the FDI flows must be placed in a global context: Africa receives relatively tiny amounts of FDI compared to the rest of the world. (See Table 4.1.) FDI inflows into Africa declined to $11 billion in 2002 and this largely reflected the two cross-border mergers and acquisitions in South Africa and Morocco in 2001, which were not repeated in 2002. In other words, the figures on FDI in Africa reflect in the main partial privatization in Morocco and the unbundling of cross-share holdings of companies listed on the London and Johannesburg stock exchanges. If one takes out these two transactions, FDI flows to Africa were about 1 percent of the global total. Compare the total FDI for Africa in 2001 to that of Brazil ($22.6 billion), Mexico ($24.7 billion), or Hong Kong ($22.8 billion).

Those countries in Africa that do attract FDI flows are—not coinciden-

Table 4.1   Regional Allocation of FDI Inflows, 1990–2001 (US$ billions)

	1990–1994 (average)	1995	1996	1997	1998	1999	2000	2001
Industrial countries	137.7	205.5	226.4	272.3	486.5	844.8	1,241.5	513.8
Developing countries	59.9	122.4	146.5	189.1	203.9	231.8	248.3	215.4
Total	197.6	327.9	372.9	461.4	690.4	1,076.6	1,489.8	729.2
Africa	2.7	5.0	5.3	9.8	7.5	9.7	7.5	17.7

Source: IMF, 2002.

tally—among the most active in promoting Nepad. (See Table 4.2.) As Table 4.2 shows, we can see that Nepad-initiating countries are those that receive top inflows of FDI: Egypt with $647 million in 2002, South Africa with $754 million, Algeria with $1.065 billion, and Nigeria with $1.281 billion. But, if one looks at the FDI figures for the whole continent, there is no real correlation between good government and democracy and FDI. For instance, Mauritius receives only $28 million, Botswana $37 million, and Senegal $93 million (IMF, 2002). Yet all are held up as paragons of democratic governance. But many of those countries notorious for malgovernance and corruption manage to obtain high FDI: for example, Chad receiving $901 million, and Angola $1.312 billion, among others. Even a country like Sudan can attract $681 million. In fact the largest portion of FDI goes to Africa's extractive sectors (mainly oil and minerals), which have tended to have a less pronounced impact on national productivity and income growth than investments in other sectors such as manufacturing and services.

Key Nepad initiators are at the forefront in advancing liberalization projects on the continent, however uneven this may be. Under Obasanjo, Nigeria has pushed ahead with liberalizing reform and is currently an anointed favorite in Washington (Odife, no date). Setting itself the goal of attracting $10 billion worth of FDI per annum; opening the telecommunications, oil, transport, and energy sectors; and pushing for a free trade area with Ghana to broaden the market for investors, Nigeria has aggressively sought to court foreign resources (see *Business Day*, Johannesburg, April 17, 2000). Cairo, likewise, is following orthodox liberalization policies in

Table 4.2   Top Ten African Recipients of FDI, 1991–2002 (US$ millions)

Country	1991–1996 (annual average)	1997	1998	1999	2000	2001	2002
Mozambique	39	–64	235	382	139	255	406
Morocco	406	1,188	417	1,376	423.2	808	428
Egypt	714	887	1,076	1,065	1,235	510	647
Sudan	18	98	371	371	392	574	681
South Africa	450	3,817	561	1,502	888	6,789	754
Tunisia	425	365	668	368	779	486	821
Chad	20	44	21	27	115	—[a]	901
Algeria	63	260	501	507	438	1,196	1,065
Nigeria	1,264	1,539	1,051	1,005	930	1,104	1,281
Angola	346	412	1,114	2,471	879	2,146	1,312

Source: UNCTAD, 2003: 249–250.
Note: a. Data unavailable.

an attempt to restructure its economy as a site of foreign investment (Mitchell, 1999). It has also seen Egyptian investors taking advantage of liberalization in other parts of Africa: in 2003 Egypt's Orascom Telecom won the bid for Algeria's global system of mobile communication (GSM) at a cost of $737 million. Algiers has been pursuing a liberalization policy since 1995, intensifying with the accession of Bouteflika.

Crucially, South African firms post-1994 have embarked on a massive expansion throughout the continent in mining, breweries, and other industries, such as telecommunications (see Games, 2003). During this period, South Africa has become one of the top ten investors in, and trading partners of, a great many African countries, often dislodging European and American companies. This has been facilitated by liberalization across the continent (and further afield):

> The timing of economic reform in Africa was in South Africa's favour. As African countries, pressured by the forces of globalization and the end of the Cold War, were pushed towards liberalization and reform during the 1990s, so South Africa's political and economic isolation ended with the advent of democratic rule and the presidency of Nelson Mandela. This allowed the South African private sector to actively look for business north of the border (Games, 2003: 6).

More of the same, as advocated by Nepad, would clearly stand to benefit South African corporations (Taylor, 2002b). For instance, both MTN and Vodacom SA have made important inroads into the telecommunication industries of a number of African countries: Vodacom, South Africa's largest cellular phone operator, now operates networks in the Congo-Brazzaville, Lesotho, Mozambique, and Tanzania. South African Breweries have bought a 64 percent stake in Miller Brewing (United States) for $5.6 billion and has acquired Birra Peroni (Italy) and Harbin Brewery (China) as well as a large variety of African breweries. South African Airways has even bought Air Tanzania and plans to build an African regional network.

The Carnegie Endowment for International Peace, through its publication *Foreign Policy,* produces an annual Globalization Index. The 2004 Index, which tracks and assesses changes in four key components of global integration (including such measures as trade and financial flows, movement of people across borders, international telephone traffic, Internet usage, and participation in international treaties) ranked nine African countries in its list of the 62 countries as being the "most globalized" (www. foreignpolicy.com).[1] There is a significant correlation between appearing on the Globalization Index and the membership of Nepad. (See Table 4.3.) These rankings are earned by those elites whom the West "can do business with," with all the attendant attention and extra resources that may flow from this position. What this means is that the key Nepad promoters in

Table 4.3   Nepad States and the Globalization Index, 2004

Country	Rank Among the 62 Countries Surveyed	Nepad Commitment/Role
Botswana	30	Member, Nepad Steering Committee
Tunisia	35	Member, Nepad Steering Committee
Uganda	38	Adherent to the APRM
Senegal	40	Founding country
Nigeria	42	Founding country
Morocco[a]	47	—
South Africa	49	Founding country
Kenya	54	Adherent to the APRM
Egypt	60	Founding country

Source: www.foreignpolicy.com.

Note: a. Morocco stands apart from most African initiatives due to its nonmembership in the African Union, based on the admittance to the OAU (and now AU) of Western Sahara as a member state.

Africa are able to pass themselves off as visionaries and globalizers precisely because of the receptivity in Western capitals to hear their reformist messages.

At the same time, African leaders must manage a more and more restless domestic population that is intensely suspicious of what liberalization actually entails if one is not part of the clientelistic loop and even though such pressures may be contained for the moment, such a position is ultimately unstable in the long run. This reality undermines the potency of Nepad's message and suggests that the call from Africa is crafted by and for a particular section of Africa's leadership who feel confident that globalization offers opportunities for them. However, such readings are based on a rather narrow conception of the global political economy, and a too easy acceptance of, and naïve belief in, the willingness of the West to compromise its power in the service of even the most ostensibly moderate and reasonable elements of Africa's leadership.

While well-placed insiders may, in the short-term, benefit through accessing resources generated through privatization and "partnerships" with investors and the donor community, the reality is that liberalization as it has been practiced on the continent so far has done little to advance broad-based economic development. In fact, tactical engagement policies by elites to maximize benefits for themselves and their clients mark out much of the liberalization processes in Africa. Because of the type of patronage systems that stake out most African polities, only already well-connected people are likely to take advantage of liberalization policies— and it is difficult to see how Nepad will change this, given its inherent limitations as outlined in previous chapters. As Hibou (2004: 8) remarks:

> The appearance of liberalisation should not deceive anyone. The links between political power and the private sector, already very close, have been made closer still . . . The classic extraction of levies . . . has not really ended; it has simply been transformed and transferred. It is now scattered among various patronage networks and numerous economic channels, licit and illicit . . . Above all, no new economic actor independent of the political sphere and acting according to considerations of long-term economic and financial profitability has established itself successfully.

Furthermore, the fact that Nepad is largely quiet on a key issue facing Africa—what has happened to its resources in the postindependence period—prompts one to suspect that a more critical stance toward Nepad's positions is urgently required. Certainly, its premium on plugging the supposed resource gap through the demand for an extra $64 billion per year in aid and investment is something that needs exploring.

The "Resource Gap" and the Dangers of Perpetuation

Nepad states that if Africa is to begin to emerge from poverty, the continent requires a GDP growth rate of 7 percent per annum, which will be apparently sourced from outside in return for African governments getting their houses in order. To achieve this amount, given Africa's present low saving and investment ratio, the continent needs to generate $64 billion annually, about thirteen percent of Africa's gross national income per year, to plug what is viewed as Africa's "resource gap." As an aside, this figure needs to be compared to the amount of foreign investment Africa received in 2003: $14 billion (UNCTAD, 2004).

However, in light of the overall analysis in this book of the broad nature of African states, there is a palpable danger that the $64 billion to plug the alleged resource gap may very well be directed not at spurring growth and development but instead toward lubricating the neopatrimonial systems upon which the bulk of African polities operate. In other words, might Nepad's call for a massive inflow of resources merely serve to invigorate the neopatrimonial state in Africa? And if so, might Nepad then merely be a cover (wrapped up in empty promises of liberalization and political reform) to bolster the position of existing predominant elites—the very same leaders who are responsible for much of Africa's woes? Rotberg notes:

> To provide $64 billion for Africa will depend on massive trust by the G8 that Africa is capable, as Presidents Mbeki and Obasanjo have promised, of taking charge and reforming itself. Many African leaders have thus far only paid lip service to the good words of Nepad. They have applauded Nepad's ambitions, but made no changes at home. Furthermore, it is not

clear that many African leaders are capable of making the abrupt governing improvements that Nepad demands and peer review mandates (quoted
in *Christian Science Monitor,* Boston, June 19, 2002).

It is interesting that Nepad's call for an increase in capital flows to Africa
has been couched as a demand for Africa's own Marshall Plan. Indeed,
"Nigerian President Olusegun Obasanjo called on fellow–African leaders
to show 'total commitment' to a 'new Marshall Plan' for the impoverished
continent" (*Daily News,* Gaborone, October 23, 2001). However, capital
inflows in the absence of economic and governmental reforms (and reforms
in global trading patterns) are unlikely to lead to sustainable economic
growth and development. Such flows may just serve to strengthen the
neopatrimonial nature of the African state. This is because it is not necessarily the lack of capital per se that prevents development, but the very
modalities of governance that divert resources away from the public
domain and into private sites, where it is used to enhance political power,
as well as consumed unproductively and/or externalized (see Chapter 3).
Indeed, revenues that might be put into the service of the public good are
often diverted: "cronyism and rent-seeking have siphoned off potential
state revenues. Taxes are not collected, exemptions granted, tariffs averted,
licences bribed away, parking fines pocketed. As a result, revenues always
lag behind expenditure" (Van de Walle, 2001: 53).

How might the sudden inflow of billions of dollars under the rubric of
Nepad alter this phenomenon, assuming for an instance that such flows will
occur? This question needs to be asked, particularly when African leaders
are suspicious of and resent the notion of conditionalities. Indeed, this leads
me to another point regarding the demand that Africa receive a Marshall
Plan. The fact is that flows from the plan had a whole string of conditionalities attached to it: stabilize exchange rates, curb inflation, balance budgets,
and so on, while calling for recipients to eliminate trade barriers, decontrol
prices, and limit state involvement in the economy. Bearing in mind that
conditionalities are routinely denounced as "neoimperialism," it is intriguing to see Nepad being touted as advocating such policies through a new
Marshall Plan. Unless, of course, the understanding of the Marshall Plan by
Africa's elites is limited to the belief that it was simply the transferral of
resources from the United States without any strings attached, something
that perhaps African leaders feel should now be practiced on the continent.
That this may be a possibility was demonstrated by the Foreign Minister of
Lesotho's assertion that finances should simply flow without *any* conditionalities, as "We do not need Western countries to tell us how to solve our
internal problems. They should assist us by injecting money . . . without
telling us how to go about it" (quoted by McAdam, 2002). Obasanjo himself has remarked that "one of the things I abhor is the threat to withhold

aid," as if conditionalities are unjustified, no matter what (*This Day,* Lagos, March 1, 2002).

If it is the case that Nepad's promoters think that Africa has missed out on an equivalent Marshall Plan then the project is based on faulty assumptions, for it ignores the huge amount of capital that has already flowed to Africa, not least in the shape of aid. In her study of aid to Africa, Lancaster estimates that between 1970 and 1996 sub-Saharan Africa received a net inflow of aid of $408.2 billion at constant 1995 prices (1999: 70). This figure, it should be noted, ignores the massive amount that flowed into Africa in the 1960s and the continued flow of aid post-1996 to date. Indeed, Africa has already received aid equivalent to six Marshall Plans (Guest, 2004: 150). The idea that Africa never received the equivalent of a Marshall Plan and thus now deserves one is thus erroneous:

> It has long been fashionable in certain circles to advocate a "Marshall Plan" for Africa . . . but in fact Africa's dismal performance has come in the context of a substantial flow of aid resources . . . [Aid increased] by an astounding annual average of 5 percent in real terms between 1970 and 1995 . . . At their peak, the Marshall Plan resources accounted for some 2.5 percent of the GDP of countries like France and Germany. By 1996, excluding South Africa and Nigeria, the average African country received the equivalent of 12.3 percent of its GDP in ODA, an international transfer . . . unprecedented in historical terms (Van de Walle, 2001: 7–8).

Indeed a look at the amount of overseas development assistance (ODA) received as a percentage of GDP reveals that most African countries collect aid way beyond what Marshall Plan recipients received. (See Table 4.4.)

Nepad is based on the premise that there has been some sort of absence of funds coming to Africa. Such a position, which is based on the idea that this Marshall Plan will arrive if African leaders cooperate and "behave," is problematic. Furthermore, as evidenced in the huge amount of capital flight that occurs in Africa yearly, as well as the misuse of capital inflows to service the neopatrimonial state and that works against good government and accountability, simply increasing flows of resources to the continent is not going to change much and may well act to bolster patronage networks which are corrupt and inimical to development. This is particularly so as Nepad's own promoters seem hesitant to practically address this problem of malgovernance, even when it is staring them in the face (see Chapters 3 and 5).

Furthermore, the whole idea of a resource gap that fatally serves to inhibit development is based on faulty economic grounds. The fact is, if an investment project is attractive enough it will get finance, either local or international. As Rimmer (2003: 475) notes, talking of the 1960s (perhaps indicating how little Nepad's approach to the "resource gap" has progressed):

Table 4.4   Overseas Development Assistance (ODA) Received
as Percentage of GDP, 1990 and 2001

Country	ODA Received as Percentage of GDP		Country	ODA Received as Percentage of GDP	
	1990	2001		1990	2001
Libya	0.1	—a	Senegal	14.4	9.0
Gabon	2.2	0.2	Guinea	10.4	9.1
Algeria	0.4	0.3	Djibouti	46.4	9.6
South Africa	—a	0.4	Zambia	14.6	10.3
Nigeria	0.9	0.4	Chad	18.0	11.2
Mauritius	3.7	0.5	Benin	14.5	11.5
Botswana	3.9	0.6	Ghana	9.6	12.3
Equatorial Guinea	46.0	0.7	Comoros	17.3	12.5
Egypt	12.6	1.3	Niger	16.0	12.7
Sudan	6.2	1.4	Gambia	31.3	13.0
Morocco	4.1	1.5	Cape Verde	31.8	13.0
Zimbabwe	3.9	1.8	Mali	19.9	13.2
Côte d'Ivoire	6.4	1.8	Tanzania	27.5	13.2
Tunisia	3.2	1.9	Uganda	15.5	13.8
Swaziland	6.1	2.3	Burkina Faso	12.0	15.6
Congo-Brazzaville	7.8	2.7	Rwanda	11.3	17.1
Angola	2.6	2.8	Ethiopia	14.8	17.3
Namibia	4.4	3.5	Burundi	23.3	19.0
Togo	16.0	3.7	Malawi	26.8	23.0
Kenya	13.9	4.0	Mozambique	40.7	25.9
Cameroon	4.0	4.7	Mauritania	23.3	26.0
Democratic Republic of Congo	9.6	4.8	Guinea-Bissau	52.7	29.4
Lesotho	22.8	6.8	Eritrea	—a	40.7
Madagascar	12.9	7.7	South Leone	9.4	44.5
Central African Republic	16.8	7.9	São Tomé and Principe	95.0	80.8

Source: UNDP, 2003.
Note: a. Data unavailable.

The supply of finance was everything, and the demand for finance taken
for granted. This suggested, at best, that not enough thought was given to
the productivity of the investment projects in view. At worst, it suggested
that these projects were generally not of the kind that investors would jos-
tle to support. The ideas were not good enough, the risks too great, the
returns too hypothetical. If finance for investment could be obtained only
by compulsion [or in the context of Nepad, a demand for an extra $64 bil-
lion], one might infer that the obstacle to development was not so much a
deficient supply as a deficient demand.

Nepad's touted "investment opportunities," which the project has sought to
sell to potential investors (twenty high-profile infrastructure projects were
offered up to the private sector), when recently taken by an analyst "to a

number of foremost project finance gurus at a number of South African private banks, all . . . only fell a little short of laughing at the complete non-viability of most of the projects contained therein" (Ruff, 2004: 24). Indeed, a report in late May 2004 noted that "not a single company has taken the bait and invested in any of these projects" (*Business Day,* Johannesburg, May 24, 2004). It seems doubtful whether investors can be persuaded to part with their capital for Nepad's projects.[2]

Yet in February 2004 Nepad Secretariat's Wiseman Nkuhlu claimed that the recovery plan was "fast gaining momentum with scores of new sponsored projects" (*Citizen,* Johannesburg, February 17, 2004). In fact, such statements were rather disingenuous. A report by the secretariat in December 2003 demonstrates the problem with Nkuhlu's assertions. The report listed as a "Nepad project," among others, the West Africa Power Market Development project (Nepad Secretariat, 2003a: 13). But this project actually stems from the decision made in December 1999 by the Economic Community of West African States (ECOWAS) to establish a West African Power Pool (WAPP). Its genesis therefore precedes Nepad quite considerably and its connection to Nepad is obscure. Similarly, the Nile Basin Initiative (NBI) is also claimed as a Nepad project—yet the NBI was launched in February 1999, that is, four years before Nepad even existed. The official NBI website (www.nilebasin.org) does not even mention Nepad. Likewise, Nepad claims ownership of projects such as the Okavango Upper Zambezi International Tourism Spatial Development Initiative (Nepad Secretariat, 2003a: 10). But Spatial Development Initiatives (SDIs) have been part and parcel of the region's development strategy since the mid-1990s (Söderbaum and Taylor, 2003). In fact, looking at one of the most recent Nepad Secretariat's communiqués, it can be seen that Nepad's promoters seek to claim credit for virtually every development project on the continent (see Nepad Secretariat, 2004). As De Waal noted, "there has been a tendency to put everything worthwhile going on in Africa under the Nepad umbrella" (2002: 466).

Yet, three years into Nepad and with not a single Nepad project receiving investments, the Nepad Secretariat suddenly, in October 2004, decided that Nepad was not about promoting development projects anymore, with Nkuhlu declaring that "You are not going to see any Nepad projects. Ours is to analyze, inspire and be a catalyst. To get things moving" (quoted in *Star,* Johannesburg, October 23, 2004). Having failed to "get things moving," the secretariat's retreat from doing what it had previously claimed as a central part of its existence was, perhaps, rather a bit too cynical, particularly since previously that same month the Nepad Secretariat had asserted that its "Flagship Projects" "would become highly visible indicators of Nepad's activities and influence" (Nepad Secretariat, 2004). Perhaps embarrassed by its failure, the Nepad Secretariat seems to have tacitly restricted itself to now acting merely as a promotion agency. It should be pointed out that Nkuhlu himself seems confused on the matter, as in December 2004 he was claiming in a South African Airways magazine that Nepad projects were being successfully piloted across the continent (*Sawubona,* Johannesburg, December 2004). Whether or not Nepad projects exist seems to depend upon the audience.

Besides all of the above, it is doubtful that the rate of development depends on expenditures labeled as "investment"; what is far more important is the productivity, not the amount of investment, and so the *demand* for capital rather than the supply is the key issue (Rimmer, 2003: 477). Aid, despite the massive quantities poured into the continent over the past forty years or so, appears not to have made much of a difference, certainly relative to the amount of capital disbursed. The problem is that for the most part aid disbursements have been transferred to state administrations, and even when the donating agencies (IFIs or actual governments) have tried to maintain some form of surveillance, the uses made by African leaders have frequently been wasteful from a developmental perspective, as have the practices of a great many aid-disbursing agencies.

Problematically, the advocates of the idea that a financial gap is the main barrier to Africa's development seem to assume that aid helps spur investment, when this is not necessarily the case: there is a big danger that aid will be consumed and diverted rather than either invested or used to facilitate conditions for investment. And in fact, there is evidence that large flows of aid over a prolonged period may actually reduce accountability and democratic decisionmaking in the receiving states, while cushioning predatory elites (Brautigam, 2000). Furthermore, investment will only generally spur growth (and certainly development) if it is made in combination with suitable technology, knowledge, productivity, and a conducive economic policy framework, which is simply not the case in most African states.

Nepad's almost sole focus on increased flows of capital (either aid, FDI, or limited debt relief) as the engine of development falls short of any authentic program to solve the inconsistencies between "good" macroconomic policies and a sustainable developmental project. As Tandon (2002) points out:

Nigeria . . . is one of the sponsors of Nepad. Everybody knows that Nigeria is "resource rich" (in oil for example). However, somehow its approximately $20 billion a year in oil revenue alone somehow gets "spirited away." So, then, it has a "resource gap" . . . which, Nepad advises, needs to be "filled" by attracting FDIs as "resources" from outside. If Nigeria is both "resource rich" (oil, etc.) and at the same time "resource poor" (in the sense that it has no money), then this should open the strategic discussion in several possible directions, and not simply the single-

minded, tunnel-visioned, monistic advice from Nepad that the way out for
Nigeria is to create conditions for FDIs to fill the "resource gap."

In short, there is not so much a resource gap in Africa as there is a governance gap. This point brings me back to a fundamental question vis-à-vis
Nepad: it fails to unpack the true nature of the postcolonial state in most of
Africa. "If Nigeria is to choose the option of opening the door to capital
resources from outside 'to fill the gap,' is it not an easy way out for its ruling elite not to do anything seriously to ensure that its domestic natural
resources (oil, for example) are not frittered away? Why should they
change their lifestyles, or their production style, if money is going to come
from outside to 'fill the gap' anyway?" (Tandon, 2002). In essence, why
should Nigeria's elites—or any other countries' elites for that matter—
address the dysfunctional (from a development perspective) nature of the
state if resource flows from external sources are to flow in, in increased
amounts, which may well end up succoring their patronage networks and
thus maintaining the status quo? Incentives for change are, in this scenario,
palpably missing.

This is not to say that Africa does not require FDI or increased capital
flows, or even that FDI cannot lead to economic growth—far from it. But
what it does say is that the environment within most African polities means
that economic growth and development will not somehow automatically
spring from such investment—however or wherever such resources are
found—as Nepad assumes. And given the political economy of most
African states, including key Nepad ones, partial reform and limited liberalization is unlikely to make a huge difference.

Concluding Remarks

Nepad's economic prescriptions are essentially based on the principles of
liberalization and privatization, though with some state involvement in promoting development. This makes nonsense of the Nepad Secretariat's claim
that "Before Nepad we had structural adjustment programs. . . . Their basic
thrust was to liberalize markets and have small governments. Nepad [has]
challenged that assumption" (*Sawubona,* Johannesburg, December 2004).
In fact, Nepad is basically a continuation of such IFI-inspired projects,
albeit ostensibly now advocated by Africans themselves. As numerous
studies have shown, liberalization has often had the effect of consolidating
the power of incumbent elites, although its results are, admittedly, mixed
across the continent (see Cornia and Helleiner, 1994). Furthermore,
because the private sector in Africa is generally weak (often due to political
reasons), privatized companies in Africa are often bought up by foreign

corporations (which does not contribute to economic independence), or are corruptly obtained by politically connected insiders (which does not add to transparency and accountability). When indigenous actors engage in the privatization process, the politics of patronage and corruption, particularly where state resources are regarded as legitimate objects for exploitation, invariably intrudes, raising the question not only about the connection between liberalization and good governance, but also about the international community's actual commitment to clean government in Africa. After all, it has been well documented (Hanlon, 2002) how elements within the state in Mozambique have obtained former national banks during the process of privatization, in the main due to the nonimplementation of supposed strictures on accountability and transparency. Yet Mozambique is held up as a star pupil and a successful liberalizer. The implications of this are that the IFIs are more anxious to ensure African governments' continued commitments to liberalization and privatization than they are to ensure publicly accountable government. The same evidence can be garnered from studies in Uganda (Tangri and Mwenda, 2001) and Zambia (Craig, 2000).

Furthermore, the claim by Nepad that "good governance" will stimulate increased investment is not necessarily correct. As has been illustrated, some of the top performers in attracting FDI are those lucky enough to sit on profitable mineral reserves, not necessarily those who practice democracy and accountability. Besides, it is wrong to argue that the G8 partners can somehow reward Nepad "good guys" by deciding to increase private capital flows to the continent. Private investors base their decisions on the market and the bottom line, not on political considerations or directions from their governments—the fact that Nepad's infrastructural projects have so far received no investment is a testament to this.

A whole host of factors inhibit long-term FDI outside of the minerals sector. These include the small size of internal African markets, decrepit infrastructures, widespread political uncertainty and turbulence, corruption, and hostile policies vis-à-vis FDI (Klein and Hadjimichael, 2002; Morisset, 2002). Fragile basic state institutions, an untrustworthy legal system open to widespread political interference, and a lack of commitment by state elites to long-term broad-based productive investment also discourage FDI.

What is remarkable is that the South African government, a key promoter of Nepad and in charge of an economy that is rapidly expanding into Africa, knows this by its own experiences with regard to its own South African business operations on the continent:

> Despite the South African government's attempts to build relationships
> with African countries based on the government's own political agenda
> and the ANC's historical ties, business has indicated that it will not be
> pressured to follow suit. The cases of Algeria and Morocco highlight this
> . . . trade with Morocco has been steadily growing despite South Africa's

low-key political relationship with the country resulting from disapproval over Morocco's handling of the Western Sahara dispute. Business ties with Angola, the DRC and now Kenya are growing despite a somewhat cool political response by the South African government to the governments in these countries (Games, 2003: 10).

If this is the case with South African investors, why do Nepad initiators presume that non-African investors will behave any differently? And if Africans themselves are not willing to invest in their continent (as demonstrated by the alarming level of capital flight out of the continent), for the reasons outlined above, why should non-Africans be expected to do so?

It is true that Nepad *may* generate some opportunities for elites in those countries that are the most globalized and integrated with the West and/or are ready to obey the requirements placed by global capital that will in turn stimulate greater integration. Such countries are, in the main, those with industrial sectors that are globally competitive. For such states, globalization and the type of message communicated by Nepad make sense. Indeed, it is conceivable that some of the proposed reforms advanced by Nepad regarding economic policy may be enacted domestically. Gradual improvements in state economic administration thus may occur, though this will vary across the continent and will be dependent upon the perceived benefits that may accrue to the leadership and their clients. "But where state office and public resources remain crucial to political leaders remaining in power then achieving 'good' governance will be a highly contested process with African rulers taking little more than token steps to attain it" (Tangri, 1999: 149). And the demand for a greater flow of resources in the form of the $64 billion has the potential of further postponing real reform across the continent. At the same time, the maintenance of subsidies and barriers to African exporters means that any nascent bourgeoisie that may well have an interest in a broader-based economy and responsible government remains stifled and frustrated. In this sense the West is culpable in fomenting patrimonial rule on the continent, particularly when it is seemingly more interested in economic liberalization than it is in genuine democratic governance and popular accountability (King, 2003).

But the key problem remains: the malady affecting the continent is not simply, or even primarily, economic, it is political. Indeed, the point is that if the logic of neopatrimonial rule dominates the policymaking process, as it does in Africa, any policies, whether they are neoliberal or *dirigiste,* will be interfered with by the persistent penchant of the elites to utilize what resources there are for private and political advantage. In a number of ways, Nepad is simply repeating the mistakes assumed by those in favor of liberalization in Africa without being cognizant of issues of political economy:

They posit that development can be "private-driven" and that African bourgeoisies can suddenly have a change of heart and become the engine of the take-off, whereas these bourgeoisies have never shown any commitment to sustained productive investment. They posit that privatization leads necessarily to rational economic decisions and that private agents are inherently more virtuous and efficient than public servants, whereas revenues derived from the sale of state assets can be stolen and squandered, and private agents are bent on defending their own selfish interests rather than the collective good. They posit that democratic governance is compatible with the imposition of full-scale austerity in an environment which is already suffering from acute material deprivation, whereas SAPs' huge social costs are unlikely to be tolerated by docile and passive populations. Finally, they posit that trade liberalization will promote more efficient African economies whereas Africa's small industrial base is incapable of withstanding and surviving foreign competition without public protection (Fatton, 1999: 4).

Indeed, those policies announced or endorsed by state elites will almost always end up being controlled and directed in the service of those who seek to preserve clientelism and patrimonialism and the advantages that accrue from such systems. The losers, of course, will continue to be the ordinary African citizens. From this perspective, Nepad falls short of proposing real solutions for Africa's renewal and may well be, as Chabal (2002: 462) avers, "in large measure at least . . . a commitment on the part of the current (and not so new) elites in Africa to the present [liberal orthodoxy] in order to guarantee a transfer of resources to Africa: a continuation with, rather than a break from, the type of relations that has guided the continent's engagement with the international community since independence." The liberalization message within Nepad seems to be more of a selling point aimed at the G8, rather than anything intrinsically part of Nepad's vision for the continent. While the call for increased market access for African products is sensible and fair, unless polities fundamentally restructure themselves to promote growth and development, taking advantage of an increased market in the West is unlikely to prove the panacea for Africa's problems. And any substantial inflow of resources, as in the demand for $64 billion a year, may only make things worse for the average African as such inflows would, as Africa currently stands, likely only benefit well-connected elites, not the broad populace.

Notes

1. Economic integration combines data on trade, foreign direct investment (FDI), and portfolio capital flows, as well as investment income payments and receipts. Personal contact tracks international travel and tourism, international telephone traffic, and cross-border remittances and personal transfers (including worker

remittances, compensation to employees, and other person-to-person and non-governmental transfers). Technological connectivity counts the number of Internet users, Internet hosts, and secure servers through which encrypted transactions are carried out. Finally, political engagement tracks each country's memberships in international organizations, personnel, and financial contributions to U.N. Security Council missions, ratification of selected multilateral international treaties, and the amount of governmental transfer payments and receipts.

2. According to Senegal's president, these include a tunnel under the Straits of Gibraltar, to be paid for by Europe, as well as a new highway connecting Morocco's Tangier and Dakar, plus a highway linking Dakar with the Indian Ocean ports on Africa's east coast.

5

Nepad and the Zimbabwe Debacle

Nepad has a great deal to say on democracy and governance. Paragraph 43 of its strategic framework document asserts that "Democracy and state legitimacy have been redefined to include accountable government, a culture of human rights and popular participation as central elements," while Paragraph 45 says that "Across the continent, democracy is spreading, backed by the African Union (AU), which has shown a new resolve to deal with conflicts and censure deviation from the norm." The norm is put forward as "accountable government, a culture of human rights and popular participation as central elements." As a result, says Paragraph 49, "African leaders will take joint responsibility for . . . promoting and protecting democracy and human rights in their respective countries and regions, by developing clear standards of accountability, transparency and participatory governance at the national and sub-national levels." Paragraph 53 then states that "The present initiative is an expression of the commitment of Africa's leaders to translate . . . .will into action." Thus, unlike the previous recovery plans and declarations, Nepad is going to be different; it is going to move beyond rhetoric and put the words into action. On the governance front, it is advanced, this is particularly imperative because "African leaders have learnt from their own experiences that peace, security, democracy, good governance, human rights and sound economic management are conditions for sustainable development" (Paragraph 71). Indeed:

> Development is impossible in the absence of true democracy, respect for human rights, peace and good governance. With the New Partnership for Africa's Development, Africa undertakes to respect the global standards of democracy, which core components include political pluralism, allowing for the existence of several political parties and workers' unions, fair, open, free and democratic elections periodically organized to enable the populace to choose their leaders freely (Paragraph 79).

Thus, "The New Partnership for Africa's Development has, as one of its foundations, the expansion of democratic frontiers and the deepening of the culture of human rights. A democratic Africa will become one of the pillars of world democracy, human rights and tolerance" (Paragraph 183).

How Nepad will do this is made clear with the statement that "Countries participating in the initiative will take the lead in supporting and building institutions and initiatives that protect these commitments. They will dedicate their efforts towards creating and strengthening national, sub-regional and continental structures that support good governance" (Paragraph 84). In other words, those countries promoting Nepad will be at the forefront in advancing democracy and human rights in Africa and are pledged to translate such lofty goals and will into concrete action. Indeed, the very objective of Nepad "is to consolidate democracy and sound economic management on the continent. Through the program, African leaders are making a commitment to the African people and the world to work together in rebuilding the continent . . . and to hold each other accountable" (Paragraph 204).

Having unflinchingly staked out its commitments to democracy and human rights, Nepad advances itself as a renewal project underpinned with a strong and forthright pledge to defend the ordinary African against the depredations of the continent's elites. This chapter aims to concentrate on holding Nepad's bold commitment to democracy—signed by African elites themselves—to account. It contrasts the actual action that various promoters of Nepad have taken (or not taken) in the aftermath of but one specific example of malgovernance and human rights abuses—Zimbabwe—with the rhetoric. In doing so, this chapter respectfully takes up Thabo Mbeki's test when he claimed that he had "been saying to the . . . developed world that they need to respond positively [to Nepad] . . . to challenge us, to say 'this is what you say but we want to see practical action from you consistent with what you are saying'" (quoted in Mbeki, 2002a: 204). This chapter investigates Mbeki and Nepad's "practical action."

It is openly acknowledged that Zimbabwe is but one case study—albeit perhaps one of the most high-profile in recent years—of human rights violations and the denial of democracy in Africa. One might easily conduct the same exercise vis-à-vis Nepad's inaction using examples ranging from Swaziland, Malawi, or Equatorial Guinea, through to Nigeria. But whether one chooses Zimbabwe or Swaziland the result is the same: rhetoric with regard to advancing democracy in Africa is compromised by the failure to do anything practical to defend and move toward it.

That the failure to do anything meaningful about Zimbabwe has impacted the project's credibility is without doubt. Even before the G8 Kananaskis meeting in June 2002 a senior U.S. official was asserting that "the sense of scepticism [regarding Nepad] really comes from the crisis in

Zimbabwe, where they had already agreed on the principles of peer review but didn't honour it in terms of coming out and questioning the fraudulent elections." The official went on to ask, "even once you have something institutional in place, will they have the capability to hold their peers accountable?" (*Financial Times,* London, June 27, 2002). The recent British House of Commons Foreign Affairs Committee report on South Africa is full of commentaries on this major lacuna (Stationary Office, 2004). Privately, many diplomats—African and Western—agree with this assessment.[1]

The Nepad framework document, when launched, did have laudable commitments to the developmental needs of the continent. It initially seemed that the attempt to penetrate the shield of sovereignty, behind which too many corrupt leaders have hidden for too long, held potential for advancing the interests of the ordinary African, rather than the elites. Because of this, there was excited talk regarding Nepad's "paradigm shift" regarding democracy and human rights and the importance this had for broad-based development. However, this paradigm shift did not last very long—the public responses by many African heads of states, including key promoters of Nepad, have seen a broad alignment with autocrats like Mugabe and against the ordinary people and—intriguingly—the "partners" in the West, upon which much of the success or otherwise of Nepad clearly hinges. Indeed, though Nepad asserts that the developed world has certain obligations to help entrench and support democracy in Africa, when Western actors do try and help and to encourage this and/or punish transgressors, they are swiftly denounced as imperialists or neocolonialists, if not racists. Zimbabwe is a case in point and it is the situation in Zimbabwe and the response by key African leaders—almost all of them ostensible backers of Nepad—to which this chapter dedicates itself.

The Zimbabwe Crisis

Much has been written on the history of land dispossession in Zimbabwe (Kinsey, 1982; Moyana, 1984; Moyo, 1987, 1995; Palmer and Parsons, 1977; Riddell, 1980; Weinmann, 1996). However, it would be false to portray the current situation in Zimbabwe as stemming simply from "the land issue." In reality, the story of Zimbabwe is the story of "the promises of liberation, shattered in the face of the politics of greed, violence and destruction" (Campbell, 2003: 1). When Zimbabwe became independent in 1980 it received extensive support and aid (though not as much as was requested) in order for it to address the legacies of both British colonial control and the subsequent (illegal) government of Ian Smith. While some commendable advances were made in the field of education and healthcare, by the late 1980s/early 1990s the postcolonial government in Zimbabwe had acquired a reputation for growing corruption (Blair, 2002; Hill, 2003; Stiff, 2000). The brutality as evidenced in the massacres in Matabeleland, where between 5,000 and 7,000 Zimbabweans were killed by the state between 1981 and 1988 (Catholic Commission for Justice and Peace in Zimbabwe, 1997), though often glossed over by contemporary accounts (Mandaza, 1986; Stoneman, 1988; Auret, 1990), also staked out, early on, Mugabe's intolerance of dissent. Thus to cast Zimbabwe as an unremitting injured party of first, colonialism and then, "neo-imperialism," is wide of the mark and has the danger of sidetracking consideration away from the systematic malgovernance of the ruling ZANU-PF regime and the government's responsibility in ruining the country through ill-advised policies (Bond and Manyanya, 2002).

As is well known, it has not simply been the land issue (i.e., the rectification of imbalances in land ownership along racial lines) that has led to the current crisis. Dissatisfaction with ZANU-PF's rule has been long-standing—the abstention of 68 percent of the voters in the April 1996 elections being a graphic example. As the economy declined, opposition grew. That this was directly linked to Mugabe's malgovernance was clear, with the debacle over compensation for war veterans from the liberation war being but one example. In April 1989, the Zimbabwe War Veterans Association (ZWVA) was established and, through sustained pressure, forced the government to start negotiations over the War Veterans Administration Bill (1991), the War Veterans Act (1992), and the War Victims Compensation Act (1993). However, the administration of compensation for victims of the war was marked by corruption and inefficiency. Controversy regarding who was and who was not a war veteran as well as increasing evidence of falsified injury claims on the part of leading ZANU-PF cadres saw the government disbursing around Z$80 million, often to well-connected individuals who did not qualify. This failure to financially compensate real ex-combatants led to the ZANU-PF summit in September 1997 where, under intense pressure from the ZWVA, Mugabe agreed to pay every genuine war veteran a lump sum of Z$50,000 (US$4,000) and a gratuity for life of Z$5,000 per month (*Herald*, Harare, September 17, 1997). Such largesse was estimated to cost the country Z$4 billion (then around US$215 million) and hastened a national financial crisis: immediately on the day the decision was announced the Zimbabwean currency plummeted from Z$11 to the U.S. dollar, to Z$21 to the dollar (Meldrum, 2004: 97).

This crisis deepened particularly after the June 1998 decision by Mugabe to send detachments of troops into the Democratic Republic of Congo to prop up Laurent Kabila. The Zimbabwean force, eventually to total 11,000 soldiers, cost the country a massive amount of money—around $1 million a day—but allowed key elites within the ZANU-PF regime to profit handsomely from looting the DRC's natural resources (MacLean, 2002; Taylor, 2003). Never mentioned by Mbeki or other supporters of Mugabe, the DRC business had an indirect link with the land issue—as landless peasants, white owners of seized farms, the donors, and the opposition pointed out—because resources spent on facilitating the personal enrichment of top Zimbabweans in the DRC could have been spent on helping to resolve the land issue. Yet Mugabe chose otherwise.

It was in fact growing dissent against Mugabe, in particular the challenges posed by both the Zimbabwe Congress of Trade Unions (ZCTU) and the National Constitutional Assembly (NCA) and by the formation of a new opposition party, the Movement for Democratic Change (MDC) that precipitated Mugabe's extreme responses and the subsequent collapse of the country. In other words, the emergence of a strong and credible alternative to ZANU-PF resulted in the methodical destruction of Zimbabwe by its ruling political elites—all in order to maintain personal power. A particular flashpoint might be identified as when the ZCTU compelled the turnaround of a deal made between Mugabe and the ZWVA to impose a special levy on the country's taxpayers in order to make available to the war veterans the package outlined above. But in doing so the burgeoning opposition stoked deep animosity from the war veterans and anyone else with a stake in the ZANU-PF patronage setup. And from this point onward the utilization of the war veterans to clamp down on ZANU-PF opposition, and the use of the state machinery to squash opposition to Mugabe, became brazen.

Of equal importance were the NCA's proposals regarding a new constitution for the country, which led to ZANU-PF convening its own National Constitutional Commission with the task of composing a new constitution. Much to Mugabe's chagrin and deep anger, the proposed constitution was rejected in a February 2000 referendum—a vote that most commentators (and Zimbabweans) regarded as a referendum on the continuing rule of Mugabe. It was during this period that the Movement for Democratic Change emerged under the leadership of Morgan Tsvangirai, the ex-head of the ZCTU. The referendum was then followed by parliamentary elections, marked by violence, murder, farm invasions, forced rallies for farm workers, and so on. The MDC only narrowly lost to Mugabe: ZANU-PF won 62 seats, the MDC 57, and one seat went to ZANU (20 nonconstituency members made up of eight provincial governors and 12 members "nominated" by Mugabe bolstered the president's majority).

But violence and intimidation on a mass scale continued, with the seizure of white-owned farms being perhaps the most prominent—*but certainly not only*—manifestation of Mugabe's attempt to punish perceived sources of opposition to his rule and distribute patronage, even if it meant destroying the country's economy. As Chitiyo (2000) noted:

> The state has pushed to extremes Zimbabwe's historical tradition of imposing short-term racial and political solutions on genuine agrarian problems. The forcible occupation of . . . White commercial farms . . . by groups of "war veterans" (many of whom are clearly unemployed youths, some who were not even born at the time of the war of liberation) is a case in point.

This background of systematic economic collapse and the abandonment of even the veneer of law and order provided the context leading up to the presidential election of April 2002 in which Mugabe was "reelected." It is this election and the subsequent events that exposed as more or less empty much of the rhetoric regarding democracy and human rights emanating from Nepad's promoters, particularly Mbeki and Obasanjo.

The Presidential Elections in Zimbabwe, 2002

Although there were repeated attempts to muddy the waters during the 2002 elections, particularly with appeals to the topic of land, the real issue was the concerted effort by President Mugabe and his ZANU-PF party to retain their hold on political power at all costs—and what was to be the reaction of Nepad's sponsors. Given that Nepad was only launched in October 2001 it was natural *and entirely reasonable* that observers, commentators, and the ordinary Zimbabwean might have expected some sort of stance on the matter—like much of the rest of the world. In many respects, it was unfortunate that it was Zimbabwe—with its racialized aspect—that was to present the initial challenge for Nepad. But then, it would be unreasonable of Nepad's adherents to pick and chose which countries in Africa should be held accountable to broad-based democratic principles and which should not. Besides, civil society and a very large proportion of ordinary Zimbabweans certainly saw the elections as a first test for Nepad—and hoped and expected that its key promoters (particularly Mbeki) would do something to help resolve the crisis (see Kagoro, 2002; Manyanya, 2003).

This was particularly so when it was quite apparent that ZANU-PF regarded both the country and its people as belonging somehow to them. All challenges to their rule were thus immediately interpreted (mischievously or otherwise) as originating from external forces—"Rhodesians," the British, the "white world," and so forth. Such an interpretation grated glaringly against Nepad's own prescriptions. Yet it soon became clear that as the crisis in Zimbabwe intensified, many African leaders—including promoters of Nepad—fell into line behind this view. In effect they positioned themselves in agreement with the view that there was a malevolent white racist conspiracy to recolonize Zimbabwe through the utilization of black stooges in the shape of the opposition and that this conspiracy aimed to turn Zimbabwe back into Rhodesia. This project was/is, supposedly, led by Britain's Tony Blair and his "gay gangsters."[2] Indeed, "the intention of the British to recolonise Zimbabwe is not an April Fool's joke but is real" according to the Zimbabwean government's newspaper (*Herald,* Harare, April 9, 2002). In this light, consider Thabo Mbeki's own comments, at the Commonwealth meeting in Australia in March 2002, that talks of ostracizing Mugabe were "inspired by notions of White supremacy," and that such moves were pursued because white political leaders apparently felt uneasy at their "repugnant position imposed by inferior Blacks" (Mbeki, 2002c). Indeed, according to the ANC's secretary-general, "ZANU-PF is not in trouble because it did not care but because it cared too much" (*Star,* Johannesburg, March 7, 2003), while Mbeki claimed that "The current Zimbabwe crisis started in 1965 when the then British Labour Government, under Prime Minister Harold Wilson, refused to suppress the rebellion against the British Crown led by Ian Smith. This was because the British Government felt that it could not act against its White 'kith and kin,' in favour of the African majority" (Mbeki, 2003c). In other words, according to Thabo Mbeki, the destruction of Zimbabwe is all London's fault and is part of a wider racist plot against a fellow African country.

This type of rhetoric is not the unique preserve of Mbeki or the ANC—it is staple fare in government-owned outlets in Zimbabwe and from the wilder shores of commentary on the matter (see for instance, the magazine *New African*). But, what is significant is that it was precisely Mbeki who had been notably active in promoting Nepad and the African Renaissance. Ironically, it was Mbeki who proclaimed at a conference on the African Renaissance in September 1998 that:

> We want to see an African Continent in which the people participate in systems of governance in which they are truly able to determine their destiny and put behind us the notions of democracy and human rights as peculiarly "Western" concepts. Thus would we assume a stance of opposition to dictatorship, whatever form it may assume. Thus . . . we say that we must ensure that when elections are held, these must be truly democratic, resulting in governments which the people would accept as being genuinely representative of the will of the people (Mbeki, 1998a).

Later, soon after the 2000 parliamentary elections in Zimbabwe, elections marred by intimidation and violence (though reflecting the clear will of the Zimbabwean people to start putting an end to Mugabe's twenty-year dictatorship), Mbeki addressed the Nigerian Institute of International Affairs and boldly stated that:

> The movement towards the consolidation and deepening of this democracy continues apace, whatever the interruptions and occasional setbacks.

Critical to this democratic renaissance in many parts of Africa has been the role of the masses of our people, acting through their formations, who have fought to end destructive and undemocratic systems of government. Through their heroic struggles, these masses have ensured that Africa experiences her second liberation in decades, while at the same time creating the possibility for the establishment of stable democratic systems of governments, political accountability and respect for human rights. Clearly, it is important that all of us should strengthen this movement towards a democratic continent and through our daily actions make certain that the democratic wave becomes an unstoppable and irreversible tide (Mbeki, 2000).

Zimbabwe provided a clear test case for such noble sentiments to be measured against and for leaders such as Mbeki to translate their courageous rhetoric into action. After all, Nepad's commitments have not been imposed: they have been designed by and then voluntarily signed up to by key African leaders, with specific practical commitments. Indeed, one of the main selling points of Nepad is its African authorship. And the chairman of the steering committee for Nepad, Wiseman Nkuhlu, is on record as saying that punitive action would be taken against countries that failed to obey Nepad rules and that "we will act against those countries that fail to respect human rights" (*South African Press Agency,* Midrand, October 25, 2001).

In the context where the notion that ZANU-PF might be peaceably removed from power through the democratic wishes of the population was rejected out of hand by Mugabe and where human rights have been systematically trampled upon for years, surely Zimbabwe provided one test for Mbeki and Nkuhlu's statements. The government consistently targeted the judiciary, the independent media, and opposition activists for repression, and Mugabe himself repeatedly flouted a series of court orders barring the seizure of white-owned farmland by state-backed "war veterans" (Taylor and Williams, 2002). In January 2001 the presses of the opposition-inclined *Daily News* were bombed and several foreign journalists were arrested and then expelled from the country. Clearly, "a stance of opposition to dictatorship" was called for. Even more so with the murder of opposition activists openly and repeatedly encouraged from the very top and with an out-of-control police force leading the country into lawless anarchy.

All of the above clearly goes against the fundamentals of Nepad, which claimed to push for Africa's development and to protect basic human rights and democracy. It certainly undermines the notion, advanced by pro-Mbeki academics, that "the democratic presumption [is] a central pillar of Mbeki's African Renaissance" (Landsberg, 2004: 161). Morgan Tsvangirai, however, recognized the problem, remarking that "you know this is the saddest thing about Africa, all these flowery declarations [i.e., Nepad's] and all without commitment. There's no commitment because there is no holding to account . . . The declarations are not worth the paper they're written on. Releasing such paper creates a feel-good atmosphere and, when leaders are reminded of what they have signed, they retreat into the defence of the sovereignty of nations" (cited in Chan, 2001: 71).

The African Response

Zimbabwe was in many ways a test case for evaluating the credibility of Nepad and a clear opportunity for enlightened African leaders to signal that they were fully committed to promoting tolerance, human rights, and democracy. As one commentator noted regarding the link between Nepad and the elections in Zimbabwe:

> [Nepad], of course, commits African states to good governance in return for better trade and aid deals. Zimbabwe had become a test case of how serious African states were about fulfilling their own pledges. However much South African officials insisted that the support of the developed countries for Nepad could not depend on the behavior of any one state, the situation was not readily passed over (Baker, 2002: 1150).

Indeed, virtually all observers (and particularly those with influence on policy) stressed the crucial linkage. As the Japanese ambassador to South Africa remarked:

> The essential is . . . how Nepad core countries representing an African conscience will react to [abuses in Africa]. The international community is very mindful on this. In this sense, it may be an important test for Nepad how core member governments react to the Zimbabwean situation. The G8 may have very much a mixed feeling in this respect. While highly appreciating the mediation efforts exerted by such countries as South Africa and Nigeria to reconcile ZANU-PF and MDC through political dialogue, the G8 feels very uncomfortable with the conclusion of the South African election observation team report, which is so remote from the international majority view. We appreciate and expect much from the introduction of peer review among African countries about the governance of each respective government. *How Nepad core members react through peer review to each incident will certainly constitute a severe test for Nepad for the real world* (Enoki, 2002, emphasis added).

In fact, African elites were enthusiastic in talking up the legitimacy of the elections. An observer team from the OAU said the elections were "transparent, credible, free and fair" (*Daily News,* Harare, March 15, 2002), while Nigerian observers in Zimbabwe endorsed Mugabe's victory, saying it had "recorded no incidence that was sufficient to threaten the integrity and outcome of the election" (*Guardian,* London, March 14, 2002). Daniel arap Moi rushed to "convey to your Excellency and dear brother congratulations and best wishes on your re-election" (*Guardian,* London, March 14, 2002), while Tanzania's Benjamin Mkapa (somewhat remarkably, given his status as a member of Nepad's HSIC) asserted that Mugabe was "a champion of democracy" and "it was up to the people of Zimbabwe to decide who should lead them, and the people of Zimbabwe have now spoken loudly and clearly" (*Guardian,* London, March 14, 2002). For its part, the Southern African Development Community (SADC) "endorse[d] the position taken by the SADC ministerial task force on Zimbabwe that the elections were substantially free and fair," Bakili Muluzi of Malawi—who then held the SADC's rotating presidency—was quoted as saying (*Star,* Johannesburg, March 16, 2002). The South African observer team blamed the long lines of voters unable to vote despite waiting many hours on "administrative oversights," drawing audible laughter from journalists and diplomats attending their press conference in Harare (*Guardian,* London, March 14, 2002). No wonder that one Zimbabwean newspaper stated that the South African "observers" were "next to useless" (*Daily News,* Harare, March 15, 2002).

The fifty-strong South African Observer Mission (SAOM), in its interim report maintained that even though the election was not adequately free and fair, "the outcome should be considered legitimate." Revealingly—and shockingly—it transpired that the report, according to dissenting members of the mission, had been drafted two days before the election by an "editorial committee" and only minor editing had occurred, without most of the observers and even members of the mission's executive seeing the released version. "We did not meet as a collective to deliberate on our experiences and to decide on the pronouncement. Even the interim statement was not distributed to us," said one member (*Sunday Times,* Johannesburg, March 31, 2002). In other words, the South African Observer Mission went to "observe" the elections in Zimbabwe with a prewritten report already endorsing the elections as legitimate.

In contrast to Nepad promoters' endorsement of Mugabe and his reelection, the Zimbabwe Election Support Network (ZESN), a network of 38 civic organizations, said that thousands of voters were deliberately and methodically prevented from voting:

> These elections violate almost all of the SADC Parliamentary Forum Norms and Standards. Voter registration was discriminatory and not transparent. Voter education was disrupted and there was insufficient time for the ESC to conduct voter education after the legislation was drafted. The fast tracking of legislation meant that there was insufficient time for the ESC to train its 22 000 monitors all of whom were civil servants in particular the army and police . . . There were disturbing episodes of violence even during the polling days—opposition polling agents and our own monitors harassed and prevented from carrying out their work . . . In summary, there is no way these elections could be

described as substantially free and fair (*The Herald,* Harare, March 14, 2002).

For his part, Thabo Mbeki stated that South Africa would help Zimbabwe, regardless of the outcome of the presidential election. Three days after the election, the South African Deputy President, Jacob Zuma, went to Harare as Mbeki's special emissary with a congratulatory message for Mugabe cheering him on his "reelection." Holding hands with Mugabe, Zuma lambasted critics of the flawed election and stated that "those discrediting Zimbabwe's electoral process should listen to what the Africans are saying" (*Star,* Johannesburg, March 15, 2002) and that his government accepted that the elections were legitimate.

The ANC later asserted that "the will of the people of Zimbabwe has prevailed," "those parties that participated in the elections need to be congratulated," and, ignoring the massive evidence of widespread and systemic violence and intimidation against the opposition in the country, that "the issue of *isolated* violence in Zimbabwe could not and should not be used as a stumbling block in the elections process in the country" (ANC, 2002, emphasis added). What was remarkable about such a statement was that this contradicted the SADC Parliamentary Forum's observer team, made up of 70 members—including 39 Members of Parliament from 11 parliaments in the region and including some ANC parliamentarians. Their report directly went against the ANC's:

> SADC's own Norms and Standards for Election Observation in the SADC Region, which Zimbabwe was signatory to, had not been met. At every level the mission found inadequacies. As regards political violence they found that it was primarily directed against supporters of the MDC: Violence was manifest in a number of hospitalized victims, numerous cases of alleged torture, arson, assault and incidences of false imprisonment . . . Acts of violence appeared to be systematically employed by the youth and war veterans . . . There are significant claims that the police have been partisan in handling of the political situation when called upon to intervene.

And rather than endorsing a blanket congratulation of the parties that took part in the elections, the Parliamentary Forum noted that:

> Whereas the ruling party's campaign was relatively uninterrupted, some of the opposition party meetings were cancelled or interrupted by opponents . . . the reduction of the number of polling stations in urban areas . . . resulted in congestion with some people spending more than 48 hours in queues . . . Well over 50 per cent of the registered voters were able to cast their vote. The major exception was the Harare Province where the voting process was excruciatingly slow . . . Further, although a large number of people voted, a significant number of the electorate was unable to vote as

a result of logistical, administrative and other impediments [and the] free movement of party agents was compromised by acts of intimidation and reported abductions in some provinces . . . [Finally] the slanted coverage the state-owned Zimbabwe Broadcasting Corporation and the Zimbabwe newspapers deprived the electorate an opportunity to make an informed choice (*Daily News,* Harare, March 13, 2002).

I would suggest that if Mbeki and the other proponents of Nepad had wished to project a solemn commitment to the principles they themselves had signed up to amid much publicity, then surely their response to Mugabe's behavior would have been different and signaled a brave commitment to Nepad's values, however uncomfortable politically that might be. After all, if one is going to unflinchingly and repeatedly state that one supports democracy and human rights, openly inviting skeptics to judge Nepad on its practical achievements, then there comes a time when such statements need to be measured against action. But African leadership solidarity won out. No wonder that Tendai Biti, an MDC MP commented bitterly on elite-produced initiatives such as Nepad, that "at the end of the day became nothing but a boy's club of little tin-pot dictators . . . For as long as Africans do not insist on uniform international standards of respect for human rights, respect for national coffers, the sacrosanct nature of elections and a commitment towards the eradication of poverty, then the noble ideas and concepts of African unity will become a pipe dream" (MDC, 2001).

In actual fact, appealing *against* "uniform international standards of respect for human rights" was the Mugabe regime's stance—calling into question the position of those African leaders who lined up to back him. Nowhere does Nepad talk of "African standards of democracy," in fact Paragraph 79 explicitly states that "Africa undertakes to respect the global standards of democracy, which core components include political pluralism [and] fair, open, free and democratic elections." Yet the government-controlled press in Zimbabwe repeatedly claimed that "in most African countries violence is prevalent" and that holding violence-free elections was "next to impossible" (*Herald,* Harare, March 25, 2002). Indeed, given the "poor logistics in any Third World country, there are bound to be small errors" in the election process (*Daily News*, Harare, March 13, 2002). Of course, Mugabe's regime would say that, but what is intriguing is how this contradicts Nepad's claim that democracy is a universal norm that is spreading across the continent and that Africa's leaders are fully committed to supporting this process. Indeed, that such lamentable justifications for wholesale fraud and violence were, by association, granted legitimacy by many African leaders—including South Africa, the de facto leader of Nepad—is peculiar. No wonder that the *Daily News* in Harare asserted that "where South African ministers assume the role of apologists for Mugabe's repression and delinquency they become part of the problem" (*Daily News,*

Harare, March 15, 2002). Indeed, the Zimbabwean opposition leader, Morgan Tsvangirai, remarked, after the elections that "If this [Mbeki and Obasanjo's response] is an expression of the so-called African solutions to African problems, or an early manifestation of the so-called Nepad peer review mechanism, then Africa is fated to remain a beleaguered and crisis-ridden continent for a very long time" (*Mercury,* Durban, January 24, 2003). Indeed, "By backing a despotic leader they [Mbeki and Obasanjo] betrayed the temporary hope they fuelled in this initiative [Nepad]" (*Zimbabwe Independent,* Harare, May 24, 2002).

Implications for Nepad

Despite Mbeki's claims that Nepad reflects "the sovereign will of the people" and the "aspirations of the masses" (quoted in *Sowetan,* Johannesburg, July 24, 2001), the whole initiative has been noteworthy for its lack of consultation with civil society in Africa. Consultation with civil society might well have produced a document with teeth that might have the potential to rein in the likes of Mugabe (see Manyanya, 2003). Instead, the collective response to Zimbabwe's crisis raises once again a raft of difficult questions about the pivotal position that Nepad affords elites in the regeneration of the continent:

> [The] assumption that African leaders share a common vision and conviction that there should be democracy and good governance, with respect to human rights, seems to be erroneous. The Nepad document is weak on strategies and methods for dealing with deviant leaders [and] makes several false assumptions: that African leaders will be impartial in dealing with each other; that they will have the political will to deal with each other; that deviant leaders will volunteer themselves for peer review. Nepad's incapacity to provide concrete mechanisms to deal with malgovernance and the erosion of democracy and human rights in deviant states appears to be a case of a failing mark on a test of enormous importance (Tsunga, 2003: 32).

The document's commitment to democracy and peace—signed by African leaders themselves—has unfavorably contrasted rhetoric with action. Even though Nepad proclaims that "development is impossible in the absence of true democracy, respect for human rights, peace and good governance," it appears that there is, sadly, little real commitment to these standards if it means having to make awkward decisions that go against elite solidarity. Indeed, the South African foreign minister has expressly said that "We will never criticise Zimbabwe," no matter what (*Mmegi,* Gaborone, February 25, 2003). But why should this matter? Surely Nepad is an Africa-originated document and should not depend on the vagaries of the West, particularly if they are trying to use Zimbabwe to throw back Nepad into its architects' faces. As the South African Minister of Trade and Industry Alec Erwin angrily said, the West "should not hold Nepad hostage because of mistakes in Zimbabwe" (*Botswana Gazette,* Gaborone, March 27, 2002). Indeed, South African government officials have repeatedly sought to separate Nepad from the situation in Zimbabwe, arguing that Nepad cannot be written off due to failings vis-à-vis Mugabe's misrule. But critics do *not* in fact declare Nepad moribund solely on the basis of inaction over Zimbabwe. Rather, the debacle is used as emblematic of the whole initiative, that is, the startling contrast between rhetoric and action. Zimbabwe is but one example—a similar chapter could have been written regarding Nepad promoters' failure to comment on malgovernance in Swaziland or Malawi or Nigeria or Cameroon or Equatorial Guinea or Gabon. As John Makumbe, professor of political science at the University of Zimbabwe, commented, the election was more than about "just Zimbabwe's future. What's at stake here is whether Africa is willing and able to police itself and is able to show the world that it is able to take that step forward to democracy and stability, rather than remain mired in the muck of autocracy and stagnation" (quoted in *Washington Post,* Washington, DC, March 12, 2002).

Interestingly, Erwin was to also complain that "If Nepad is not owned and implemented by Africa it will fail and we cannot be held hostage to the political whims of the G8 or any other groups" (quoted in *Botswana Gazette,* Gaborone, March 27, 2002). But of course, there lies the rub: while the document may have been written in Africa, it most certainly is not "owned" by Africa. It is owned, in a sense, by select African leaders and, more importantly, its very logic makes Africa dependent upon huge injections of aid and financial resources. It is difficult to see how it could be implemented, given the project's own approach to the continent's problems, if the West ever decided to walk away from the "partnership." This issue is of major relevance, as Nepad requires an injection of $64 billion a year to meet commitments outlined in the document. In short, it is all very well for African elites to try and reject linkages between Zimbabwe and Nepad but, however much those in Pretoria or Abuja may wish otherwise, Zimbabwe—and the African response to it—*was* a test of the continent's leaders' commitment to democracy. As a commentary in the British House of Commons report on South Africa notes, "South Africa's kid glove handling of Zimbabwe's governing elite has served as a reality check for many of Africa's developmental partners, in terms of their expectations of Nepad and prospects for the African Peer Review Mechanism" (Stationary Office, 2004: Ev109).

If donor support does not materialize, what if any contingency plans exist for advancing Nepad *without* huge financial injections? There is no evidence of any and so I return to a fundamental issue: if African elites *voluntarily* commit themselves to certain conditions, and hinge their entire renewal project on a quid pro quo basis (in essence, good governance and democracy in return for more resources), then these same elites are rather hypocritical to turn around and lament that their agreed conditions are now being held against them. As Chanda Chisala put it:

> A few weeks before the G8 meeting [in June 2002] at which the rich nations were supposed to endorse Nepad plan, the African presidents failed the first test, even before the plan took off. According to Nepad, African presidents are supposed to isolate any nation on the continent that would not adhere to certain ideals of good governance and political stability. That particular week there were elections in Zimbabwe which were clearly replete with intimidation, violence and possible rigging by the party of the country's . . . dictator, Robert Mugabe. The same people who have been peddling the Nepad plan were in the forefront praising and defending Robert Mugabe. Then when the rich nations failed to show enthusiasm for the plan (they did not pledge as much as they were expected to and did not sound too optimistic about the whole thing any more), the African leaders everywhere condemned the G8 for not being serious— for not putting their dollars to their words (Chisala, 2002).

After the Kananaskis Summit, a member of the British House of Lords, the Earl of Caithness, put it similarly, reflecting the way in which inaction over Mugabe threatened to tarnish countries such as South Africa:

> Mr. Mugabe has taken about 18 billion U.S. dollars from thousands of private investors. That was done with the tacit support of leaders of neighboring countries [i.e., South Africa] and is in direct contravention of what they signed up to at the recent G8 summit . . . I want to know what, if any, good reason there is to invest in or trust those countries in the future? (cited in Hansard: House of Lords London: Government Printers, July 4, 2002, column 339).

Curiously, in a speech to a "Review Workshop" on Nepad in January 2002, Mbeki boldly stated that "if we cannot unite through an initiative that can permanently reshape this continent and bring about sustained improvement in the lives of our people, then we would have lost an opportunity that will not arise for some time" (quoted in *Botswana Gazette,* Gaborone, January 25, 2002). Yet the damage caused to Nepad's credibility by inaction over Zimbabwe was compounded by the subsequent debacle over Zimbabwe's suspension from the Commonwealth—a situation that again exposed key Nepad promoters to widespread condemnation, if not derision—and which is likely to have a profound impact upon how seriously Nepad is now taken in the West, leading some to ask if indeed Nepad has "lost an opportunity."

The Commonwealth and Zimbabwe's Suspension

Almost immediately after the flawed elections in Zimbabwe, the Commonwealth moved to suspend the country. The decision was made on behalf of the 54-nation group by the leaders of South Africa, Australia, and Nigeria after studying the Commonwealth Observer Mission's report on the elections. At the Commonwealth Heads of Government meeting in March 2002, Mbeki had sought to defend Mugabe by saying that any notion of punishing him for his malgovernance was "inspired by notions of White supremacy." However, Mbeki was ineffective in his defense and, rather embarrassingly for him, was mandated, along with Obasanjo and Australian Prime Minister John Howard, to come to a decision regarding the Commonwealth's reaction to the elections—dependent upon the Commonwealth observers' mission report. The observer's report was highly critical and should have left Mbeki and Obasanjo with no space to continue defending Mugabe. For instance, the report asserted that:

> The Presidential election was marred by a high level of politically motivated violence and intimidation, which preceded the poll . . . most of these were perpetrated by members/supporters of the ruling party against members/supporters of the opposition . . . We were concerned that the legislative framework within which the elections were conducted, particularly certain provisions of the Public Order and Security Act and the General Laws Amendment Act, was basically flawed. Limitations on the freedom of speech, movement and of association prevented the opposition from campaigning freely (*Star,* Johannesburg, March 31, 2002).

However, despite such condemnatory, clear-cut language, the eventual agreement to suspend Zimbabwe from the Commonwealth for twelve months was marked by foot dragging. Certainly, the way in which the two African leaders eventually agreed to the suspension did not exactly inspire confidence in them. En route to London, Mbeki and Obasanjo had stopped in Harare and tried to convince Mugabe and Tsvangirai to form a government of national unity. This was, in the circumstances, a perfectly reasonable—if in retrospect quixotic—thing to do. But having failed to achieve this, Mbeki and Obasanjo then exerted themselves in defending a leader who had been condemned as illegitimate by the very organization of which they were members.

The decision to suspend Zimbabwe took place after three hours of deliberations where there was a lot of "pushing and shoving and cajoling and pleading," with ten-minute phone calls being made to Mbeki by Blair (*Mmegi,* Gaborone, March 22–28, 2002). In fact, "in London Mbeki faced intimidating phone calls from the British and Canadian prime ministers, both of whom told him bluntly that they would not continue to back Nepad if there was no action on Zimbabwe from him" (Baker, 2002: 1151). Finally, at the announcement of the suspension neither Mbeki nor Obasanjo said anything and left immediately, refusing to answer questions (Taylor and Williams, 2002). None of this behavior, I would argue, reflected well on the two African leaders, and it was precisely this sort of conduct that led to calls for "Nepad [to] be withdrawn, pro tem, from the agenda of the G8 summit until there is a full buy-in by African states of its stance on human rights and democracy" (*Financial Mail,* Johannesburg, March 22, 2002). While Walter Kansteiner (U.S. Assistant Secretary of State for African Affairs) commented that the suspension "had saved the position" of Nepad on the agenda at the G8 summit for June 2002 (quoted in *Business Day,* Johannesburg, April 10, 2002), the issue was not over. Indeed, damage to Nepad's position was exacerbated by the controversy surrounding the renewal of the suspension one year later.

The Commonwealth Heads of Government Meeting (CHOGM), held in Abuja, Nigeria, in December 2003, was always going to be dominated by the question of whether or not Zimbabwe should be readmitted to the organization after its initial twelve-month-long suspension following the fraudulent presidential elections. This became more and more clear in the months preceding the meeting when it seemed to become apparent that Obasanjo, and later Mbeki, were pushing for Harare's readmission.

According to reports, at the start of 2003 Obasanjo had declared that he saw "no need" for the Commonwealth's measures to continue beyond the initial year. In a letter to his fellow troika member, John Howard, Obasanjo claimed that "land occupation by demonstrators ha[d] ended," which at that time was untrue. Obasanjo lauded Mugabe's seizure of commercial farms as "remarkable" while dismissing the mass violence and terror as being somehow condonable as, after all, "it is reasonable to expect that a major reform on this vast scale would be attended by some measure of corruption together with complaints of unfairness." In the letter, Obasanjo also claimed that Mugabe had "confirmed to me that he had in place procedures for receiving complaints," while "all those found guilty of malpractices have been brought to book"—something at odds with what all other observers on Zimbabwe were saying at the time. Obasanjo also stated that "the Zimbabwean government gave land to those who intended to utilize it for farming purposes," rather than—as has been well documented—to, amongst others, ZANU-PF politicians and members of the army, who then proceeded not to bother farming their newly acquired estates. The Nigerian leader also sought to dodge the issue of political violence, claiming—just as the South African Observer Mission had done during the elections—that "if there is some [violence] coming from government agencies then there is certainly some coming from non-government agencies."[3] Finally, Obasanjo attempted to frame the situation in Zimbabwe as having been "exacerbated" by the "unhelpful media war between Britain and Zimbabwe" and demanded that Tony Blair "discourage the media offensive against Zimbabwe from the UK side," betraying a lack of awareness of how the British media operates (all quoted in *Business Day,* Johannesburg, February 13, 2003).

Later, in an interview with the BBC, Obasanjo claimed that "human rights abuses . . . had largely ended" but that anyway, "during a massive land redistribution we should expect a certain amount of disruption before things come back to normal" (quoted in "Readmit Zimbabwe to Commonwealth," *BBC News Online,* February 17, 2003). Such comments came at a time when Zimbabwe's people were literally starving and where non-Mugabe supporters were being routinely denied food aid; when illegal farm invasions were still occurring; when political violence was continuing unabated; and when the opposition leader was being tried on a charge of treason with the possibility of a death sentence at the end.

But, unlike Mbeki, Obasanjo's position began to change as Abuja neared and as Mugabe's intransigence frustrated any efforts to move the situation forwards. In the run-up to the meeting, Obasanjo flew to Harare to offer Mugabe, who was apparently frantic to attend the CHOGM, a last-minute opportunity to obtain an invitation. Obasanjo "left the country angry and exasperated" (*Zimbabwe Independent,* Harare, November 21, 2003). Mugabe rejected out of hand Obasanjo's attempt to put together a meeting with the MDC leader, Morgan Tsvangirai, in order to break the political impasse. Any such meeting would have helped Obasanjo (and Mbeki) to claim that Mugabe was serious about dialogue with the opposition—something that Mbeki had been repeatedly claiming for months. During his visit to Harare, Obasanjo first met with Mugabe who "claimed he was a victim of a racist campaign by the 'White Commonwealth,'" but that he was trying to sort out Zimbabwe's crisis (*Zimbabwe Independent,* Harare, November 21, 2003). Mugabe also claimed that there had been informal talks between ZANU-PF and the opposition, something that Mbeki had been also falsely claiming. But, after meeting Mugabe, Obasanjo went to see the MDC leader:

> Sources said Obasanjo's first words were: "What's happening Mr. Tsvangirai?" to which the MDC leader replied: "since your last visit to Zimbabwe [with Mbeki in May 2003] nothing has changed, except for the worse." "Obasanjo looked surprised because Mugabe had given him the impression there was progress" a source close to the talks said (*Zimbabwe Independent,* Harare, November 21, 2003).

As a result, Obasanjo left Zimbabwe angry and disappointed with Mugabe and refusing to extend an invitation to attend the CHOGM unless there was positive—and rapid—movement forward. It was from this point onward, after apparently being hoodwinked by Mugabe, that Obasanjo's position on

Zimbabwe began to diverge from that of Mbeki's. For his part, Mbeki continued to insist on Zimbabwe's readmission "even though it was clear to all that Harare had not made any attempt to meet the concerns set out in the Marlborough House Statement of March last year following President Robert Mugabe's disputed re-election" (*Zimbabwe Independent,* Harare, December 19, 2003). Previously, Mbeki's spokesman had said that it "did not regard the extension of further sanctions against Zimbabwe as valid" because "the Commonwealth imposed the maximum penalty on Zimbabwe by suspending it for one year in March last year." As a result, said Pretoria, "there is no reason for the continued exclusion of Zimbabwe from the Commonwealth" (*Mail and Guardian,* Johannesburg, October 1, 2003).

Thus the Commonwealth convened in Nigeria. Striking what was now a well-known pose, Mbeki made a strong speech on the very eve of the summit about democracy and human rights. Starting off with the statement that "I think we must accept that in good measure we [African leaders] have made a mockery of the gift of independence," Mbeki went on to assert that:

> None of us can prosper in peace if our African neighbor is weighed down by misery . . . We have to act together to ensure that our continent becomes a continent of democracy and human rights . . . The struggle for democracy is a struggle to enable every African to play a role in deciding the future of our countries and continent. It is driven by the commitment we must all make to respect and promote the dignity of all Africans . . . We should not allow the fact of the independence of each one of our countries to turn us into spectators when crimes against the people are being committed . . . We cannot speak of African renewal and allow the situation to persist that some among us abuse their positions of authority and power to steal from our countries and the masses of our people. I am convinced that if we sustain the initiatives represented by the African Union and its development program Nepad, as we must, we will advance towards meeting the goals I have already stated (Mbeki, 2003b).

These forthright comments were made on the eve of the CHOGM, offering up a very quick test of the seriousness of Mbeki's rhetoric. Indeed, Mbeki himself noted, in the same speech, that "the taste of the pudding is in the eating. Practice will tell the extent to which all of us have internalized the concept of the new partnership" (Mbeki, 2003b).

Yet within twenty-four hours of making the above comments, Mbeki devoted his entire energies to defending Mugabe and, in the process, not only dangerously split the Commonwealth over the matter but also alienated larges swathes of the organization (including his partner, Obasanjo) and, crucially, further undermined the credibility of Nepad. Mbeki insisted on Zimbabwe's readmission and sought to garner support for his stance. In addition, Mbeki attempted to force out the incumbent Secretary-General

Don McKinnon by lobbying for a Sri Lankan candidate, Lakshman Kadirgaman. The attempt, widely seen as vindictive—if not racially inspired—on the part of Mbeki, who had always opposed the New Zealander McKinnon's upholding of Commonwealth standards regarding democracy and human rights when applied to Zimbabwe, failed. The Sri Lankan was beaten by eleven votes to McKinnon's forty and an analysis of the voting pattern suggested that only four Asian and seven African states voted for Mbeki's candidate. South Africa expressed deep anger at this exposure of Mbeki's failure to rally African support, with Mbeki's spokesman calling the publication of the election results "un-Commonwealth" (*Mail and Guardian*, Johannesburg, January 9, 2004). But as the London *Guardian* noted:

> Mbeki tried to do something that would have been regarded as pretty amazing had it not been attempted inside an organization that many wrongly regard as belonging to the backwaters of international life. He tried simultaneously to depose its secretary general and restore full membership to a country that by common consent is even further derelict in democratic practice, the observance of human rights and good government than it was when suspended in early 2002 (*Guardian*, London, December 12, 2003).

Those who wanted Mugabe to stay suspended argued, with evidence, that Zimbabwe was in clear material breach of basic Commonwealth principles such as the Harare Commonwealth Declaration, the Millbrook Commonwealth Action Program on the Harare Declaration, the Marlborough House Statement, and the Zimbabwe Mid-Term Review Statement. The Marlborough House Statement was released when Zimbabwe was initially suspended, while the Zimbabwe Mid-Term Review Statement, which proposed ways of settling the ongoing situation in Zimbabwe, was issued by the Commonwealth troika of Mbeki, Howard, and Obasanjo in September 2003. When Zimbabwe was suspended, Mugabe was obliged to tackle matters such as real political dialogue, implementation of the recommendations of the Commonwealth election observer group, the establishment of an equitable and sustainable land reform program and, importantly, a continued engagement with the Commonwealth Secretary-General Don McKinnon. In fact, Mugabe barred McKinnon from Zimbabwe and refused to move on the rest of the above.

In seeking Zimbabwe's readmission, "Mbeki's argument—which ironically was similar to that of apartheid apologists—was that if Mugabe remained in isolation he would create a more repressive system and no one would be able to influence him to change." British Prime Minister Tony Blair, however, argued that "if Mugabe was readmitted without complying with Commonwealth demands he would actually think what he was doing was acceptable" and thus refused to endorse Mbeki's stance. Blair also questioned the fact that Mbeki had never been able to influence Mugabe and thus "it was not clear why he thought this time round he would succeed" (*Zimbabwe Independent,* Harare, December 12, 2003). The arguments over Zimbabwe continued through a two-day closed-door retreat and delayed the departure of Blair and others. In addition, Mbeki's haggling and obstruction in defense of Mugabe meant that other issues on the CHOGM agenda, such as efforts to promote democratic ideals, fashion a common position on global trade, and also HIV/AIDS, were scrapped.

In order to break the stalemate, Kenya (acting on a suggestion by Canada's Jean Chrétien) suggested that an ad hoc committee made up of six countries (South Africa, Mozambique, India, Jamaica, Australia, and Canada, later joined by Nigeria) be established to resolve the matter. The result however was a humiliation for Mbeki, as all the countries, except South Africa, voted to continue Zimbabwe's suspension. In response, Mugabe announced that Zimbabwe was leaving the Commonwealth.

With Mbeki's diplomacy in tatters, a statement "on behalf of the SADC" was released accusing Commonwealth members who had voted for Zimbabwe's continued suspension of being "dismissive, intolerant and rigid" (*Mmegi,* Gaborone, December 10, 2003). This statement was greeted with widespread shock. One commentary put it that "the SADC stance is likely to make a mockery of the democratic principles espoused in Nepad. The principles of promoting good governance on the continent have clearly been thrown out of the window by SADC leaders because they have shown that they will not act to uphold them" (*City Press,* Johannesburg, December 14, 2003).

Interestingly, the SADC statement was delivered by South Africa on behalf of Lesotho, which then chaired the SADC Organ on Politics, Defense and Security. This however prompted claims regarding "the question of whether [the South African] government, instead of formally consulting all SADC governments about the issue, simply put pressure on [its] most pliant neighbor to take a unilateral stance that purported to represent a multilateral consensus within the group" (*Star,* Johannesburg, December 11, 2003). Indeed, this appeared to be the case as it transpired that Botswana distanced itself from the SADC statement saying that it was not present in drawing up the communiqué. Nigeria's president meanwhile described the statement as "unethical" (*Mmegi,* Gaborone, December 19, 2003).

It became apparent that Mbeki and Obasanjo had widely divergent stances on the matter, with Obasanjo reported to have requested southern African leaders not to make their statement on Nigerian soil (*Mail and Guardian,* Johannesburg, January 9, 2004). Yet at the same time, the South African Foreign Affairs Department began feeding the media spin, "questioning" the future of the Commonwealth, with Abdul Minty, the Foreign Affairs Deputy Director-General, claiming that now that South Africa had been embarrassed over its support for Mugabe, there were somehow "serious concerns about the Commonwealth's future" (*Star,* Johannesburg, December 11, 2003). A stream of letters to the media from key Mbeki aides proceeded, reaching a nadir when Bheki Khumalo, Mbeki's personal spokesman, wrote that "Zimbabwe has held regular elections ever since its independence in 1980," without commenting on their quality or fairness. Khumalo went on to state that "Neither has there been a military coup that has placed President Mugabe in his position [thus] we find it difficult to understand what you [critics of Mbeki's policies] mean when you refer to a dictator" (*Saturday Star,* Johannesburg, January 3, 2004). Thus, according to the South African government, "the coverage of the Zimbabwe elections [was] driven by a 'colonial agenda,'" where "racism pervades other aspects of Whitehall's (London's) approach" to Mugabe (*Saturday Star,* Johannesburg, January 3, 2004). Such racialization of the issue, implicit in Mbeki's approach to Zimbabwe throughout the crisis, was also shared by analysts from the government-funded Africa Institute of South Africa, with Korwa Adar fulminating that the Commonwealth was "dominated by White racists," that Abuja had exposed the "hidden agenda of the White Commonwealth," and that the only issue was the "fact" that "White Zimbabweans are worried about the land issue . . . because once their land has been taken away they will have nowhere to go" (quoted in *Citizen,* Johannesburg, December 10, 2003). Such comments took their cue from Mbeki's own expressed positions on the affair.

Concluding Remarks

What is intriguing regarding the Zimbabwe affair is the way that Mbeki, as chief promoter of Nepad, has emerged diplomatically diminished. This is worrying, as Hussein Solomon of the University of Pretoria noted: "I don't think it is in [South Africa's] national interest that President Mbeki has no credibility as a leader because he is not prepared to stand by the principles that he is espousing in terms of Nepad and a vision of an African renaissance" (*Mail and Guardian,* Johannesburg, December 8, 2003).

Certainly, Mbeki's stance not only severely damaged the integrity of Nepad but also divided Africa and stimulated profound tensions between both the key supporters of the renewal project and alienated key external supporters. On the internal front (within Nepad), "Details have emerged of how Mbeki's divisive posturing embarrassed Obasanjo, for whom CHOGM was the most important political function on home soil during his term in office. There was 'anger and disquiet' at Mbeki's stance, say highly placed

Commonwealth insiders" (*Mail and Guardian,* Johannesburg, January 9, 2004). As a result, "South Africa's President Thabo Mbeki begins [2004] alienated from his most powerful ally in Africa, Nigeria's President Olusegun Obasanjo, because of South Africa's obstinate support for Zimbabwe at the Commonwealth Heads of Government Meeting . . . The rift has large implications for African unity. It may hamper coordinated peace-keeping efforts on the continent and the implementation of Africa's economic recovery plan, the New Partnership for Africa's Development" (*Mail and Guardian,* Johannesburg, January 9, 2004).

Indeed, Mbeki's behavior "left Africa more divided than ever on Zimbabwe. Obasanjo, who still favors rapprochement with Zimbabwe, is now likely to work with Kenya, Botswana, Ghana, Mauritius, and Tanzania. Each country supports the reintegration of Zimbabwe into the fold of nations, but they have consistently maintained a stronger position on the rights abuses by President Robert Mugabe's government than countries like South Africa" (*Mail and Guardian,* Johannesburg, January 9, 2004). "Analysts say it will take nimble political footwork to repair the relationship with Obasanjo, a partnership that is a key to advancing Nepad" (*Mail and Guardian,* Johannesburg, January 9, 2004). Likewise, Mbeki's behavior is believed to have seriously alienated Tony Blair and other ostensible partners. What is surprising is that analysts were long warning that Zimbabwe was undermining Nepad's support in the West—yet Mbeki still pressed on with his stance.

Immediately after the Abuja meeting diplomatic sources were saying that Blair had had enough of Mbeki's posturing and, in the words of one British diplomat, "the doors were now closed to Mbeki" (personal conversation with author). A later report seemed to confirm this, asserting that "Whitehall analysts are now concerned over the effect of Abuja on the Blair-Mbeki relationship, and the future of Nepad" (*Business Day,* London, December 11, 2003). As a result of Mbeki's stance, "Once-close allies, especially Britain . . . are dumbfounded. Britain's prime minister, Tony Blair, who has supported Nepad since its inception, is said to be losing his enthusiasm for Mr Mbeki" (*Economist,* London, December 20, 2004). While "No-one will actually say they don't believe in the plan [i.e., Nepad] anymore . . . it will be hard not to conclude that the promise of accountability and good governance has fallen at the first hurdle" (Western diplomat, quoted in *Guardian,* London, March 18, 2002).

Such feelings have been exacerbated after the extraordinary response by Mbeki, published soon after Abuja on the ANC website, to the whole CHOGM decision (Mbeki, 2003c). Foreign diplomats in Pretoria were said to have "reacted with dismay to what they called Mbeki's 'deeply offensive' remarks written in his weekly electronic letter" (*Sunday Independent,* Johannesburg, December 14, 2003). In his missive, Mbeki made a number of claims that were not true, in addition to peppering his whole letter with racially loaded references á la Mugabe to "White settler colonial 'kith and kin.'" For instance, Mbeki claimed that the Commonwealth's Secretary-General, Don McKinnon, had never explained what he meant by the "broadly held view" of member states when extending the suspension and also claimed that the Zimbabwean government had never been given a chance to reply to the Commonwealth election observer team's report on the presidential elections. This was simply not true; the Zimbabwean government was given plenty of chances to react to the report and to meet with McKinnon to discuss such issues—what Mbeki failed to bring up in his letter was that McKinnon and his envoys had actually been refused visas to enter Zimbabwe.

Mbeki made the statement that, quoting the South African Observer Mission's report, "the outcome of the [2002 presidential] elections represent[ed] the legitimate voice of the people of Zimbabwe" and that "We accepted this determination and have no reason to conclude that the eminent South Africans who came to this conclusion were wrong." In other words, post-Abuja, Mbeki—the chief promoter of Nepad—came out in the open and endorsed the fraudulent Zimbabwean elections of 2002 as legitimate.

However, it was on the subject of land reform in Zimbabwe that Mbeki's letter revealed the South African leader's desire to defend Mugabe, come what may. According to Mbeki, the finances pledged by the British and the West at Lancaster House "never materialized. The land dispossession carried out by the settler colonial 'kith and kin' through the barrel of the gun had to be sustained" (*Sunday Independent,* Johannesburg, December 14, 2003). This is untrue; London actually made available over £47 million during the period 1980–1985 for land reform but very few of the farms acquired went to the landless and most went to Mugabe's inner circle (Chikuhwa, 1998). In fact, in 1998 the United Nations Development Program decided that land reform in Zimbabwe was not satisfactory and was corrupt and as a result donors pulled out of funding the program. Yet, despite such problems (unacknowledged by Mbeki) when the South African president visited Blair in London in 2000 he was told that London had set aside a further £36 million for land reform if the UNDP approved a transparent, corruption-free land reform project. Mugabe was unable/unwilling to give such assurances and so the funds were never released.

Mbeki also lamented the fact that "those who fought for a democratic Zimbabwe . . . have been turned into repugnant enemies of democracy" (Mbeki, 2003c). But as the *Zimbabwe Independent* noted, "that is perhaps because they *have* become repugnant enemies of democracy!" (*Zimbabwe Independent,* Harare, December 19, 2003). Indeed, it was on the whole issue of democracy that Mbeki, one of the key promoters of Nepad—a project underpinned by its commitment to democracy—arguably exposed himself. As a result, "no longer an honest broker, South African President Thabo Mbeki has become part of the Zimbabwe problem" (*Sunday Independent,* Johannesburg, December 19, 2003). In his letter, Mbeki appeared shocked that the United States should try and "foster the infrastructure of democracy, the system of a free press, unions, political parties, universities and allow people to choose their own way." In fact, Mbeki appeared to suspect that human rights were simply a tool "for overthrowing the government of Zimbabwe. . . . In modern parlance, this is called regime change" (Mbeki, 2003c). Thus, according to Mbeki, concern over human rights abuses in Zimbabwe was simply motivated by a desire to replicate the example of Saddam Hussein's removal. Such notions permeate the ANC and take their cue from Mbeki. Thus in November 2004, Malusi Gigaba, a member of the ANC National Executive Committee, claimed that "apparently, in Zimbabwe, the rule of law and democracy means the unfettered right of the propertied classes that are almost wholly White to property ownership and economic domination . . . If the ZANU-PF . . . threaten this . . . then they would have transformed themselves into eternal enemies of the propertied classes, which, because they have lost domestic power in Zimbabwe . . . call upon their governments in Britain and the United States to fight their battles for them . . . Those whose principal task is to advance the interests of their kith-and-kin in Zimbabwe have nothing to teach us as to what we should do" (Gigaba, 2004). Indeed, echoing Mbeki's own racialization of the whole Zimbabwe situation, Gigaba goes on to add that "the UK/Australia faction of the White Commonwealth has seized on [the lack of democracy in Harare] to construct its anti-Mugabe platform" (Gigaba, 2004). How all this connects to Nepad is noted below:

> Mr Mbeki's big idea [is] the New Partnership for Africa's Development (Nepad), where African leaders take responsibility for good governance and stamping out corruption in exchange for Western investment . . . But there is a gaping hole in this record, called Zimbabwe. The more President Robert Mugabe abuses human rights and destroys his economy the more he is coddled by Mr Mbeki. Where the leaders of Botswana and Kenya speak out against this regional despot the president of South Africa is silent . . . Maybe events will vindicate Mr Mbeki but so far there is no evidence: no substantial talks between Mr Mugabe's party and the opposition, no improvement in human rights or economic management. Mr Mbeki has allowed Zimbabwe to shred his and Nepad's credibility (*Guardian,* London, January 13, 2004).

It is in this context that, as with HIV/AIDS (see Chapter 6), Mbeki—along with others—has helped undermine the potency and credibility of Nepad. But why is this so? Why did Mbeki see fit to go against everything in his rhetoric and his own pet project for African renewal? A number of reasons might be advanced.

One reason might be that Mbeki has been disinclined to confront Mugabe due to the fear that such actions might precipitate wholesale economic collapse in Zimbabwe and produce negative repercussions in South Africa. Zimbabwe has long been a significant economic partner for Pretoria and, even though its economy is now in ruins, Harare still remains important. Furthermore, despite South Africa's economic and political might, deep reluctance to be seen to be overtly flexing its muscles and a sensitivity (perhaps over-sensitivity) to being seen as the regional hegemon means that Pretoria does not wish to deploy the resources at its muster. This then ties in with elite politics within southern Africa whereby South Africa is seen as the new arrival and Mbeki is viewed by many of the leaders in the region as little more than a nonentity arriving late to the party. As Landsberg remarks, "all these liberation movement leaders—whether it's Dos Santos or Nujoma or Mugabe—belong to the same generation. They are all 70 years old. They literally treat Mbeki like the upstart, the new kid on the block . . . like the young boy whom we've groomed and who spent time at Sussex while we were liberating our countries" (quoted by *Radio Netherlands,* Hilversum, September 19, 2003). As Aguilar (1998) has noted, the politics of gerontocracy is of profound importance in Africa, often trumping rational arguments based on merit and judgment.

A further reason for Mbeki's actions may be that he regards himself as the consummate politician, adept at behind-closed-doors negotiations and diplomacy. Despite the fact this strategy has failed in Zimbabwe, Mbeki would be reluctant to admit this because, as Lodge notes, "Mbeki never likes to admit that he's wrong" (quoted in *Mmegi,* Gaborone, December 9, 2003). One need only think about the debacle surrounding the HIV/AIDS issue in South Africa and the scandal surrounding Mbeki's dissident views (see Chapter 6) to see that the South African president will not be swayed by others, even if it means undermining Nepad.

In addition, however erroneously, Zimbabwe's denouement has been portrayed by both Mugabe and Mugabe's apologists as a rectification of colonial ills and, more crudely, one in the eye both for white citizens living in southern Africa and to the "arrogant" West in general. Such a stance fits neatly with Mbeki's Africanism and his repeated racialization of most political debates. Witness his contemptuous disdain for Zimbabwean citizens who happen to be white (many of them third or fourth—even fifth—generation Zimbabweans) as mere "settlers" worthy of no respect or consideration—or rights. Shutting his eyes to human rights abuses, legitimizing fraudulent elections, and supporting one of Africa's more heinous dictators, all in the name of "good neighborliness," is thus the order of the day. But as Alden and Schoeman (2003: 28) put it:

Good neighborliness, in the end, is a strategy or tactic, not a principle. Sometimes it is not possible to be all things to all states, and South Africa may have ended up, with its policy on Zimbabwe, paying too high a price for its broader continental goals whilst once again bowing to the pressure of the "racial dichotomy." As long as African leaders use the adjective "racist" or "Western" with reference to liberal values in order to protect themselves from criticism and to manipulate support from amongst their continental peers, South Africa's claims to a commitment to these values, and its hope of fostering good governance on the continent will come to naught.

Furthermore, intra-elite solidarity within some sort of brotherhood or family and a profound reluctance to criticize fellow African leaders, as well as an entrenched regard (some might say, a convenient over-regard) for notions of state sovereignty and noninterference in one another's affairs, has traditionally staked out continental relations, even more so, debatably, than in other parts of the world:

> [The OAU/AU's] values for long [have] served to protect brotherly interests alone, which implicitly legitim[izes] the maltreatment of those not considered as kin . . . The result [is] that the suffering inflicted by state elites on the unprivileged masses of Africa's domestic political orders [meets] with the OAU's [and now AU's] culture of silence (Van Walraven, 1999: 377).

Suspicion and sensitivity toward the West—the past colonial masters— compounds this and may further account for Mbeki's reluctance to try and influence Mugabe openly. And this history is influential in another way in that both ZANU-PF and the ANC are liberation parties who came to power after fighting white minority governments.

Finally, the sort of "quiet diplomacy" and nonconfrontational diplomacy that Mbeki practices vis-à-vis Mugabe has an added advantage, as the MDC's secretary-general, Welshman Ncube notes:

> The beauty of quiet diplomacy is that it can't fail in the minds of its architects, and the reason is simple. If it does not deliver, it is the fault of the megaphone diplomacy of others. If somehow there is a settlement in Zimbabwe and that settlement is because of the pressure created by others, quiet diplomacy will claim victory (quoted in *Africa Today,* London, vol. 10, no. 2, 2004).

But even if all of the above is noted, the practical results of Pretoria's "quiet diplomacy" towards Mugabe has been to produce a policy that "is so vague, so subtle, so nuanced, that it scarcely amounts to being a policy" (*Mmegi,* Gaborone, December 9, 2003). Yet, "What is perhaps more surprising is that, even as they implore the rich to bankroll their plans, Mbeki and company do not stop to consider the harm their continued association with the likes of Zimbabwean President Robert Mugabe does to their cause. That is, what harm this relationship does to the image they want to cultivate of themselves as an African leadership imbued with fresh thinking" (*Mail and Guardian,* Johannesburg, July 12, 2002). This has direct and highly negative implications for the African recovery plan, leading a South African analyst to lament that:

> We can't afford it [Mbeki's stance on Mugabe] for economic reasons. We can't afford it for social reasons like the refugee crisis, et cetera, and we can't afford it for political reasons, because so long as Zimbabwe exists, Nepad and the AU are non-starters because nobody takes them seriously . . . we can't afford Zimbabwe to continue in the way that it is (Adam Habib, quoted by *Radio Netherlands,* Hilversum, September 19, 2003).

Indeed, Nepad Secretariat's David Malcomson, responsible for international liaison and coordination, has openly admitted that "Wherever we go, Zimbabwe is thrown at us as the reason why Nepad's a joke" (*Business Day,* Johannesburg, March 28, 2003). While I would not say it is a joke, I would concur with the broad-based NGO alliance Crisis in Zimbabwe Coalition (2002: 9–10) that has remarked that "Zimbabwe is . . . an important test case for Nepad. The sincerity of African governments' commitment to democracy and state legitimacy must be tested against what they have done, are doing and are prepared to do in order to ensure the restoration of democracy and good governance in Zimbabwe. That is a return to legitimacy." From this perspective—the perspective of ordinary Zimbabweans—Nepad has failed the test.

Notes

1. Based on discussions with diplomats in Gaborone, Harare, London, Lusaka, Port Louis, and Pretoria.

2. In October 1999 gay activists ambushed Mugabe's car outside his London hotel and tried to exact a citizen's arrest. Mugabe, his dignity affronted, immediately accused Tony Blair of setting "gay gangsters" on him in revenge for his "land reforms" (*Guardian,* London, November 9, 1999).

3. Obasanjo's comments should be put in the context where the Zimbabwe Human Rights NGO Forum had found that up to the end of August 2001, MDC members had perpetrated 55 assaults while in comparison ZANU-PF supporters, members of war veteran militias, the police, the army, and the Central Intelligence Organisation (CIO) had carried out 1,163 assaults. This general trend was to continue with the presidential election (see Crisis in Zimbabwe Coalition, *Zimbabwe Report,* Harare: Crisis in Zimbabwe Coalition, 2002).

6

Missing Dimensions: Gender and HIV/AIDS

I n Africa, Acquired Immunodeficiency Syndrome (AIDS) has a woman's face, and the female half of Africa's population is the most oppressed and disadvantaged. Although it is problematic to make generalizations regarding the status of women on an entire continent, "most African women live in poverty. They have little or no economic control, and therefore virtually no say in sexual relationships" (*Women's International Network News*, Winter, 2000: 44). Of course, differences that class, social status, location—even ethnicity—make in a woman's overall experience of gender oppression are of fundamental importance, and the issue of gender oppression on the continent needs to be disaggregated along such lines. Having said that, it would be true to say that women on the continent overall still need to overcome "the barriers that women face in exercising their human rights in the face of increasing poverty, abuse of power, gender discrimination and patriarchy" (Kitunga and Rusimbi, 2000: 61). At the same time, HIV/AIDS continues to ravage the continent, with doomsday scenarios staking out predictions for the continent's future, while the general lack of sexual autonomy makes HIV/AIDS a gender-based illness. In this light, any African recovery plan that does not seriously seek to tackle the pandemic and mainstream gender upliftment is incomplete, to say the least.

This chapter examines and analyzes Nepad's stance on both key issues (recognizing that they cannot be realistically separated). Light will be cast on how far Nepad fails to tackle some of the key developmental challenges facing Africa in the new century, the prejudices and positions held by crucial promoters of Nepad, and the extent to which such leaders undermine any coherent and sustainable African renaissance project. The chapter is divided into two sections, the first half on broad gender issues, the second on the HIV/AIDS pandemic. The posture of Nepad's framework document and the opinions of key Nepad initiators toward both issues are discussed.

Gender

Underrepresentation and the exclusion of women from decisionmaking powers is a major subject both in African civil society and, more broadly, the world. Primarily, "a government by men for men can't claim to be a government for the people by the people" (Lowe-Morna, 1999: 13). In the context of Nepad, we can add that a recovery plan devised by (elite) men for (elite) men cannot claim to be a recovery plan for all the people. While access is important, what is required is not just increased participation, but concrete actions that will result in a transformation of institutions and power relations in the whole of society (Rai, 1998). In other words, structural changes need to be promoted within society in order to improve the position of women. In this light, a practical and serious plan for Africa's renewal *must* mainstream gender and address the day-to-day problems facing the continent's women and the wider structural issues surrounding gender inequality. Unfortunately, as Longwe puts it, "Nepad is better understood as being in the category of empty lip-service to principles of gender equality. In principle Nepad is much in favor of equal rights for women, but in practice it proposes almost nothing in the form of action to realize these principles" (Longwe, 2002a: 15).

It is certainly true that Nepad starts off with some declarations on the necessity of promoting gender equality. Nepad makes sporadic mention of women in its framework document but the most detailed and telling view of the place assigned to women is to be found in Paragraph 49, where it is stated that Africa's leaders will take joint responsibility for:

> Promoting the role of women in social and economic development by reinforcing their capacity in the domains of education and training; by the development of revenue-generating activities through facilitating access to credit; by assuring their participation in the political and economic life of African Countries.

But the immediate point here is this: African leaders (universally male) have generally failed to advance the status of women in Africa over the past forty or so years since independence (Parpart, 1988). Why then should they suddenly be now taken seriously on this matter, and why is it only now that these male leaders are "assuring" the participation of women in African society? And how are they going to do this? Paragraph 67 states that Nepad's goal is "to promote the role of women in all activities," but as one commentator notes:

> The pro-women add-on, as the second long-term objective, is not matched by any concrete commitments to gender equality in Nepad, suggesting that it is a contentless, politically-correct gesture of window-dressing,

probably required by donor "partners." The natural gender concerns of Africa's patriarchal leaders are reflected in the fact that virtually none have lifted a finger to improve women's conditions (Bond, 2001: 51).

Such gestures are seen again in Paragraph 68, which states the admirable but over-ambitious target "to make progress towards gender equality and empowering women by eliminating gender disparities in the enrolment in primary and secondary education by 2005." Like much of Nepad, such sentiments are pretty mainstream and uncontroversial at face value and certainly talk the talk that donors like to hear. But in doing so, Nepad replicates previous declarations, such as the *Abuja Declaration on Participatory Development: The Role of Women in Africa in the 1990s*. This declaration was signed in 1989 and was aimed at ensuring the full participation and involvement of African women in the design and implementation of development programs. Little has been achieved so far and for all intents and purposes the Abuja Declaration has died a quiet death (for an early overview see United Nations Economic and Social Council, 1993). In this light, pledges by Nepad somewhat lose their potency when one considers how the actual implementation of enforcing gender equity in Africa is to be pursued within the framework provided—or not—by the document or, of course, how such declarations are to be implemented under the current conditions on the continent and given the lack of serious attention paid or resources put into past proclamations regarding gender equity on the continent. At the risk of being denounced as an "Afro-pessimist," I doubt that Nepad will eliminate gender disparities in educational enrollment by 2005.

In actual fact, though gender is mentioned in Nepad, its place within the overall document and the stance taken by Nepad is quite vague. It is perhaps unsurprising that there is not sufficient identification of precise problems regarding gender issues and no prioritization of such issues, or that there are no meaningful strategies or anticipated procedures to tackle them. Nepad's pronouncements on gender empowerment could be seen to be following a well-worn path that has emerged over the past decade or so whereby the rhetoric of empowerment is inserted into texts as a legitimization device, but little more. As Longwe (2002b: 9) notes, this is not simply the malaise of African leaders, but is apparent from the behavior of the donor community as well:

> There is a pervasive problem that development agencies and national governments exhibit a lack of political will in addressing gender policies. Instead there tends to be much vague lip-service, involving ill-defined phrases such as "gender-sensitive" and "gender-aware implementation" of development programs, when in practice these programs neither identify nor intend to address the important gender issues which affect all women in Africa. Instead their programs employ "watering down" strategies that serve to overlook, sideline or compartmentalize gender policy imperatives.

The language of empowerment began to appear in documents from the IFIs from the mid-1990s onward. The inclusion of such language was illustrated by the 2001 *World Development Report,* which devoted an entire portion of the report to "Empowerment." But does the inclusion of terms regarding gender empowerment, whether in the World Bank's documents or in Nepad actually mean much? We should not be too cynical but it is true that, as with the Nepad document, if one examines the *World Development Report* we can see that top-down (male) leadership is assumed almost without question and that certainly, gender equity requires little if anything to be done at the state level, let alone the global. Furthermore, Pheko (2003) notes this top-down trend within Nepad where "[from] the outset [it] states that African leaders are implementing it on behalf of their people and not with the African people. This is a significant nuance." And as Parpart (1999) notes, while "alternative development" advocates declare their backing for the transformation of society by means of empowerment, they are often guilty of top-down approaches that are likely to replicate, not transform, power relations.

If Nepad was to act decisively and move beyond Longwe's notion of it as mere lip service, it would need to tackle serious problems regarding women's control over their own labor and their ability to gain access to, and exercise management over, resources. Only through this, through the social and economic empowerment of women, can Africa's sexual division of labor, which relegates most women to the further fringes of an already exploited and oppressed labor force, be addressed. This in itself would require a comprehensive effort to tackle the structural causes of women's marginalization, be they cultural values (a sensitive and crucial subject and one that very few state-sponsored initiatives—such as Nepad—ever dare address), or inequitable laws and customs. After all, in many parts of the continent, even the most qualified and professional woman's sexual identity is treated as more important by her male colleagues than her competence (N'Galy et al., 1988; Siziya et al., 1996; Siziya and Hakim, 1996).

This is being slowly challenged throughout Africa, mainly through women's self-organization, but on the main it remains true that attitudes towards women continue to be hidebound. And custom and tradition often act to hold back women's self-fulfillment and development: "customary law (or the local version of Sharia law) maintains and enforces women's subordination. Typically the overall pattern is that women are treated as legal minors, cannot inherit property, and cannot own land. Rather than own property, they are *part of the property which is owned* by men, often in polygamous marriage" (Longwe, 2002b: 2). Yet, nowhere in the entire document is there mention of how such practices undermine gender equity. In Paragraph 21 there is the comment that "Colonialism subverted hitherto traditional structures, institutions and values," but it is unfortunately left at that—no explanation, no interrogation of what this means, and certainly no evaluation of how this may or may not have impacted Africa's women. And what Africa's rulers have done to redress this after independence is omitted. In other words, what gender oppression that exists is presumably, forty years on, still the fault of the colonialists. Furthermore, there is no recognition that "tradition" is not fixed but is mutable and contingent. Equally, tradition is often invoked—particularly by male elites—as being static if and when it suits the powerful and almost invariably in situations where females are subordinated before men. In Kenya, as Gough ("Wives Challenge Custom," *Guardian,* London, December 31, 1998) showed, "custom" was frequently invoked when a man was arrested for beating and brutalizing his wife.

As mentioned above, despite the fact that Nepad has acknowledged that promoting gender equity is one of the project's long-term objectives, the implementation of this lofty goal is vague and equivocal. For instance, Paragraph 49 states that Nepad will be advancing and "promoting the role of women in social and economic development by reinforcing their capacity in the domains of education and training; by developing revenue-generating activities through facilitating access to credit and participation in the political and economic life of African countries." Yet this in itself exposes the problem inherent in the program's approach to gender. As Longwe (2002b: 10) remarks: "the vocabulary is very revealing of the mindset of the authors. 'Promoting the role of women' is a well worn phrase which insultingly suggests that women are not sufficiently 'playing their part' in the development process!"

Indeed, Nepad seems to hold the view that gender equity can be achieved by simply advancing technical solutions, problem solving as it were, without touching on the essence and reality of gender discrimination, which is far more than an instrumental problem but is more structural, attitudinal, and deep seated. As White (1996: 7) notes, for both participation and gender: "What began as a political issue is translated into a technical problem which the development enterprise can accommodate with barely a falter in its stride."

For instance, facilitating access to credit is all very well, but what difference that will make in environments where development policies are in the main constructed by and for males, where land reform is prevented— often violently and often at the behest of traditional rulers—if and when it challenges male domination, and where in any case, women's roles and status, particularly in official decisionmaking, are trivialized as encroaching upon the preserve of "men's work," is unclear. Besides, "credit may not be the most appropriate tool for poverty eradication among the very poor, [the majority of which are women] without complementary access to resources necessary to convert an asset into a profitable enterprise, access to credit cannot form the basis of the longer term movement out of poverty" (Mbilinyi, 2001). Thus access to credit, while not in itself a bad thing, would be radically undermined by other key questions facing African women, in particular equal access to resources such as time and property rights, but also their overall position in society. Indeed, as Longwe (2002a: 6) points out:

> Nepad's near complete lack of internal coherence, where principles do not follow through into goals, and goals don't follow through into objectives, the subject of gender, small to begin with, soon fades away entirely. In its little mention of gender issues the document does not acknowledge the prevalence, or even the existence, of the many serious issues of structural and institutionalized gender discrimination. The unsatisfactory attempt to formulate a gender goal in the area of "gender equality and women's empowerment" merely reveals the authors' implicit belief that women's subordinate position is due to their own inadequacies. So they recommend more education!

Yet, "the work assigned to girls in Africa is so stressful that many abandon education after the first four years" (*Women's International Network News*, Spring 2001: 75). Therefore, few advance to secondary education.

As Randriamaro (2002) notes, "Nepad sees gender equality to be achieved by micro women-specific projects, as opposed to tackling the fundamental structural causes of women's poverty and inequality such as discriminating laws, cultural norms, male-biased development priorities, land reform, or public expenditures, and macroeconomic policies, just to name a few." In essence, Nepad's approach to gender, seen mostly as a technical problem whereby "partnerships" with the North might aid African (male) elites to become more or less "gender friendly" eerily resonates with the now largely discredited notions of modernization theory (Rostow, 1960) whereby pursuing a set of laws would lead to modernity and progress. That a supposed African-devised project should be returning to such approaches to development is intriguing, to say the least.

Indeed, as one participant at the NGO Forum preceding the 32nd Ordinary Session of the African Commission on Human and People's Rights in Gambia in late 2002 remarked, the lack of attention to gender issues within Nepad must be seen in the context of the African Union, "which is seen as a collection of patriarchal states with a record in this area of high level commitments and low level action. For action on gender issues, the Nepad document is not seen as a turning point, but rather as a continuation of the previous miserable strategies" (*Daily Observer,* Banjul, October 16, 2002). Without a doubt, such a situation is compounded by the highly elitist nature of Nepad and the politics of elite noninterference that has traditionally staked out postcolonial relations between African states. In this light it is scarcely conceivable that questions regarding gender inequality will be raised by one African male leader against another African male leader. As one African gender activist remarks, "for patriarchal men, the question of 'how we treat our women' is definitely an internal matter, even at the domestic level, never mind the national level!" (Longwe, 2002b: 9).

This is perhaps a key problem in taking Nepad's commitment on gender, however vague, seriously. In the light of its excessively top-down genesis and history to date, how can the male elites of Africa, who have never previously shown much regard for women's equality, now be taken on their word? After all, a recent report on the state of education in Africa, conducted by the University of Dar-es-Salaam, squarely "blames the governments of sub-Saharan Africa for making little effort to erase the gap between girls and boys in primary education [and] according to the authors of the study, the majority of countries have failed to eliminate the discrepancies in the areas of access to secondary and higher education" (*Women's International Network News*, Spring 2001: 75). As Longwe (2002b: 2) notes:

> The huge gender gaps in literacy, education, wealth and access to power are the result of discriminatory practices. These practices do not exist only at the social and traditional level. To different degrees, in all African countries, these discriminatory practices are entrenched in law, in the administration of the law, and in the general regulations governing government and corporate bureaucratic practice. It is governments who are the principle perpetrators of discrimination against women, and the enforcers of their continued oppression.

Unfortunately, as Goetz (1995) has noted, there is a well-established pattern by a good number of African governments to publicly champion gender equity, confident in the knowledge that they will rarely be held accountable or judged—even by the donors—for their failure to implement the assurances they have made.

In addition, according to Randriamano (2002) a conspicuous confirmation of the apparent gender-blindness of Nepad is the fact that it does not take into account the overwhelming effect on African women (and other exposed sectors of the population) of SAPs. Indeed, in Paragraph 119 Nepad advocates the position that Africa must:

> Work with the World Bank, the International Monetary Fund (IMF), the ADB, and the United Nations (UN) agencies to accelerate implementation and adoption of the Comprehensive Development Framework, the Poverty Reduction Strategy and related approaches.

Yet, a study by Zuckerman and Garrett (2003) found that only three out of thirteen Poverty Reduction Strategy papers (PRSP) addressed gender issues commendably, if not completely (these were for Malawi, Rwanda, and Zambia). All others either applied the outdated Women in Development approach, defining gender issues as reproductive health and girls' education, or neglected gender altogether. Rwanda's was the only PRSP that tried to engender expenditures wherever possible; the others did not break down the numbers of men and women consulted or indicate whether their surveys included gender-related questions or even a budget for any gender-specific projects. Furthermore, according to Zuckerman and Garrett, the majority of Joint Staff Assessments that go together with PRSPs to the Bank and Fund Boards contained superficial gender analyses. Yet Nepad asserts that one of its recommendations is to accelerate implementation and also the further adoption of PRSPs. That it can advance such a position illustrates the gender-blindness of Nepad and also that, as is well known by now, the document was drawn up with no consultation with African civil society. After all, "besides being gender blind, [Nepad] has experienced a very low profile among the rank and file at the national and even continental level. The idea according to the managers of this initiative is to hand it over to a marketing company that can begin to raise awareness about it among the African people. This brings into question the nature of this 'partnership.' A plan that is supposed to fundamentally change our lives has curiously not been a part of the discourse and the subject of debate within African communities from its conception" (Pheko, 2003). That is why those elements within African civil society that wish to remain engaged with the document are having to play catch-up and seek to justify—often to a skeptical audience—the merits of Nepad (see Butegwa, 2002). Yet, had it engaged and tapped into the growing wealth of talent in advancing gender activism on the continent (Tripp, 2001) then we might have seen a much more comprehensive and inclusive document.

Having said that, as Van de Walle (2001: 148) notes, "although [African] governments have often criticized the social cost of adjustments in international forums, concern about poverty and inequality do not seem otherwise to weigh much on the national policy agenda." In Nepad's prescriptions for gender upliftment, the document does not even go as far as that—remarkable in that it has long been acknowledged that even basic concepts such as gender awareness are integral to any coherent development project (Longwe, 1991). As a result, "*In principle* Nepad is much in favor of equal rights for women, but *in practice* it proposes almost nothing in the form of action to realize these principles" (Longwe, 2002b: 7).

HIV/AIDS

A decade ago, HIV/AIDS was regarded primarily as a health crisis. Today, it is clear that HIV/AIDS is a development crisis and is fast becoming a global crisis. Since its appearance in the early 1980s, HIV/AIDS has arguably become the most severe epidemic to affect the world. As is well known, the human immunodeficiency virus (HIV), which causes AIDS, has resulted in a global pandemic. In 1991, UNAIDS and the World Health Organization's (WHO) Global Program on AIDS estimated that by 2000 some 9 million people would be living with HIV/AIDS and that 5 million would have died. By the time the December 2000 UNAIDS report was released the true figures were considerably worse.

Globally, there is a great deal of variability in the trend of infections (increasing, stabilized, decreasing), mode of transmission, and the extent of the spread of the pandemic in the general population. In Africa, and increasingly in South and Southeast Asia and Latin America, the epidemic is becoming generalized, that is, most infections are due to heterosexual and mother-to-child transmission, although the pandemic is a complex and regionally specific phenomenon (Kalipeni et al., 2004). In parts of Latin America, Eastern Europe, and high-income countries the epidemic is still concentrated in sub-populations, in particular intravenous drug users and homosexual men.

In 2003, the total number of people in the world living with HIV/AIDS was 40 million, of whom 2.5 million were children under 15 years of age. The number of people newly infected with HIV in 2003 was 5 million, and 3 million people died of the disease (UNAIDS, 2003a: 3). The developing countries are by far the worst affected, with sub-Saharan Africa having the highest prevalence. Between 25 and 28 million people in Africa are living with AIDS, between 3 and 3.4 million people in Africa were newly infected with HIV in 2003, and between 2.2 and 2.4 million people died of AIDS there in that year (UNAIDS, 2003: 5). Certainly,

> In a belt of countries across Southern Africa, HIV prevalence is maintaining alarmingly high levels in the general population. In other sub-Saharan African countries, the epidemic has gained a firm foothold and shows little sign of weakening—with the exception of some positive indications from mostly urban areas in a few countries in eastern Africa. The trend offers no comfort. The epidemic in sub-Saharan Africa, in other words, remains rampant (UNAIDS, 2003a: 4).

The gendered nature of the pandemic is clear: "Unlike women in other regions in the world, African women are considerably more likely—at least 1.2 times—to be infected with HIV than men. Among young people aged 15–24, this ratio is highest: women were found to be two-and-a-half times as likely to be HIV infected as their male counterparts, according to six recent national surveys" (UNAIDS, 2003a: 7).

National adult HIV prevalence exceeds 30 percent in Botswana, Lesotho, Swaziland, and Zimbabwe, and other countries face rapidly rising levels of infection. Why this is so, particularly in southern Africa but also throughout the continent, is blamed on the legacy and practices associated with the migrant labor system whereby unsafe sexual practices became entrenched (Bassett and Mhloyi, 1991; Hunt, 1996). Increased mobility of populations has intensified the pandemic's geographic spread (Lyons, 2004). But whatever the causes for the high levels of infection, in brief, the epidemic is worsening faster than humanity can mobilize action against it, and two decades after its discovery, some would argue that we have not yet reached the peak of the epidemic (Barnett and Whiteside, 2002). Certainly, we have not felt the full consequences of an epidemic that is slow in taking its toll, but is now becoming more and more apparent.

According to the World Bank and UNAIDS, HIV/AIDS in the hardest hit countries of Africa is directly responsible for an annual loss of 0.5–1.2 GDP. This is in a continent that must achieve a growth rate of 7 percent to meet the United Nations Millennium Development Goals of halving poverty levels by 2015 (Akukwe, 2002). By 2020, heavily infected countries may lose up to 20 percent of their GDP to AIDS. HIV/AIDS is also fingered as a major factor in the current life expectancy in Africa of 47 years, instead of 62 years without AIDS. The impending death of up to 25 percent of all adults in some African countries will have an enormous impact on national productivity and earnings. Labor productivity is likely to drop, the benefits of education will be lost, and resources that would have been used for investments will have to be used for health care, orphan care, and funerals. Savings rates will decline, and the loss of human capital will affect production and the quality of life for years to come. USAID estimates that Kenya's GNP will be 14.4 percent smaller in 2005 than it would have been without AIDS. The disease is similarly expected to hinder growth prospects throughout Africa as well. Socially, a whole generation of orphans will develop, with attendant social problems that may act in quite unexpected ways (Guest, 2001).

In the light of such grim statistics, what does the new continental recovery plan have to say about what constitutes a—perhaps *the*—major threat to Africa's long-term future? The answer is, not a lot. Indeed, HIV/AIDS is mentioned—briefly, and in passing—only four times in the whole document. Paragraph 49 merely comments that "African leaders will take joint responsibility for . . . Revitalizing and extend[ing] the provision of education, technical training and health services, with high priority given to tackling HIV/AIDS, malaria and other communicable diseases." Paragraph 189 goes on to note that "Recognizing the need to sequence and prioritize, the initiating Presidents propose that the following programs be fast-tracked, in collaboration with development partners: (a) Communicable diseases— HIV/AIDS, malaria and tuberculosis; (b) Information and Communications Technology; (c) Debt reduction; (d) Market access." Thus the pandemic is seemingly lumped together with the need for more computers in Africa and advancing liberal reforms.

Paragraph 127 asserts that Nepad should "Lead the campaign for increased international financial support for the struggle against HIV/AIDS and other communicable diseases." In other words, it seems that "the struggle against HIV/AIDS" is something that is to be sourced and driven not from within Africa, but from outside. That possibly one of the greatest threats to the continent's future is to be left to the success or otherwise in mobilizing international financial support is massively problematic, I would argue.

All of the above is despite the fact that in Paragraph 129 Nepad admits that "One of the major impediments facing African development efforts is the widespread incidence of communicable diseases, in particular HIV/AIDS, tuberculosis and malaria. Unless these epidemics are brought under control, real gains in human development will remain a pipe dream." As a South African newspaper notes, "National, regional and global partnerships against AIDS would give Nepad an enormous boost. Failure could doom Nepad" (*Sunday Times*, Johannesburg, August 11, 2002). Yet, as mentioned, Nepad itself mentions AIDS but four times and nowhere is there anything remotely like any suggestion on how to implement strategies to cope with and combat the pandemic. Furthermore, there is no mention of the fact that women have become the main victims of the AIDS crisis and are now classified as a high-risk group.

So, how is this possible? How can it be that an ostensible African recovery plan mentions HIV/AIDS—in passing—precisely four times and not once in relation to gender? And why is it, when it is clear that HIV/AIDS is going to have a massive impact upon virtually all of Nepad's lofty goals, that the recovery plan "lacks a serious focus on the HIV/AIDS epidemic in Africa"? Akukwe (2002). That "Nepad boasts African leadership but, unlike with the Congo crisis, South Africa has so far chosen to follow rather than lead the public in the war against HIV/AIDS" (*Sunday Times*, Johannesburg, August 11, 2002) provides a clue. In part, it can also probably be explained with reference to what is now a familiar path trod by the male leadership in Africa, which, as Nzioka (1994) showed in Kenya, has systematically sought to ignore the AIDS crisis. But specifically vis-à-vis Nepad, I suggest that we can pinpoint the failure to treat AIDS as a serious problem to the beliefs and prejudices of its key initiator Thabo Mbeki, who has obfuscated and prevaricated around one of Africa's key developmental challenges.

HIV/AIDS, Thabo Mbeki, and Nepad

It seems, despite the strenuous denials and smoke-and-mirrors that have sought to confuse the issue, that the president of South Africa does not actually either believe that HIV/AIDS exists or that HIV leads to AIDS.

This is the only conclusion one can make following the debacle over Mbeki's stance on the pandemic and key statements made by him on the matter:

> "Personally, I don't know anybody who has died of AIDS," Mbeki said. Asked whether he knew anyone with HIV, he added quietly: "I really, honestly don't" (*Washington Post,* Washington, DC, September 25, 2002).

This is from a president of a country where nearly five million people are infected with HIV and more than 600 people die of AIDS every day. And from a man whose own presidential spokesman, Parks Mankahlana, died of AIDS-related complications. Furthermore, it is well known that Peter Mokaba, who had declared that HIV "did not exist" and that anti-AIDS drugs were "poisonous," was a member of the ANC Executive (i.e., a very close colleague of Mbeki) and was appointed by Mbeki as head of the party's planning for the 2004 election campaign. Mokaba died in 2002 of "acute pneumonia and respiratory problems" in 2002—code words (alongside a "short/long illness") in the region for AIDS. It was also reported that "Mbeki [had] personally talked him out of using anti-retroviral drugs" (*Mail and Guardian,* Johannesburg, June 14, 2002). Yet now Mbeki claims that he has never known anyone with HIV.

The history of the debacle around AIDS and Mbeki goes back a long way. Within South Africa, prior to the 1990s very little was done by the apartheid government to combat AIDS besides the 1985 establishment of an AIDS Advisory Group. In those days, AIDS was seen as a "black disease," and in the perverted racist world of apartheid, a disease that seemed to strike almost exclusively the black population was heaven sent. It was only in 1992, at the tail end of the apartheid era, that the National AIDS Coordinating Committee of South Africa was established to develop a national AIDS strategy. When the new nonracial government took office in 1994, Mandela's administration adopted the AIDS plan. Commentators later noted that "the bulk of the plan could have been effectively implemented in less than two years" (Van der Vliet, 2003: 2). Unfortunately, the plan was largely neglected, and South Africa saw its HIV prevalence rate in annual antenatal clinic surveys go up from 2.2 percent in 1992 to 26.5 percent in 2002.

Controversy almost immediately embroiled the new government over its handling of the pandemic. In 1996 a large portion of the AIDS budget was spent on a critically panned musical play titled Sarafina II that was meant to spread awareness of the disease. Not only was the play regarded as unsuccessful but the proper tendering procedures were not followed, resulting in the European Union demanding a refund from the finances it had put up for the show. One of the main characters implicated in this scandal was Nkosazana Dlamini-Zuma, then health minister and currently South Africa's foreign minister.[1]

Later, in 1997–1998 senior members of the South African government—including then Deputy-President Thabo Mbeki—began championing a locally produced treatment known as Virodene. Whereas antiretroviral (ARV) triple therapy, which entailed the use of three drugs in tandem, cost more than twelve hundred dollars a month, Virodene cost six dollars. Health Minister Dlamini-Zuma attempted to fast-track the drug, seeking to avoid normal medical procedures, which, according to one report, meant that: "Failure by government and its leadership to go through the proper channels opens them up to corruption, abuse of power, bureaucratic anarchy and the charge of maladministration" (*Business Times,* Johannesburg, March 29, 1998).

Controversially, the researchers behind Virodene had dodged the usual scientific tests. In fact, they had been refused a license by the Medicines Control Council (MCC) on the grounds that the drug was possibly dangerous. Later, it emerged that Virodene's main ingredient was dimethylformamide, an industrial solvent that produces acute liver damage if ingested and that could actually activate the HIV virus (*Mail and Guardian,* Johannesburg, March 20, 1998). The company producing the drug was planning to offer a 6 percent share of the profits to the ANC (*Sunday Times,* Johannesburg, September 26, 1999). When all this was exposed, not only did Mbeki refuse to admit his mistakes but he and other ANC officials, such as Dlamini-Zuma, immediately labeled the chorus of criticism over the debacle as "racist." Yet as one commentator noted:

> It is beyond understanding how Health Minister Nkosazana Zuma, as a medical doctor herself, could have been party to this disgraceful abuse of ministerial power. It was her duty, in which she failed miserably, to advise her cabinet colleagues against their involvement in a delicate matter such as research into drugs that can be dangerous, and even lethal, if the proper channels are not followed (*Business Times,* Johannesburg, March 29, 1998).

Later, in 1998 Minister Dlamini-Zuma announced that the South African government would no longer provide the medicine AZT to pregnant women, despite the well-established medical evidence that the drug was known to lessen the danger that babies would be born with the HIV virus if their mothers were infected. The rationale was that AZT treatment was "unaffordable" and that AZT was "dangerous." The announcement provoked a storm of protest, with one newspaper commenting that "By refusing to fund AZT for pregnant mothers, the government is once more discriminating against the poorest and most vulnerable" (*Sunday Times,* Johannesburg, October 11, 1998). Despite worldwide evidence to the contrary, the government—at the behest of Mbeki—maintained that AZT was "toxic," despite the fact that AZT has been around for thirty years and was accepted by South Africa's MCC more than a decade ago. Intriguingly, when Dlamini-Zuma was replaced, the new minister (Manto Tshabalala-Msimang) asked the MCC to look again at the risks of AZT; when the council concluded in two separate reports that the benefits offset any risks, the minister disregarded the reports.

This was somewhat surprising as when, in June 1999, Tshabalala-Msimang was appointed as the new Health Minister, she pledged to work "endlessly" against the pandemic and was actually welcomed by the very same people who had been systematically marginalized and vilified by Dlamini-Zuma. Indeed, at the end of 1999 the Health Department released a five-year plan with a policy for putting a stop to mother-to-child transmission. That same year, Pretoria became free to produce generic drugs after the Clinton administration removed South Africa from its sanctions watch list. However, such movement as it was, was rapidly thwarted by the activities of the president. Mbeki began to make statements about the toxicity of AZT and that it was being challenged by court cases in the United States, Britain, and South Africa. The manufacturer, Glaxo Wellcome, however, proved that there were no such court cases and that the drug was fully licensed under South African, U.S., and other countries' laws. Where Mbeki found his "evidence" of AZT's toxicity soon became apparent: the Internet. Apparently, Mbeki had a "thick set of documents" from the Internet about the perils of AZT, according to his media liaison officer, Tasneem Carrim (*Citizen,* Johannesburg, November 1, 1999). Carrim was quoted as asserting that "the president goes into the Net all the time." Indeed, it was stated that "Mbeki stumbled onto a Web site supporting dissident theories on AIDS during a sleepless night nearly two years ago, according to some of his closest advisers" (*Washington Post,* Washington, DC, October 19, 2001).

Soon, Mbeki became the center of a national and indeed global scandal as his unorthodox opinions regarding AIDS became more and more public. In April 2000 Mbeki sent a letter to U.S. President Bill Clinton, UN Secretary-General Kofi Annan, and the heads of state of Germany, France, and the United Kingdom expressing support for AIDS dissidents (*Sunday Times,* Johannesburg, April 23, 2000). Tragically, the letter coincided with the release of South Africa's AIDS statistics for 1999, which confirmed that nearly 10 percent of its population (around 4.2 million people) was infected with HIV. In the letter, Mbeki equated the dissidents who denied that AIDS existed or that HIV did not lead to AIDS with the antiapartheid struggle, saying that "Not long ago, in our own country, people were killed, tortured, imprisoned and prohibited from being quoted in private and in public because the established authority believed that their views were dangerous and discredited." Mbeki went on to say that "the day may not be far off when we will, once again, see books burnt and their authors immolated by fire" (*Sunday Times,* April 23, 2000). Thus, according to Mbeki, "we are now being asked to do precisely the same thing that the racist apartheid tyranny we opposed did." Apparently diplomats were so shocked by the tone and contents of the letter that "some United States officials were, at first, concerned that the document was fraudulent" (*Mail and Guardian,* Johannesburg, April 28, 2000). Ironically, in light of Nepad's later assertion that finances to fight the pandemic should be sought from overseas, Mbeki in his 2000 letter stated that "as Africans, we have to deal with this uniquely African catastrophe" and that there was a "specific threat that faces us as Africans" (*Mail and Guardian,* Johannesburg, April 28, 2000). In response, commentaries noted that:

> The letter is deeply disturbing. It demonstrates a capacity for justifying the most unreasonable of positions by a brew of implausible appeals to populist sentiments and prejudices. It suggests a racial-based perspective, not uncolored by paranoia . . . But, more importantly, the mode of discourse reflected in Mbeki's letter is no stranger to South Africa. Sober, reality-based assessment is cast aside in favor of ideologically driven rhetoric—as if the intensity of verbalized belief can supersede objective fact and rational argument, and displace any unwelcome, internal doubts (*Mail and Guardian,* Johannesburg, April 28, 2000).

That same year Mbeki set up a Presidential Advisory Panel where he invited AIDS dissidents to sit with acknowledged scientific experts on AIDS in order to "advise" him on appropriate responses to the pandemic. Problematically, the dissidents' positions ranged from the view that AIDS was not caused by the HIV virus (something that Mbeki came very close to saying on a variety of occasions); to the notion that drug treatments to delay the onset of AIDS were toxic; to the idea that AIDS did not actually exist in Africa; to the rather less controversial idea that AIDS possessed sociological and political aspects to it. Later, in Mbeki's opening speech of the 13th World Conference on AIDS, held in Durban in July 2000, he refused to admit that HIV causes AIDS, attributing it to poverty and coming "perilously close to endorsing the dissident view that AIDS is not caused by the HIV virus, but by environmental factors" (*Sunday Times,* Johannesburg, July 16, 2000). As a side note it should be remarked that if HIV/AIDS is characterized as simply an issue relating to poverty, then behavioral issues, particularly relating to male sexuality, are neatly sidestepped and the gendered nature of the pandemic is conveniently overlooked.

Just before the Durban conference, a declaration signed by 5,000 important international scientists (including twelve Nobel prize winners), stating that HIV had been scientifically proven to be the sole instigator of AIDS, was published in the journal *Nature* (July 6, 2000). The declaration was a strong condemnation of the dissident theories on AIDS. Mbeki's office responded on the eve of the conference with the presidential spokesman Parks Mankahlana declaring that the declaration "belongs in the dustbin" and that "If the drafters of the declaration expect to give it to the president, or the government, it will find its comfortable place among the dustbins of the office" (*Star,* Johannesburg, July 4, 2000).

As South Africa's infection rates continued to climb, the messages given by the president and his key government ministers responsible for combating the pandemic were confused, contradictory, and, I would aver, increasingly absurd. "In insisting that violence and accidents, and not AIDS, [were] South Africa's primary causes of death, Mbeki based his assertion on information in a five-year-old mortality study by the World Health Organization. In a subsequent letter to his health minister that was leaked to the media . . . Mbeki used the statistics to call for a review of government spending on the pandemic" (*Washington Post,* Washington, DC, October 19, 2001). In August 2000 the Health Minister gave to provincial health ministers a memorandum marked "Top Secret: For African Ears Only." The document was also distributed to all premiers by Tshabalala-Msimang's parliamentary officer Johannes Kgatla "on the instructions of the minister" (*Sunday Times,* Johannesburg, August 3, 2000). Accompanying the memo were excerpts, without comment, from the book *Behold a Pale Horse*, by William Cooper (1991). Cooper's book claims that the Illuminati are involved in a global conspiracy to take over the world and that they introduced AIDS into Africa to reduce the African population. According to the book, although the cure is known, it is being kept secret until enough Africans have died. The memorandum that Tshabalala-Msimang attached to the excerpts also included the comments that "The AIDS virus could definitely be in any vaccine that has been donated and/or bought [into] your country. Test all vaccines bought outside Africa to ensure that no AIDS virus was planted in the vaccines that you are giving to the good people" and that "After reading, you might be able to figure out why Africa has the majority of AIDS cases in the world. PLEASE WAKE UP NOW!!!!!!!!!!" (quoted in *Harper's Magazine,* New York, December, 2000).

Tshabalala-Msimang henceforth became an easy target for the media who were bent on exposing her unorthodox ideas. This was perhaps understandable given that Mbeki rarely deigned to talk to the press. Thus at a media briefing in September 2000, the Minister of Health was asked by a reporter: "Can you tell us, yes or no, whether your government believes HIV causes AIDS." The minister responded with the following: "Why do you say 'your' government? Isn't it our government? I think a little patriotism would be good . . . I don't want people to put words in my mouth. I have a certain way of answering questions. I am not a baby, a child or a schoolgirl" (*Sunday Times,* Johannesburg, September 24, 2000).

Yet worse was to come. In March 2002 at the ANC's National Executive Committee meeting on AIDS a policy document entitled *Castro Hlongwane, Caravans, Cats, Geese Foot and Mouth and Statistics: HIV/AIDS and the Struggle for the Humanisation of the African* was sent out by the ANC—with the full approval of Mbeki—to its party structures.[2] The anonymous 114-page document made several claims. One was that the late presidential spokesperson Parks Mankahlana *had* AIDS, but was actually killed by toxic anti-retrovirals. In addition, the document asserted that AIDS was a conspiracy pressed onto Africa by an "omnipotent apparatus" and rejected "as baseless and self-serving the assertion that millions of our people are HIV positive," in fact, it rejected "the claim that AIDS is the single largest cause of death in our country." In addition, the document claimed that white South African scientists had experimented with anti-retroviral drugs on black pregnant women, who subsequently died.

What was particularly worrisome was that not only did the document exhibit strong similarities in style with other public writings by Mbeki, but it found itself in the hands of the press as an electronic attachment and the *Mail and Guardian* newspaper was able to prove that the electronic signature on the document was recorded as, "Author: Thabo Mbeki" and "Company: Office of the President" (*Mail and Guardian,* Johannesburg, April 19, 2002). The president refused to comment on the authorship of the document when asked.

The storm of outrage at Mbeki's stance, however, began to reach worrying proportions for the government; every time Mbeki traveled overseas or was interviewed the key questions being asked were about his stance on AIDS. This became increasingly problematic as "If Mbeki was to appear as a credible leader on the international stage, he had to avoid the situation where, for instance, journalists at press conferences ignored his views on Nepad and Africa's recovery plan, and went straight for the AIDS jugular" (Van der Vliet, 2003).

Thus, Mbeki began to take a less and less vocal stance on the issue. However, it rapidly became apparent that the Health Minister Manto Tshabalala-Msimang was now the new spokesperson for both Mbeki and the dissidents. Earlier, she had announced in March 2002 that the ANC government would not abide by a court ruling ordering the government to provide the anti-retroviral Nevirapine. In April the Constitutional Court issued an interim order that the government must provide the ARV Nevirapine, yet the state continued to refuse, with the minister pronouncing in July that anti-AIDS drugs were "poison" that were killing "our people" (*Star,* Johannesburg, July 10, 2002). As a result, tens of thousands of pregnant HIV-positive women needlessly transmitted the HIV virus to their babies. Later that same month the government blocked a R720 million (approximately US$120 million) grant from the UN Global Fund for AIDS Prevention to KwaZulu-Natal and attacked the Global AIDS Fund as an entity that was trying to "bypass a democratically elected government" (*Star,* Johannesburg, July 20, 2002).

The situation got even worse when in December 2002 Tshabalala-Msimang was quoted as saying South Africa could not afford anti-AIDS drugs because it needed submarines to deter attacks from nations such as the United States (*Business Day,* Johannesburg, December 18, 2002). "Look at what Bush is doing. He could invade," the minister was quoted as saying. Critics pointed out that compared to the government's $6 billion arms deal (which could cost South Africa $62 billion by 2019), the amount needed for ARV treatment was minimal. And indeed, compare the cost of $41 million for implementing the drug Nevirapine (offered free by drug companies to South Africa due to lobbying by the Treatment Action Campaign) as part of a mother-to-child transmission prevention strategy, to Mbeki's brand new $50 million presidential jet.

The new year (2003) saw Tshabalala-Msimang inviting Roberto Giraldo, a scientist and AIDS skeptic, to South Africa to deliver a presentation. Giraldo, a member of President Thabo Mbeki's AIDS advisory panel, declared that "the transmission of AIDS from person to person is a myth" (*Sunday Times,* Johannesburg, March 9, 2003). Giraldo believes AIDS is caused by nutritional deficiencies. Later, South Africa's health minister, in charge of the health of a country with the highest number of people infected with the HIV virus in the world, announced that South Africans with HIV/AIDS would not get ARVs but should instead eat garlic, onions, olive oil, and African potatoes to boost their immune systems. "Thanks to our scientists . . . we know that traditional and nutritional supplements work as well," Tshabalala-Msimang said (*Star,* Johannesburg, August 4, 2003). The minister repeated her medical advice in February 2004 with the comment that "I think garlic is absolutely critical. Lemon is absolutely critical to boost the immune system. Olive oil is absolutely critical—just one teaspoon, it will last the whole month" (*Business Day,* Johannesburg, February 10, 2004).

Yet in August 2003 it had seemed that the government had somewhat changed its stance when, after an 18-month delay, Pretoria signed an agreement with the Global Fund to Fight AIDS, TB, and Malaria—giving South Africa access to $41 million for the struggle against the pandemic. The government agreed to begin planning a national treatment program. But the suspicion that the government had not really changed its mind over AIDS remained strong. A week after the announcement, Tshabalala-Msimang warned that there would be "delays" in rolling out the anti-AIDS plan (*Star,*

Johannesburg, August 18, 2003). A few days later, a visiting delegation of six U.S. senators in southern Africa to study AIDS prevention and treatment programs was snubbed by the health minister, and in early September 2003 the head of the World Health Organization, Jong-Wook Lee, expressed misgivings about the depth of Mbeki or his government's commitment to the new plan or to fighting the pandemic (*Citizen,* Johannesburg, September 1, 2003). Within a month Lee's fears seemed confirmed when Defense Minister Mosiuoa Lekota complained about "All this noise every day about HIV/AIDS and so on . . . There is no alarm in this country" (*Business Day,* Johannesburg, October 8, 2003).

Then, the perception that there had been a real change of mindset was crushed with the interview with Mbeki in the *Washington Post,* mentioned previously, where he denied knowledge of knowing anyone with AIDS. It again seemed very clear that the president still did not believe that HIV/AIDS either existed or killed people. And as one commentator noted regarding the genuineness of Mbeki's about-face:

> Cynics . . . have suggested that the prospect of an election, which must be held before the beginning of September next year, has concentrated politicians' minds. While issues like the lack of jobs, houses and land can be dealt with in debate, there is no way the government can explain away its failures on the AIDS front. Voters, unlike the President, know many people close to them who are dying of AIDS (Van der Vliet, 2003).

Indeed, while the March 2004 announcement that the Health Department would give the option of ARV treatment to people whose CD4 count (a measure of the spread of the virus in the body) had dropped below 200 was warmly welcomed, many saw it as a cynical attempt at vote winning just weeks before the general election in April 2004.

As if to add insult to injury, Mbeki's stance towards sexual violence, something which most observers think helps spread HIV/AIDS, was exposed in late 2004—again calling into question his fitness to lead Nepad. An official report showed a minor drop in South Africa's rape rate—the rape rate declined from 115.3 per 100,000 in 1994 to 113.7 per 100,000 in 2003/04 (in the United States the rape rate in 2000 was around 32 per 100,000). A white female journalist, Charlene Smith, who had herself been the victim of rape, questioned these figures and, as an aside, argued that gender relations and the subordination of women tended to encourage sexual violence. Mbeki's response? On the ANC website, Mbeki accused Smith of being a racist who thought that "every African man [was] a potential rapist" and that Smith thought that "African people [are] barbaric savages." It should be noted that Smith's article did not even mention race at all. Mbeki went on to dismiss the fact that South Africa had one of the—if not *the*—highest rates of rape in the world, as, according to Mbeki, this was simply based on the racist assumption that "we are an African country, and therefore have the men conditioned by African culture, tradition and religion to commit rape" (Mbeki, 2004).

This is not an isolated incident. When the UNAIDS deputy executive director, Kathleen Cravero, asserted that "most of the women and girls, as much in Asia as in Africa, don't have the option to abstain [from sex] when they want to," something which most experts agree on, Mbeki implied that Crevero was simply a racist who apparently saw African men, as "violent sexual predators" (*Cape Times,* Cape Town, October 1, 2004). That the leading promoter of Nepad dismisses concerns over rape, gender imbalances, and sexual violence as "racist" is a major cause for concern. It certainly makes a mockery of such statements that "Mbeki is extremely principled about race" (Landsberg, 2004: 160).

Implications for Nepad

So what is the point of all the above? Are Mbeki's policies on AIDS a domestic matter that has no bearing on Nepad as a continental recovery plan? I would argue differently. Nepad is for all intents and purposes a South African creation and is primarily promoted by Mbeki, with bit parts played by Obasanjo and, occasionally, others. Yet, this recovery plan not only pays minimal attention to the AIDS pandemic—because, it is suggested, of Mbeki's stance on the issue and his guiding hand in Nepad's formulation—but is spearheaded by a leader who has repeatedly blocked and confused what is one of Africa's worst problems and appears—if one judges him by his actions—not to view the AIDS catastrophe as anything particularly momentous. It is no wonder that Bond (2001: 113) comments that "Pretoria's failure to address HIV/AIDS, in part by promoting dissident analysis in South Africa's Presidential Commission on AIDS . . . suggest that Nepad's own authors are not serious about [the AIDS] problems."

As a result of all of the aforementioned, any serious and credible African recovery plan would need to recognize, analyze, and then operationalize measures to both uplift half of the continent's population and acknowledge and do something about the gendered nature of the AIDS pandemic. It would have to understand how gender identities manipulate women (for good or for bad) and how this influences their approaches to and behavior in sexual relationships. Yet Nepad does not even recognize such commonsense notions that "the second-class status of women in economic, social and civic life has fueled the [AIDS] pandemic in much of the world," Africa included (Human Rights Watch, 2001). We have seen how Mbeki regards such comments.

At the risk of falling foul of the South African president, I would concur with the general view that within Africa, the vulnerable state of many women means that the negative economic costs of ending high-risk relationships with unfaithful partners is often seen as more severe than the obvious health risks of remaining in the relationship. And the social stigma of being a woman who has "abandoned" her husband further acts to keep women locked into dangerous (health-wise) relationships. In addition, due to the economic structures that stake out much of the social and economic frameworks within which African women must live, women are unduly impacted if/when a male head of the household succumbs to AIDS. Economic dependency and the concomitant susceptibility that this may bring regarding HIV infection—plus the social barriers restricting women's ability simply to say "no" to either sex or sex without condoms, further makes women vulnerable. In addition, "in many societies, motherhood [which, of course, implies practicing unsafe sex] represents the only route to status, identity and personhood, and ultimately security and support in old age" (Doyal, 1994: 20). To make such a situation even worse, gender-related discrimination (unrecognized, it should be noted, by Nepad) is underpinned by the law, which often prevents females from possessing land and property (Downs and Reyna, 1988).

Of course, the situation varies throughout the continent, but it cannot be denied that women are much more vulnerable to AIDS infection than men and that their structural position in society is, in general, less than their male counterparts (Tembo and Phiri, 1993; Akeroyd, 2004). Ideas of masculinity and the refusal to blame certain constructions of male sexuality compound this and further marginalize women, particularly when such conversations stimulate an exaggerated defensiveness vis-à-vis male sexuality and "dignity" (e.g., Oppong and Kalipeni, 2004). In fact, due to the deadly impact of AIDS on women and girls in Africa, analysts have come to argue that AIDS can be seen as a form of mass femicide (Russell, 2001). As a result, writers (see J. Relly, "Societal Norms, Poverty Blamed for Rapid Spread of AIDS," *San Francisco Chronicle,* February 26, 2001; M. Schoofs, "AIDS, the Agony of Africa, Part 5: Death and the Second Sex," *Village Voice,* New York, December 1–7, 1999) have made a specific linkage between male domination and the construction of gender in Africa and the spread of AIDS on the continent. Schoof links the highly gendered pattern of AIDS infections and deaths to the way in which male dominance plays out on the continent. Russell (2001) also notes the gendered nature of HIV infection rates and argues that a number of variables, more or less common across the continent, impact upon the pandemic's effect on women. The refusal by many males to practice safe sex while having multiple partners is seen as central, as is the failure to inform female partners about nonmonogamous relationships. The often coercive nature of sexual relationships, particularly when the husband is exercising his conjugal "rights," also contributes to the high infection rate, especially as this is usually done without protection (Russell, 2001). Research conducted in Zambia and Tanzania found that the ABC (Abstinence, Be faithful, and use Condoms) strategy, a cornerstone of HIV/AIDS prevention efforts in many African countries, does not protect females "because they have not been allowed by men to practise this strategy. To fight AIDS successfully and to protect girls, the debate has to be broadened to tackle the issues of gender inequality, harmful cultural practices, discrimination and sexual violence" (Zulu, 2004). The former director general of the World Health Organization, Gro Harlem Brundtland, agrees, noting the gendered nature of the HIV/AIDS pandemic:

> The way women's roles, in many of the countries that are mostly affected, develop; the human rights of women; the respect of women and sexual practices that are respectful of women, more of a choice about how many partners they want to have, being more economically independent is what matters. I feel that unless we get a change to the better with regard to education of women, the rights of women, the roles of women, respect for women, if we haven't seen a major change in that in the positive direction in the next 10 or 15 years, I'm afraid that it will be worse for the development of the epidemic (UNAIDS, 2003b).

That such a situation has arisen has been disastrous. And that it has undermined Nepad's coherency if not credibility is also not in doubt. In an interview with UNAIDS director Peter Piot, the official expressly stated that the "New Partnership for African Development (Nepad) did not get the support from the G8 it hoped for because it failed to adequately address HIV/AIDS" (quoted by *South African Press Association,* Johannesburg, July 5, 2002). In the interview, Piot said, "this [was] the first time there has been a comprehensive plan for African development, and yet, although HIV, with armed conflict, is one of the most significant challenges in Africa, there is not a significant approach to dealing with HIV/AIDS in that development plan."

What this has meant is that commentators such as Stephen Lewis, the HIV/AIDS Advisor to Kofi Annan, the UN's Secretary-General, are fundamentally correct when they note that:

> It seems to me that there's a critical flaw at the heart of the Nepad document. For all its talk of trade, and investment, and governance, and corruption, and matters relating to financial architecture, there is only a pro forma sense of the social sectors, only modest references to the human side of the ledger. And in a fashion quite startling, in fact, disturbingly startling, Nepad hardly mentions HIV/AIDS at all. But how can you talk about the future of sub-Saharan Africa without AIDS at the heart of the analysis? The failure to do so leads to a curious and disabling contradiction (Lewis, 2002b).

Indeed. And when HIV/AIDS is mentioned, it is in the context of other diseases, thereby blurring the particular imperatives needed to combat the pandemic. As Cohen and Smith note, "It is . . . inexplicable that the only mention of AIDS in Nepad is in the context (very brief) of communicable diseases, as if AIDS were indistinguishable from other diseases such as malaria. To address the issues in this way totally fails to note the complex ways in which the HIV/AIDS epidemic undermines sustainable development" (Cohen and Smith, 2002).

Problematically for Nepad as a serious document of renewal but one that neglects the AIDS crisis, the connection between health, the reduction in poverty, and the concomitant opportunities for sustainable economic growth are strong. HIV/AIDS undoubtedly acts to further stymie growth and development and has to be dealt with head on in any recovery plan worth its salt. While the prevention of HIV/AIDS is at the end of the day a personal matter—one that can be influenced by education and awareness—the delivery and management of treatment is a social and political duty. Yet not only does Nepad duck this issue, but the key state advancing the recovery project is headed by a president who seems not to believe in the medical world's understanding of the pandemic. This is doubly unfortunate, particularly when concerted efforts to check and treat the pandemic would no doubt stimulate greater labors to develop the public health structures in countries and thereby provide momentum to a wider project of renewal.

Concluding Remarks

In summary, although Nepad is a recovery plan for the whole of Africa, it fundamentally fails to speak to and about half of the population, leaving commentary on gender issues as mere add-ons with the appearance of being afterthoughts. Such a reality continues long-term trends in Africa's various recovery plans whereby questions around gender and women's rights are broadly ignored or sidelined. Given the excessively elitist nature of Nepad's origins, this is unsurprising. But given the pivotal role Nepad (as a plan) is afforded in reinvigorating the continent, this is unforgivable. Not only that, but in the context where the AIDS pandemic has a profoundly gendered aspect to it, the disease is barely mentioned at all and when it is, is invariably lumped together with other health problems such as malaria. It thus ignores the fact that it has been largely women who have borne the main burden in the share of infection rates, mortality levels, and the social and financial responsibilities of caring for the disease's victims. Yet such an overlooking of the disease's ramifications neglects the reality that virtually all studies comment in depth on the serious social, economic, and development implications of the disease:

> In regions where HIV/AIDS has reached epidemic proportions, it destroys the very fabric of what constitutes a state: individuals, families, communities, economic and socio-political institutions, and the military and police forces, which guarantee the protection of state institutions. AIDS and global insecurity coexist in a vicious cycle . . . HIV/AIDS is both a cause and effect, initiator and beneficiary of instability and conflict (www.unaids.org).

This neglect is quite remarkable and reflects a massive gap in the overall coherency of Nepad. Simply put, unless Africa manages to tackle the AIDS crisis seriously, all of the lofty goals of Nepad will come to nothing. And yet, perhaps reflecting one of its authors' own predilections, the disease receives short shrift from what was supposed to be a "holistic" regeneration project. As De Waal puts it, "Reflecting Thabo Mbeki's reluctance to face this [AIDS] problem, Nepad accords HIV/AIDS no greater status than that of a problem of health—a conventional approach that has signally failed to treat the pandemic with the seriousness it deserves" (De Waal, 2002: 475). This has meant that:

> Nepad represented an opportunity, but is at the same time an [indication] of the distance still to travel in persuading African leaders of the enormous threat that HIV/AIDS poses for sustainable development . . . [It] is clear that an understanding of the issues is more or less missing from Nepad (Cohen and Smith, 2002).

Indeed, regarding the AIDS crisis and the gendered nature of the pandemic Nepad is lamentable. Perhaps, given the fact that Nepad springs from an exclusively male club of elites, it is no surprise that patriarchal structures are not interrogated. This has been long-standing (Stichter and Parpart, 1988). In addition, one might suppose that, given that women suffer proportionally more from HIV/AIDS, it is no surprise that the pandemic receives short shrift, particularly given the fact that one of the document's key authors has unorthodox views on the whole matter. Mbeki's comments in March 2004 that he would "beat his sister if she told him she had fallen in love with an opposition leader" (*Star,* Johannesburg, March 23, 2004) or the aforementioned attack on an anti-rape campaigner as a "racist" surely raises eyebrows.

Certainly, Mbeki's penchant for racializing AIDS is troubling. It is apparent that Mbeki seems to think that concern over the pandemic in the West is motivated by the idea that Africans are somehow immoral: "We are blamed as criminals and seen as human beings of a lower order that cannot subject its passions to reason . . . as natural-born, promiscuous carriers of germs, unique in the world, doomed to a mortal end because of our unconquerable devotion to the sin of lust" (Mbeki, quoted in *Economist,* London, February 21, 2002). Yet reflecting on Mbeki's outburst, Guest (2004: 17) comments:

There is a simpler explanation. People who worry about AIDS in Africa do so because the disease threatens to kill more people than all the continent's wars put together and multiplied by ten. And in countries where a quarter of the adult population is infected, it is clear that someone is having unprotected sex. Without frank discussion of what exactly people are doing in bed and behind bushes, it will be impossible to curb the epidemic.

It is axiomatic that "the HIV/AIDS pandemic is the number one survival threat both to Africans as individuals and to African countries and their prospects for development and governance. If, as seems probable, the economic and governance impact of HIV/AIDS will be far greater than has been anticipated hitherto, it will be necessary to move HIV/AIDS to the head of the Nepad agenda" as well as openly discuss the pandemic (De Waal, 2002: 475). However, as it stands, the lack of any earnest attention paid to gender and to the HIV/AIDS pandemic fundamentally undermines Nepad as a serious document of regeneration and renewal.

Notes

1. Tipped by some to be Mbeki's successor as president of South Africa.
2. Castro Hlongwane was a 17-year-old thrown out of a KwaZulu-Natal holiday resort by its white owner, who supposedly claimed that the teenager had AIDS and would rape other campers. The use of his name in the document was presumed to illustrate the alleged "racist agenda" of anyone who opposed Mbeki's stance on the pandemic.

7

Another False Sart?

This volume has sought to evaluate Nepad as the latest plan aimed at promoting the African continent's renewal. Overall, it has advanced the argument that Nepad needs to overcome both a great deal of skepticism *and* needs a heavy dose of realism. This skepticism is based largely on an understanding of how politics in Africa works and the subsequent conviction that the type of governance strictures that make up Nepad cannot be hurriedly implemented—as Nepad demands—without undermining the basis upon which most African presidents and their followers base their rule. In other words the empirical state in Africa does not conform to Western conceptions of the Weberian state, something that Nepad fails to acknowledge. Indeed, it is precisely the rational-bureaucratic state that is taken as an assumed given within Nepad. This is hugely problematic as many of the accepted features of a democratic state are simply not present in large swathes of the continent, even though African elites have been adept at appropriating the external guarantees for their states (Clapham, 1996a). While it may be true that it is our (Western) conceptions of the state in Africa, rather than the state itself, which has failed (Dunn and Shaw, 2001) this overall does not really help the average African, mired in poverty and all too often susceptible to autocratic impulses and predatory rule by her leaders, despite the promises made by Nepad. Indeed, "alternative" formulations of the state in Africa, which may take the form of emphasizing the informal and those activities outside of the "normal" functions of the state as a solution to Africa's impasse, are somewhat problematic. As Leys (1994: 36) remarks:

> Contrary to the wishful thinking of some observers [the increase in the informal] is part of the pathology of Africa's collapse, not a seed-bed of renewal. Anyone who believes that, for example, carrying sacks of cocoa beans on bicycles along devious forest tracks to sell them illegally across the frontier is more promising for the economy than taking them directly

to the port by truck, is not to be taken seriously. People resort to the second economy for survival, to escape the predations of the corrupt and parasitic state machinery, that is all: they bribe the police to look the other way, they pay no tax, and the roads still get worse.

Equally problematic however is the fact that "enforcing basic democratic rights in Africa would mean reviewing and replacing practically every government in Africa. With less than five exceptions, Africa's governments are dictatorships, whether this fact is proclaimed openly and proudly or quietly enforced through manipulating elections and jailing opponents" (Van der Walt, 2003). And the chance that such elites will commit effective class suicide in the furtherance of Nepad is viewed with some doubt. That perhaps Nepad's own promoters implicitly recognize this might be seen in Mbeki's rather defensive dismissal of the notion that "Africa's political leaders cannot be trusted to promote and entrench democracy and human rights" (Mbeki, 2002d).

Some defenders of Nepad are quick to label such skepticism as "Afropessimism" (Maloka, 2002). This is rejected as I believe that an honest appraisal of the current situation on the continent is far more useful to the reader than some naïve celebration of Nepad based, seemingly, on what elites say, rather than what they do (e.g., Kanbur, 2001; Akinrinade, 2002; Hope, 2002). One of the leading promoters of Nepad at least appears to recognize this, with Wade complaining in October 2004 that:

> I am disappointed [with Nepad]. I have great difficulties explaining what we have achieved when people at home and elsewhere ask me that question. . . . We're spending a lot of money and, above all, losing time with repetition and conferences that end and you're not quite sure what they've achieved (*Cameroon Tribune,* Yaoundé, October 25, 2004).[1]

In addition, criticism that concepts such as democracy and accountability are "Western" imports and/or culturally specific, implicit in ZANU-PF's defense of its thuggery or Obasanjo's dismissal of accusations of electoral impropriety, are also rejected, as is the idea that concepts originating from outside of the continent cannot be useful in understanding Africa. Of course, recognition that we must be careful in applying "non-African" ideas to the study of Africa is conceded, but:

> We must reject outright any attempt to assign a particular conceptual category as belonging only to the "West" and therefore inapplicable to the African situation. For millennia, Africa has been part of Europe as Europe has been part of Africa and out of this relation, a whole series of borrowed traditions from both sides have been and continues to be brewed and fermented. To deny this inter-cultural exchange and reject all theoretical imports from Europe is to violate the order of knowledge and simultane-

ously disregard the contribution of various Africans to European cultural
and intellectual history and vice-versa (Bakare-Yusuf, 2002: 11).

Besides, incredulity vis-à-vis Nepad can be reversed through the production and demonstration of concrete results, even if such moves—criticizing
Mugabe rather than openly endorsing him, for example—may well only be
gestures in the short term. Of course, the project is a renewal program for
the whole continent and, even if successful, would take many years to show
noteworthy results, but it is surely imperative that the elites associated with
Nepad demonstrate some commitment to what they have signed up to quite
soon. This is not impossible, nor unreasonable. But this is also where
grounds for the skepticism shown so far toward the plan are largely self-
created by the project's own initiators. Open support of Mugabe has cast
Nepad's high-sounding rhetoric regarding democracy and good governance
into sharp relief—and rightly so. After all, "It [is] hypocritical of Mbeki to
punt Nepad while he is scuttling its founding premise: financial reward for
good governance" (*Citizen,* Johannesburg, February 14, 2003). Indeed:

> African states have to appreciate that they cannot unilaterally rewrite the
> Nepad contract and attempt to detach its economic benefits from the
> accompanying political obligations, "cherry picking," as it were, those
> aspects of the project they find most appealing while disregarding the oth-
> ers. African states, and South Africa in particular, have objected to what
> they see as a Western fixation with Zimbabwe at the expense of the bigger
> African picture and they particularly resent the threat to inflict collective
> punishment on Africa for Mugabe's failings. However, this is to miss the
> point, for the two issues are inextricably tied. The lessons that Western
> governments and potential foreign investors are drawing from African
> states' complicity with the Zimbabwean outcome is that Mugabe style
> behaviour is a very real possibility in those states too and that peer pres-
> sure on fellow African leaders to adhere to democratic norms is virtually
> non-existent (Hamill, 2002: 18).

But Zimbabwe is but one case and critique should not—cannot—be limited
to that alone.

Far more important in my mind is the fact that many of Nepad's stalwarts do not practice what they are now preaching, either to the rest of
Africa nor to the international community. It is unreasonable that the likes
of Omar Bongo or Denis Sassou-Nguesso sit on Nepad's HSIC and (presumably) sign off on pledges towards democracy and clean government.
And it is remarkable that the likes of Dorothy Njeuma sit on a so-called
independent Eminent Persons panel, while being a member of Paul Biya's
political party and openly canvassing for him in "elections." The Nepad
summit held in Algiers in late November 2004 graphically illustrated this
absolute disjuncture between rhetoric and practice. Obasanjo, we are told,

informed the conference that "things are on the brighter side" and that "it is clear that the success of the peer review mechanism will considerably increase the credibility of African countries in their efforts to ensure growth, development, stability and democracy" (*Nigeria First,* Abuja, November 25, 2004). Assembled in the audience as part of this credible group of leaders interested in development, stability, and democracy? No less than Dos Santos of Angola, Sassou-Nguesso of Congo-Brazzaville, and Bongo of Gabon.

As the South African writer Breyten Breytenbach asks, "The sham of recognizing a regime irrespective of how it came to power, makes the members of the [Nepad] club partners in infamy and the greed for power at all costs. Will Nepad escape the double-talk?" (Breytenbach, 2002). And lest observers argue that Bongo or Biya's membership of the HSIC is nothing more than regional representation or symbolic buy-in, note Mbeki's comments that "implementation of the plan will commence as soon as briefings have been completed and commitments made by a critical number of African countries . . . Countries that are not ready will be welcome to join later" (cited in Nabudere, 2002: 6–7). This implies that, at least as far as Mbeki and Nepad promoters are concerned, Bongo, Biya, Sassou-Nguesso, Dos Santos, and others have all presumably made believable commitments to good governance and are actually ready and willing to move forward along the lines prescribed by Nepad. As a result of such illusory rhetoric, the notion that Nepad is simply a show, like other aspects of political life on the continent (Cruise O'Brien, 2003), soon gains credibility. But if this is so, then what of the substance that seemed to promise so much in the run up to the launch?

The disjuncture between rhetoric and reality is probably why the G8 has adopted a wait-and-see attitude and has not rushed to embrace Nepad beyond—again—rhetorical flourishes, as Mbeki, Obasanjo, and others had hoped.[2] Key promoters of the program have had to learn the hard way that simply announcing a plan, as "paradigm changing" as it may be on paper, is not enough, particularly when, as Chapter 2 demonstrated, Nepad is but the latest in a long line of African recovery plans. Aware of this history, the G8 has held back from committing the massive resources demanded by the Nepad framework.

Indeed, as Chapter 2 detailed, all previous recovery plans have failed due, in part, to a distinct lack of political and financial commitment by those African leaders who signed up to them. I have already detailed my doubts about the true commitment to Nepad from a political angle, but from the financial side it looks as if Nepad is going the same way as other previous plans. A report in November 2004 supports this analysis, pointing out that up to late 2004, only $4 billion has been collected for Nepad "out of a colossal sum of 64 billion dollars required each year." In fact:

Heads of State [will] have to tackle the tricky issue of raising money to support their projects, which appears to be the most difficult puzzle to get Nepad going. After three years trying to lay the groundwork little appears to be on track, at least, financially. Out of the four billion dollars collected about 2.5 billion has been made available by the World Bank. This implies that contributions from member States have been insignificant. Furthermore, the World Bank's assistance to the project has been earmarked for a specific sector—energy development in the South African region. This leaves much of Nepad projects on the drawing board . . . [Yet] at birth, it was agreed that African countries would contribute towards Nepad, taking the challenge into their hands to pay for the projects while seeking foreign assistance, through partnership (*Cameroon Tribune*, Yaoundé, November 23, 2004).

Just as with investment within the continent, if Nepad's own promoters and leaders have so little confidence in the project that they refuse to contribute financially to its success, it seems strange that they expect the outside world to somehow bankroll the whole thing: "It may be pertinent to let the Heads of State and Government in the continent know that Africa's development partners and prospective donor-nations will not throw in their hard earned money if they do not see corresponding evidence of seriousness by those who should be most enthusiastic about the programme" (*Daily Champion*, Lagos, December 8, 2004). The report in November 2004 that Pretoria's Foreign Affairs Minister, Nkosazana Dlamini-Zuma, was being sent to the Middle East "to persuade the Arab nations to invest in Africa" and to market the recovery plan "because there's a lot of pessimism about Nepad" reiterates the need for African leaders to invest African capital, rather than scurrying around the world in the hunt for finance (*BuaNews*, Pretoria, November 26, 2004).[3]

This brings me to another issue. The philosophical premise that African elites should be essentially rewarded for *not* being predatory and/or preventing development is somewhat interesting, as is the notion that the extra $64 billion per year is required not only to plug the alleged resource gap but also to kick-start growth and development on the continent. After all, the barriers to Africa's development are not fundamentally financial— they are political and institutional, and simply introducing more financial resources into the continent will not generate too many results unless fundamental changes are made. But this is the crucial issue facing Nepad. Can these major changes be made as swiftly as Nepad authors seem to believe, in order to release significantly more resources into the continent? And, are all those who have so publicly signed up to making such reforms prepared to go through with the profound implications such commitments demand, particularly when a good deal of them are seen by many as the "principal obstacle to qualitative changes in Africa"? (Bathily, 1994: 68). The answer is, almost certainly, not, with even those countries that have signed up to

Nepad exhibiting very little real commitment to its strictures and resolutions:

> Nepad has gained nominal support from African heads of state but support is very shallow . . . South Africa's president is the only one to have spent any significant time promoting the plan. Heads of state signed the document but have done little to promote it or its pledges of good governance within their societies. Many African states appear to have adopted a posture of waiting to see what if any money Nepad offers before taking action to embrace and sell its principles of reform (Herbert, 2003).

The Governance Problem

The key problem facing the continent is the ability or otherwise of governance and development initiatives such as Nepad to successfully operate in the context of neopatrimonialism and Big Men politics. As Chabal (2002) notes, any cool evaluation of the political situation on the continent undermines the potency of the renewal project as a means toward better governance. I have already remarked that "rewarding" leaders with extra resources for *not* undermining human rights and not preventing democracy is flawed. This is because in my mind good governance should not be dealt with as a tradable commodity or some sort of bargaining chip with the outside world. Shouldn't African leaders be encouraging the practice of good governance irrespective of the stance of the industrialized states? And besides, "good governance is something African leaders owe first and foremost to their own people," rather than, as Nepad promoters have framed it, "a condition of their relationship with the continent's creditors" (*Sunday Times*, Johannesburg, September 22, 2002). As Seepe rather bitingly put it:

> Nepad's subtext is: "We African leaders, having failed to consolidate democracy, to ensure sound economic management, and to bring about people-centered development in our countries, come before you chaps in the G8 to enlist your support. If you give us money, we promise to honor the commitments we made to our people. We need to be rewarded for what we should have been doing in the first place" (quoted in *Mail and Guardian*, Johannesburg, July 12, 2002).

A Zambian writer goes further and states that:

> The Africans [promoting Nepad] are asking the rich countries to bribe them to practice democratic governance and to pursue policies of economic and political stability . . . There is no reason whatsoever for the people of Africa to be proud that their leaders are now offering to sell their "good governance" commitment for a few billion dollars . . . Why should our leaders be paid to do the right thing? Don't they have a conscience of their

own to simply know that it is wrong for them to tolerate corruption and general bad governance, with or without developmental aid from the rich? Why can't they simply be [good leaders] even when it does not involve any money? (Chisala, 2002).

Indeed, in such a case, if the $64 billion that is required as part of Nepad does not arrive, then does that mean that notions of accountability and democratic rule will be quietly dropped?

Be that as it may, there has been very little concrete progress or substance vis-à-vis Nepad beyond a host of meetings, summits, pronouncements, and speeches. One commentator links this to the very nature of Mbeki's politicking:

> Despite Mbeki's clear intellectual ambition . . . there [is an] inconsequentiality to his presidency. Endless initiatives [are] announced with grand éclat—a policy co-ordination unity here, an integrated rural development policy there—but within a short time these initiatives [are] abandoned, for there [is] no follow-through. It [is] as if Mbeki enjoy[s] giving the inaugurating speech for such initiatives but [loses] interest once the speech [is] over. The two greatest examples are his Nepad . . . and the African Union (Johnson, 2004: 222).

In practical terms, whatever Nepad's intentions are, and a good number of these, particularly regarding democracy and good government, are praiseworthy, any short-term successes are likely to be hidebound—if not prevented—by Africa's well-established governance problems such as personal rule, clientelism, corruption, and the unwillingness of the majority of state leaders to engage with nongovernmental organizations or expend resources on broad-based development projects. The logic of neopatrimonialism underpins politics in Africa and rules out the very type of policies that Nepad advocates, such as accountability and good governance. As Clapham (1985: 186) noted, some twenty years ago now:

> The problem is not where you should be trying to go, but how you should get there. And the most evident tragedy of third world states lies in the fact that many of those comparatively few states that have managed to build effective institutions on the basis of shared values have dramatically failed to do so. . . . In these cases the most evident sources of the problem . . . has been the refusal of those elites which control the state to accept the diminution in their position of privilege which accountability would imply.

Most previous commentaries on Nepad have ignored this reality. In brief, and recapping a general theme of this volume regarding Nepad and its appropriateness to the current African milieu, in spite of the façade of the modern state, power in most African politics progresses informally, between patron and client along lines of reciprocity. This system is deeply personalized and is generally not implemented on behalf of the general populace, but rather key constituencies that are strategic to maintaining patronage arrangements. Most African countries broadly follow this pattern, including such ostensible Nepad stalwarts such as Nigeria, Angola, Gabon, Congo-Brazzaville, Cameroon, and so forth. Indeed, very few countries have avoided such a state of affairs, and this is perhaps the fundamental problem facing Nepad's credibility:

> One cannot imagine that a union designed by the beneficiaries of state power . . . would be allowed to work to any other advantage than that of the dominant political class. And this raises an absolutely fundamental point: that in the global scheme of things we assume that the state apparatus exists largely to protect the security of its citizens. Across much of Africa . . . this is simply not so . . . To succeed, even moderately, Nepad is going to demand the commitment of political leaders . . . to policies that may cause them considerable discomfort . . . It is, in a way, a self-denying ordinance (Cornwell, 2000: 94, 95).

As noted in Chapter 1, under neopatrimonial systems of governance the separation of the public from the private is recognized (even if in practice only on paper) and is certainly publicly displayed through the theatricalities of power (Cruise O'Brien, 2003: 141–154). However, in practical terms the private and public spheres are habitually not separated. Such neopatrimonial practices are deeply entrenched within society (Chabal and Daloz, 1999), and there are profound obstacles for any initiative—Nepad or otherwise—to deal with questions of governance and development through the reconfiguration (i.e., democratization) of power when clientelism and patronage politics are so firmly deep rooted. The implications for Nepad may mean that it is little more than an instrument calculated to gain Western endorsement of certain elites and the continuation of resource flows (Chabal, 2002). Furthermore, there is the very real danger that rather than implementing genuine reforms, Nepad may evolve into yet another institutional structure but one with very little influence. That seems to be the implication already, if one looks at the various elaborate structures being proposed by Nepad's Secretariat. And concomitant with this, there is the danger that Nepad's promoters are seeking to turn it into some sort of giant pan-African co-coordinating agency for expected inflows of FDI and aid. Yet, Nepad, as it is progressing, is becoming more and more problematic:

> It is in dire danger of becoming a mechanism for aid-funded projects, a sort of mega-NGO, distinguished by the fact that its governing board consists of heads-of-state. What's happened to the government-citizens partnership? . . . Governments should implement the reforms necessary to realize Nepad goals . . . Nepad should be about policy . . . Nepad is not an

implementing agency. If it were to become so, it would be a competitor to existing ministries and departments and would rightly be shunned. Nepad has no business in projects. It has no business handling resources (De Waal and Raheem, 2004: 3–4).

In fact, the Nepad Secretariat until recently was quite active in showcasing itself as an implementing agency and claiming all sorts of credit for a multitude of initiatives and projects, most of which actually have nothing to do with the recovery plan. Now, as remarked earlier, it is denying that there are in fact any such "Nepad projects." Confusion and contradiction seems to be the order of the day, causing Senegal's president to remark: "We have not had one project that has been realised. It is time to reflect . . . We are spending lots of resources on conferences and we still don't know our objectives" (*Saturday Star,* Johannesburg, October 23, 2004).

But returning to the theme of this volume, "It beggars belief that a gathering of men [i.e., Nepad elites] who benefit from disorder will help unravel . . . disorder; that they will pave the way for good government in their countries; that they will give up their cash cows, surrender power and, with it, their means to a livelihood" (quoted in *Mail and Guardian,* Johannesburg, July 12, 2002). Certainly, it is suggested that trying to enlist the support of elites who are expected to undermine their own positions and the positions of their supporters is naive. And even if there exists a particularly visionary leader, one of Africa's supposed "New Leaders" (Ottaway, 1999), then how the strongest societal obstacles to reforms are to be overcome is left unspoken. There have been a series of case studies that demonstrate that bureaucracies and parliaments in particular stall reform the most (Haggard and Webb, 1994: 13–15). In Africa it is fairly well established that states present bureaucrats with access to patronage and power (World Bank, 2000). Reforms, as advocated by projects such as Nepad, threaten this access and stimulate resistance. Thus even if political will and visionary leadership is present (and this is doubtful vis-à-vis perhaps most of the signatories to the APRM or even HSIC), the types of relationships that are embedded within and around most African state machineries (who are, according to Nepad, to be the key implementers and promoters of the renewal project) can prevent the very same sorts of governance strictures advocated by the program. This means that analyses of Nepad that move beyond agential explanations—a must for any coherent study—will come up against the structural impediments of governance reforms that the recovery plan demands.

In addition, Nepad also stresses a functioning, administrative state with a competent, committed, and non-corrupt bureaucracy. This simply does not exist across whole swathes of the continent: "The state [has] long ceased to perform as a mechanism to meet peoples' long-term survival needs" (Reno, 2004: 108). Certainly, the type of development policies articulated by Nepad would require major infrastructural needs to be addressed, such as education, communications, the maintenance of a conducive political and economic environment, a reliable legal framework, the assurance of public order, and the sort of milieu that can encourage and guarantee long-term FDI. But, "if these functions cannot be efficiently performed, as is unquestionably the case for a large number of African states, then development policies which depend on them will fail" (Clapham, 1996b: 822).

Africa's economic predicament has continued for now over two decades because, in large part, state elites have fallen short of executing thoroughgoing economic and political reforms and overseeing a capable administrative state. This is because, whether they are presidents or powerful bureaucrats, the continent's leaders have continued with clientelistic politics that safeguard their advantaged positions within society and provide access to resources, even while development remains trapped and the broad masses suffer. There is very little evidence, despite the pronouncements contained in Nepad, that this situation has fundamentally changed, even if the democratization waves of the late 1980s/early 1990s have created—in part—somewhat different environments within which elites on the continent must navigate their control. Indeed, what is alarming vis-à-vis the supposed reformist (political or economic) impulses that have enervated the continent recently is the "partial reform syndrome" that stakes out much of Africa. Characterized by continued economic crises and typified by enduring clientelism and a pattern of ongoing foreign aid disbursements (even though many African elites are demonstrably failing to implement meaningful reforms), the continent's leaders continue business pretty much as usual, even if they have had to learn new skills to do so (Van de Walle, 2001).

A good number of the democratic transitions have not only been very limited in scope and invariably confined to electoralism, but also have often been hijacked by civilianizing military dictators, returnee Bretton Woods employees, or recycled elites who held positions in previous (now derided as undemocratic and corrupt) regimes. Indeed, what is striking in a great many countries that have undergone "democratization" over the past twenty years or so is that in many of them the political terrain is dominated by a very narrow group of elites who have been at the apex of the system for years, often since independence. However, "the outcome of the elections has been to confer on those leaders an aura of 'democratic' legitimacy that, ironically from the perspective of Western donors, has strengthened their patrimonial claim to rule" (Chabal, 2002: 462). Certainly, such African leaders have been able to carry on as aid recipients even though they ignore much of the conditionalities that have been supposedly imposed as part of SAPs. And where they do implement them, this is invariably partial in nature if not subverted entirely so that reform strictures in point of fact strengthen neopatrimonial practices.

Much of this, it is suggested, is because African elites have been remarkably adept at learning what the donors want to hear, and making their pronouncements fit accordingly, even if they are rhetorical add-ons with little concrete commitment. The inclusion of gender in Nepad, as detailed in Chapter 6, is a case in point. Nepad's strictures on gender certainly talk the right language but, as various commentators have noted, there is very little practical detail on how gender inequality on the continent is going to be addressed. Of course, Nepad is a general document of intent, but even so, the approach taken to gender empowerment stands out as little more than rhetorical additions. Certainly, "in common with most high-level [i.e., male elite] African initiatives, the involvement of women has been at best marginal, and commitments to gender equity such as those adopted in Beijing have not been accorded mainstream status within Nepad" (De Waal, 2002: 73). As for HIV/AIDS, one of the greatest threats facing the African continent, this is barely mentioned at all—a remarkable omission and one that may come back to haunt Nepad when, in years to come, commentators will reevaluate the project's progress.

But overall, if the analysis of postcolonial state formations in Africa within this book is correct then its operations are largely based on and directed by the imperatives of privatized patronage and the prohibition and erosion of real, functioning democracy—in other words, broad accountability. Long-term development and broad-based inclusivity—including gender empowerment—is more or less off of the agenda in most countries. Practically, implementing and operating by Nepad's rubric of "good governance" would inevitably damage the incumbent elites' own personalized grip on the system and reduce their ability to service their clients, probably leading to their replacement by others. As a result, the speedy implementation of Nepad's measures on governance and accountability, which are really preconditions for the continent's future development, is viewed with some doubt. After all, it is not simply about reordering politics on the continent and thus "getting the politics right," but is rather much more deeply rooted and contextual and there are no easy solutions nor shortcuts.

The Role of the Developed World

Nepad is quite explicit in its ambition to obtain from the developed world the resources needed for the continent's development. We have already seen in Chapter 4 the problematic point of departure that this demonstrates regarding the "resource gap" in Africa. While governments often claim to not have enough finances to invest in development, patrimonial and predatory administration is the main cause of this shortage and lack of capacity or will to implement policies.[4] As Herbert (2003) remarks:

There is a common line of argument that poor governance in Africa is the result of a lack of capacity. Lack of capacity in turn is blamed on poor education and poor salaries, which are blamed on lack of money. Too often African politicians dismiss their lack of delivery by blaming those two things—lack of money and capacity. There are some technical fields in which education matters [but] African governments have for too long failed to abide by even basic standards of service delivery. President Moi, for example, show[ed] great intelligence in manipulating the political system to his advantage and [was] able, when it suit[ed] him, to mobilise thousands of government agents to his purposes. Surely if that same cleverness were applied to delivering better services, things would improve. As a result, I submit that the fundamental failure in many African nations is not lack of money as much as lack of political will.

Where Nepad is on firmer ground is in its quest for a fairer global trading system, particularly with regard to attaining greater access to global markets for the continent's exporters. And this is where the developed world, if it is serious about trying to aid Africa's situation, can help, particularly with regard to opening up markets for African agricultural products and improving the quality of technical aid (Alden, 2002). Much of this, however, is dependent on the results of tariff negotiations with the EU and the U.S. and on the willingness of African state machinery to eliminate internal obstacles to African producers.

However, the limited nature of Nepad reveals some shortcomings on this score. There is certainly a too easy acceptance and naïve belief in the willingness of the G8 to compromise its power and core interests, and there is a definite link between how "globalized" a country is and its stake in Nepad. This reinforces the idea, put forward in Chapter 4, that the driving force behind Nepad's initial establishment is this linkage between export-driven trade policies and the interests of key elites in strategically important African countries with growing interests in an economically liberalized continent. As Melber (2002a) notes, there is the perception that "Nepad offers the opportunity for South African capital to expand further in Africa by creating new market access. Nepad is hence considered as a lubricant for a South African expansion into other parts of the continent, which under an Apartheid regime until the mid-1990s would have not been conceivable" (see also Naidu, 2003).

I would argue that a thorough overhaul of the international financial system is a prerequisite if Africa is to even begin tackling its lack of development, setting aside the very real internal problems of neopatrimonial rule that have been identified as holding the continent back. As part of this overhaul, the subsidies for agricultural producers in the North would need to be addressed, as such structures effectively close off the developed world's markets to African exports. As Christian Aid (2002) notes:

Currently, even the most democratic of African governments in Africa find trade rules are stacked against them. Western markets are closed to many of their exports, and yet they are forced to open their own markets to subsidized imports from the rich world. At the same time they are forbidden from adequately supporting or protecting their own vulnerable producers in the way that almost all Western countries do.

However, much of the debate on market access within Nepad focuses on tariffs and quotas but misses the essential point. Of course, tariffs and quotas are important for already active traders and investors. But, the issue of subsidies is far more important. Any development plan that claims to support agriculture in Africa and help alleviate rural poverty has to directly target the subsidies in the West. After all, it is estimated that sub-Saharan Africa's annual loss from exports over the past 30 years has been calculated at $68 billion (Subramanian and Tamirisa, 2001: 3).

Such facts beg the question, why was it that Nepad received such an initially positive response from the G8? It is partly because Nepad does not ask deep questions regarding the structural arrangements of the global economy and because it can fit more or less neatly within the ongoing liberalizing discourse. Furthermore, it would have been politically unthinkable for any Western leader simply to turn his back on an initiative coming out of Africa, despite any misgivings. Besides, sympathetic hearings do not cost too much. And as argued in Chapter 4, there was an increasing realization as the twentieth century drew to a close that poverty in the developing world constituted more of a systemic threat to the liberal global economy than perhaps had been previously realized and that increasing protests against "globalization" at all the elite meeting points needed some form of reply. Mbeki and others seized this opportune moment and latched onto what at the time seemed favorably disposed social democrats in key Western countries (primarily Britain and Canada). Thus dressing up Nepad as Africa's own contribution to the Third Way sought to build on space opened by some quite specific contextual impulses.

Yet, this space, dependent as it was upon the receptiveness of the likes of Blair and Chrétien, was brutally narrowed by the events of 9/11 and the consequent shifting of priorities away from Africa (unless it fitted somehow into the ongoing War on Terror). The invasion of Iraq and the consequent massive diversion of resources into first that campaign and the subsequent rebuilding project, let alone the continuing skirmishes in Afghanistan and elsewhere, has seen Africa's place on the global agenda rapidly slide. The new main concerns of security cooperation and anti-terrorism, rather than the type of absolute support for Africa's leaders that Nepad essentially advocates, are now the order of the day and certainly places serious questions around the sustainability of Nepad as it currently stands, dependent as it is on external largesse. At the same time, the debacle in Zimbabwe very quickly (perhaps prematurely) held up Nepad to its first test, which as Chapter 5 suggested, it failed in a rather spectacular fashion. As Hamill (2002: 18) remarks, "the first major opportunity for African governments to demonstrate their commitment *in practice* to the principles of Nepad came . . . with the presidential election in Zimbabwe and it was a test that, in the main, they failed lamentably."

What this has provided to the continent is a notable lesson in self-reliance, which may in the long run actually be quite positive. Certainly, Africa's recovery plan would have been far more advised to construct a plan that sought to mobilize the continent's own private and public resources as a means to pay toward any recovery project, while advancing an agenda to address major structural barriers to African trade, rather than naively relying on the West as the external motor of recovery. After all, it is estimated that 40 percent of wealth created in Africa is invested outside the continent (*This Day,* Lagos, December 4, 2003). As the Port Harcourt-based Center for Advanced Social Science (CASS) noted: "the goals of Nepad are laudable. However . . . Nepad is predicated on the notion that foreign assistance is indispensable to national development. That presupposes that the forces of development are largely exogenous. Such a notion negates the experiences of developed countries. There is no substitute for development forces that must come from within" (CASS Newsletter, 2002: 2). But of course, relying on endogenous resources would need serious interrogation into the levels of capital shifted outside of Africa. Addressing capital flight would have meant an indirect (or perhaps, direct) attack on the corruption and squandering of the continent's resources by Africa's elites and their international partners. And as the Zimbabwe case has shown, such full opposition to the continent's Big Men very quickly loses its steam.

But this is where the nature of the continent's politics again comes into play. Africa's own trade structures, often subordinates—if not sabotages—African producers, sacrificed before the needs of the elites to maintain power and prevent the emergence of potential rivals. This can generate more damage than tariffs imposed from abroad (Wang and Winters, 1998). Certainly, as Bates (1981) showed, most African states adopt policies that are damaging to broad-based agriculture as part of a strategy to pacify urban residents and avoid disturbances in the urban areas. In other words, political expediency goes before agricultural development. And where policy does not erode the agricultural productivity of a country (as in Kenya, see Bates, 1989), this is because the state was intimately linked to the interests of a rural farming elite. In other words, policy is not the outcome of an optimization process altered and influenced by interest groups within a structured and transparent political process but is rather, within the politics of clientelism and patronage, the tactics of actors able to deploy their resources and/or call in favors so as to manipulate aspiring and incumbent politicians and hence the political system. As long as the logic of neopatrimonialism more or less directs policymaking, this is unlikely to change, in spite of Nepad's pronouncements on governance. Thus again, how politics is practiced in large parts on the continent reveals the extent to which Nepad's ambitious goals are contrary to the reality on the ground.

Identifying Allies for Development?

If the analysis relating to the nature of governance modalities on the continent is accepted, then Nepad appears perilously divorced from the actualities that stake out fairly large parts of Africa (including most Nepad participants). Certainly, the dynamics of many state formations in Africa serve to limit the ability for reform and development (and hence sabotages Nepad). With such forms of governance, in effect, "shadow states" (Reno, 1999), dominating large parts of Africa, it is doubtful whether many of the current elites who head such states will line up behind Nepad if and when it moves beyond rhetoric to practical action. In cases where state elites use the mantle of sovereignty to help bolster their own patronage networks and weaken those of potential challengers rather than to promote the collective good, relying upon the very same elites to end such practices and embrace Nepad in a meaningful fashion will be inherently problematic.

That is why Africa's renewal depends not on the Obasanjos or Bongos of this world but on the development of working relationships between reform-minded and serious state elites and associations on the continent, be they formal or informal, that promote welfare and public services. Mutual accountability between the two may stimulate greater responsibility and chart a new way forward for Africa, although where Nepad fits in, with its elitist nature and its failure to gain approval from virtually all grassroots organizations on the continent, is questionable. This is tragic for any African-led initiative, given that NGOs and grassroots organizations are more and more important as actors in their own right promoting development and can, if circumstances allow, spur an interesting synergy between state and society (Tripp, 2003). And in situations where the state is so predatory yet at the same time inefficient in promoting growth and development, local networks can reduce transaction costs using culturally based formations (Brautigam, 1997). Further, it is in the ordinary people that the struggle for democracy and accountability is grounded (Harrison, 2002), not, in the main, with the elites, despite what Nepad claims. As Young (2004: 48) remarks, "the empirical state . . . is likely to fall well short of the praiseworthy standards of the African renaissance version," but of course, this is a key problem. In this light it is thus entirely predictable that an elite-led initiative such as Nepad should shut out nonstate voices, particularly as "a bottom-up approach will immediately reveal what the nature of a state is and how committed it really is to Nepad" (*Sunday Times,* Johannesburg, December 28, 2003).

Yet, as part of any meaningful partnership, the G8 should devise a partnership with the peoples of Africa, not its venal elites, and should encourage the development of this "reconfiguration" of state power across the continent (Boone, 1998; Joseph, 1999), while at the same time balancing this by providing technical resources to those states that are genuine in their reform efforts (i.e., those who fulfill agreed conditionalities) (Mills and Sidiropoulos, 2004). Providing assistance to serious state elites should continue, while those who lack such credentials should be provided with advice, but no resources (Guest, 2004: 162). Harmonizing aid amongst donors and making it more accountable (through perhaps outcomes-based evaluations) would help. Slippage will occur and it will be a long journey. Indeed, "it is unrealistic to think that countries in Africa can suddenly reverse course and institutionalize stable democratic government simply by changing leaders, constitutions and/or public mentalities. If progress is made toward developing democratic government, it is likely to be gradual, messy, fitful, and slow, with many imperfections along the way" (Diamond, 1989: 24). But we should not give up hope.

Serious African state elites genuinely interested in broad-based, long-term development and democracy need sustained encouragement (however this may transpire) to construct genuine relations with their own citizens, rather than as at present, mainly either with international actors (donors, corporations, bankers, foreign governments, investors, etc.) or with fairly narrow circles of clients within the domestic patronage system—the two sets often overlap (Bach, 1999; Callaghy, Kassimir, and Latham, 2001). Humanitarian aid and technical assistance must continue, but mutual answerability (and accountability to the citizens in both granting and recipient states) needs profound strengthening, as does the African state's legitimacy (Englebert, 2000). As Scott (1998: 273) notes:

> As long as public officials or businessmen can conspicuously display their enormous wealth that cannot be attributed to their innovation, business acumen, hard work, inheritance, winning the lottery etc., without any fear of being asked by the appropriate authorities to account for their wealth, inefficiencies and corruption will continue to flourish. The average African must first realize that the luxury automobiles or the villas arrogantly displayed by a public servant may be connected with his or her poverty and deplorable living conditions.

Indeed, at the end of the day, fundamental political changes must come from within Africa, with backing from outside playing a supportive role. This is certainly possible: Africa has an enormous potential and its current state is *not* due to some inherent "Africanness" that holds the continent back. Its predicament has political rather than intrinsically cultural roots, and the future is not closed, nor inevitable. It is the task for the continent's peoples to build on its own rich human, mineral, and agricultural resources. The international community *can* play an accommodating role, particularly in helping build capacity and supporting Africans' efforts to exercise responsible power through legal channels and through rehabilitating the state into something capable of pursuing developmental goals—a tall task, admittedly, but not unattainable (Stein, 2000). But picking who to work with needs to be far more selective than at present. Certainly, there should be a complete refusal to lend and donate to state elites where there is an absence of the rule of law, good governance, and sensible economic policies (Rotberg, 2000).[5]

With regard to future engagement with Nepad by key Western allies, this is looking less certain, although as this is written it is perhaps too early to say—and it may not necessarily be wholly negative. Certainly, the announcement by British Prime Minister Tony Blair in early 2004 that he is setting up a Commission for Africa to take a fresh look at the challenges Africa faces in the context of the global forces in play in the twenty-first century is not good news for Nepad or its credibility (*Star,* Johannesburg, March 29, 2004). After all, if Nepad was deemed to be working and credible, why would the British establish a separate entity that duplicates it? The new commission is supposed to discuss Africa's development challenges in the areas of the economy, education, conflict resolution, peace building, health, the environment, HIV/AIDS, governance, and culture—all more or less within Nepad's remit. The implications of the new initiative are that the British government does not have full confidence in Nepad: "Virtually every major theme of [the British] commission is a major strategic objective of Nepad. Is the British government letting the cat out of the bag regarding G8 intentions towards Nepad?" (*Business Day,* Johannesburg, March 24, 2004). Indeed, the commission suggests that "the British government is getting impatient with the pace of political and economic reforms in Africa, and may be signaling a new paradigm in Africa-G8 relations, whereby Western democracies bypass normal channels in Africa in the bid to assist Africans in need" (*Business Day,* March 24, 2004). In other words, have the British given up on most of the elites in Africa as agents of positive change? Certainly, the "new Commission signals impatience and lack of confidence with Africa's home-grown development paradigm" (i.e., Nepad) (*Business Day,* March 24, 2004). The fact is, if Prime Minister Blair had real faith in Nepad as a serious partner in achieving the Millennium Development Goals, surely he would not have felt the need to set up his Commission for Africa, which, cynics might say, is yet another talking shop on Africa's problems.

The American Millennium Challenge, which distributes extra aid and assistance to those countries pursuing approved (i.e., liberal) policies, also suggests that "rather than give general political backing to initiatives like [Nepad], U.S. officials say the Millennium Challenge initiative is a way of backing countries that show commitment to Nepad-style policies" (*Business Day,* Johannesburg, May 10, 2004). The effect of this is to bypass, if not ignore, the APRM and the HSIC, and deal directly with what are perceived to be countries serious about reform. In other words, the Millennium Challenge suggests that Washington has very little confidence in Nepad's ability to make the necessary distinctions between genuine reformers and those who pay mere lip service—and the setting up of Blair's Commission suggests the same. As the Zimbabwe case showed, there is not yet the political will among Africa's elites to shun even the most heinous regimes. In such circumstances, external actors, either through the Commission for Africa or the Millennium Challenge, will pick and choose who to "reward," effectively making Nepad increasingly redundant. But through picking serious leaders, a demonstration effect may be initiated that in the long run is probably far more useful than having a pan-continental recovery plan that pretends that Biya, Bongo, and Dos Santos are earnest in their desire for reform and development. Indeed, drawing a dividing line between the sober leaders and the rest—and focusing efforts and resources on the former—is perhaps the best chance the continent has.

Concluding Remarks

Ultimately, the achievements of Nepad will not be calculated in terms of the amount of conferences and workshops that it generates but in measured increases in democracy, clean government, and economic growth and development. The contention of this book has been that the neopatrimonial nature of most African states is fundamentally deleterious to broad-based development and good governance and it is this that may well ultimately sabotage the high aspirations contained in Nepad. This is because Nepad is an elite-driven, top-down project that has had negligible input from ordinary Africans and that continues to have minimal engagement with the continent's peoples. Furthermore, it has been argued that the credentials of a good number of Nepad's promoters and adherents are highly dubious and in a number of cases are the antithesis of what Nepad is supposed to be about. Why they have been included is because Nepad seeks to be as inclusive as possible, following on from the long-established traditions of pan-African elite solidarity. However, this solidarity, although it may have served Africa well during the dark days of colonialism, apartheid, and the Cold War, is now surely a negative impulse, holding the continent down to the lowest common denominator, despite Nabudere's (2002) protestations to the contrary. Africa desperately needs to move beyond such elite solidarity. After all, "As much as an European Union (EU) has to position itself towards the Jörg Haiders and Silvio Berlusconis in its ranks, an AU . . . and even more so a Nepad has to do so vis-à-vis its culprits" (Melber, 2002a). That is why selectivity by the donor community and external actors about who to work with is absolutely imperative if change in Africa is to be brought about.

What is intriguing here is that on the one hand leaders such as Mbeki lament the fact that the world seems to treat Africa as an undifferentiated mass, so that what happens in Zimbabwe is presumed to happen in Ghana or Botswana. Yet on the other hand the very same leaders insist on African elite unity and that the world affords the same treatment to the entire continent (i.e., the generous disbursal of aid and resources), whether one is a Bongo or a Kabila, or a Wade or a Mogae. Such a stance is ambiguous and untenable: "When Africa's leaders suggest they should not tolerate bad rule, they should walk the walk. They should stop openly hobnobbing with (at least) the worst tyrants among themselves" (*Mail and Guardian,* Johannesburg, July 12, 2002). Yet this elite unity continues to trump any real commitment to democracy and human rights. Consider the vote in November 2004 by the UN General Assembly's human rights committee. Resolutions that would have condemned human rights abuses in Sudan and Zimbabwe were sunk "after nations led by South Africa made their opposition clear." "Just as the two resolutions were introduced, South Africa interrupted and called 'no action' motions—procedural moves that put off consideration of the topic until the next year's General Assembly session" (*South African Press Agency,* New York, November 24, 2004). Britain's UN Ambassador condemned the procedural motions, saying "It is anathema that members of the General Assembly should be prevented from expressing their views," while the U.S. Ambassador remarked, "One wonders, if there can't be a clear and direct statement on matters of basic principle . . . what are we all about?" (*South African Press Agency,* New York, November 24, 2004). I might add, paraphrasing the ambassadors, that it is anathema that leading promoters of Nepad actively prevent criticism of heinous regimes such as in the Sudan and Zimbabwe—if there cannot be a clear and direct statement on matters that are supposedly basic principles of the recovery program, what is Nepad all about?

In this light, grand pronouncements regarding the importance of good governance and democracy or of economic liberalization are made redundant by the behavior and actions of the very same people responsible for drawing up and/or committing themselves to such aims. Again, the divorce between rhetoric and reality is stark and more and more unpalatable. And with regard to Nepad as a new framework for the continent's rebirth, as De

Waal (2002: 465) remarks "Africa doesn't need grand new paradigms: what it needs is a proper application of lessons already learned, and a replication and broader application of existing best practices."

While one needs to be fully aware of the structural constraints on the African state's development, history has sufficiently demonstrated that harmful exogenous influences may pale to insignificance against the destructive talents of homegrown elites in Africa and that simultaneous economic and political change on the continent is exceedingly complex and difficult (Callaghy and Ravenhill, 1993). Without the construction of transparent and accountable government, the rule of law and basic norms such as democracy, Nepad's ambitious economic plans, whatever their own weaknesses, are a nonstarter. It is true that Nepad—as promoted in its initial stages—had a seemingly firm commitment to resolving the governance problem. However, the failure to act in any meaningful way about violations of the principles of sound governance and human rights makes Nepad an unlikely tool to advance Africa's regeneration, compounded by the program's failure to take either AIDS or gender seriously. Uncertainties about what exactly is novel or different regarding the APRM, as well as the failure to engage African civil society, also undermines its credibility (Van der Westhuizen, 2003: 394).

Critical voices from within Africa indeed echo this prognosis, questioning "its optimistic expectations of foreign resource inflows, its analysis of globalization, its gender blindness, the ambiguity and tensions in its relations with existing continental organizations [and] its governance defects" (Graham, 2002: 3). This sort of confusion has marked the developmental discourse for years, and has ominous implications for Nepad:

> African leaders . . . are saddled with a strategy that hardly any of them believes in and that most of them condemn [including Nepad?] . . . Lacking faith in what they are doing and caught between their own interests, the demands of their external patrons, and their constituents, African leaders tend to be ambivalent, confused and prone to marginalize development and even their role in its pursuit. The development of Africa will not start in earnest until the struggle over the development agenda is determined (Ake, 1987: 41).

In the end, Nepad's level of success will depend on one's perspective. As an attention-grabbing reaction to donor fatigue and an attempt to secure more resources for the continent's elites, Nepad may achieve some limited success. In that way it is simply a continuation of the continent's "extraversion" (Bayart, 2000) whereby Africa's elites seek to use external resources to maintain internal power. Indeed, Nepad might be best understood as a strategic response by African leaders to diminishing investment and interest in the continent (Melber, 2002b), and a desire to continue and increase such flows. And as a means to raise the profile of Africa—even if momentarily—then it has succeeded. But thus far, as a grand framework to reconfigure the entire continent and to reconstitute relations with the outside world, Nepad seems an unlikely source to promote Africa's regeneration in the new millennium.

Notes

1. The announcement in December 2004 of a "Nepad-inspired musical," entitled "Sing Africa Dance," to be launched in May 2005, probably did not allay Wade's concerns. See *Sunday Times,* Johannesburg, December 12, 2004.

2. The news that Reatile Mochebelele, the adviser to Nepad on water affairs and sanitation, has been named by the government of Lesotho as the recipient of more than $678,000 in bribes during his tenure as head of the Lesotho delegation on the Highlands Water Commission reinforces this notion that the link between rhetoric and reality is less and less credible with regard to Nepad. Mochebelele, it should be noted, has represented Nepad at many international forums, where he has talked of the need for zero tolerance on corruption and investment in Africa (see *Mercury,* Durban, December, 13, 2004).

3. It was recently revealed by the director of the AU's Peace and Security Division that the organization currently spends only $1.6 million a year on resolving conflicts throughout the entire continent. Given the numerical membership of the AU, this means that each state in Africa contributes less for resolving conflict in Africa—surely a major obstacle to the continent's development—than the price of *one* mid-range automobile (*Cape Times,* Cape Town, July 6, 2004).

4. On a related matter, one is always struck by how no African country rushed to stop the genocide in Rwanda in 1994—pleading lack of finances, capacity, and so on—yet a whole host of countries were able to rustle up the finances and abilities to intervene in the Congolese war (Clark, 2002). That these armed forces were used to indulge in wholesale looting and profiteering on behalf of state elites, rather than doing anything so mundane as saving ordinary Africans' lives, is something rarely commented on.

5. This is *not* a call for neoliberalism, but rather economic policies capable of tapping Africa's immense human capital and economic potential. On "good governance," I would argue that this basically places emphasis on linking rights and responsibilities between the leadership and its citizens. Improving how government works, advancing involvement in the democratic process, promoting gender equality, putting together policies to promote the broad welfare of the people, and strengthening public services such as health and education would be intrinsically part of this process.

Appendix: Nepad in Brief

1. What is Nepad?
The New Partnership for Africa's Development (Nepad) is a vision and strategic framework for Africa's renewal.

2. What are the origins of Nepad?
The Nepad strategic framework document arises from a mandate given to the five initiating Heads of State (Algeria, Egypt, Nigeria, Senegal, South Africa) by the Organization of African Unity (OAU) to develop an integrated socioeconomic development framework for Africa. The 37th Summit of the OAU in July 2001 formally adopted the strategic framework document.

3. What is the need for Nepad?
Nepad is designed to address the current challenges facing the African continent. Issues such as the escalating poverty levels, underdevelopment, and the continued marginalization of Africa needed a new radical intervention, spearheaded by African leaders, to develop a new vision that would guarantee Africa's Renewal.

4. What are Nepad's primary objectives?
- To eradicate poverty
- To place African countries, both individually and collectively, on a path of sustainable growth and development
- To halt the marginalization of Africa in the globalization process and enhance its full and beneficial integration into the global economy
- To accelerate the empowerment of women

5. What are the principles of Nepad?
- Good governance as a basic requirement for peace, security, and sustainable political and socioeconomic development
- African ownership and leadership, as well as broad and deep participation by all sectors of society

• Anchoring the development of Africa on its resources and the resource-fulness of its people
• Partnership between and among African peoples
• Acceleration of regional and continental integration
• Building the competitiveness of African countries and the continent
• Forging a new international partnership that changes the unequal relationship between Africa and the developed world
• Ensuring that all partnerships with Nepad are linked to the Millennium Development Goals and other agreed development goals and targets

6. What is the Nepad program of action?
The Nepad program of action is a holistic, comprehensive, and integrated sustainable development initiative for the revival of Africa, guided by the aforementioned objectives, principles, and strategic focus.

7. What are the Nepad priorities?
a. Establishing the conditions for sustainable development by ensuring
• Peace and security
• Democracy and good, political, economic, and corporate governance
• Regional cooperation and integration
• Capacity building

b. Policy reforms and increased investment in the following priority sectors
• Agriculture
• Human development with a focus on health, education, science and technology, and skills development
• Building and improving infrastructure, including information and communication technology (ICT), energy, transport, water, and sanitation
• Promoting diversification of production and exports, particularly with respect to agro-industries, manufacturing, mining, mineral beneficiation, and tourism
• Accelerating intra-African trade and improving access to markets of developed countries
• The environment

c. Mobilizing resources by
• Increasing domestic savings and investments
• Improving management of public revenue and expenditure
• Improving Africa's share in global trade
• Attracting foreign direct investment
• Increasing capital flows through further debt reduction and increased ODA flows

8. What are the immediate desired outcomes of Nepad?
- Africa becomes more effective in conflict prevention and the establishment of enduring peace on the continent
- Africa adopts and implements principles of democracy and good political economic and corporate governance, and the protection of human rights becomes further entrenched in every African country
- Africa develops and implements effective poverty eradication programs and accelerates the pace of achieving set African development goals, particularly human development
- Africa achieves increased levels of domestic savings, as well as investments, both domestic and foreign
- Increased levels of ODA to the continent are achieved and its effective utilization maximized
- Africa achieves desired capacity for policy development, coordination, and negotiation in the international arena, to ensure its beneficial engagement in the global economy, especially on trade and market access issues
- Regional integration is further accelerated and higher levels of sustainable economic growth in Africa are achieved
- Genuine partnerships are established between Africa and the developed countries based on mutual respect and accountability

9. What are the key priority action areas?
- Operationalizing the African Peer Review Mechanism
- Facilitating and supporting implementation of the short-term regional infrastructure programs covering transport, energy, ICT, water, and sanitation
- Facilitating implementation of the food security and agricultural development program in all subregions
- Facilitating the preparation of a coordinated African position on market access, debt relief, and ODA reforms
- Monitoring and intervening as appropriate to ensure that the Millennium Development Goals in the areas of health and education are met

10. What does the structure for implementing Nepad look like?
Nepad is a program of the African Union designed to meet its development objectives. The highest authority of the Nepad implementation process is the Heads of State and Government Summit of the African Union, formerly known as the OAU.

The Heads of State and Government Implementation Committee (HSIC) comprises three states per AU region as mandated by the OAU Summit of July 2001 and ratified by the AU Summit of July 2002. The HSIC reports to the AU Summit on an annual basis.

The Steering Committee of Nepad comprises the personal representatives of the Nepad Heads of State and Government. This Committee oversees projects and program development.

The Nepad Secretariat coordinates implementation of projects and programs approved by the HSIC.

Source: www.nepad.org/en.html.

Acronyms

AAF-SAP	African Alternative Framework to Structural Adjustment Program for Socio-Economic Recovery and Transformation
ADB	African Development Bank
AEC	African Economic Community
AIDS	Acquired Immunodeficiency Syndrome
ANC	African National Congress
APPER	Africa's Priority Program for Economic Recovery
APRM	African Peer Review Mechanism
ARV	anti-retroviral
AU	African Union
AZT	Azidothymidine
CASS	Center for Advanced Social Science (Nigeria)
CHOGM	Commonwealth Heads of Government Meeting
CODESRIA	Council for the Development of Social Science Research in Africa
CPDM	Cameroon People's Democratic Movement
CSSDCA	Conference on Security, Stability, Development and Co-operation in Africa
DPGI	Democracy and Political Governance Initiative
DRC	Democratic Republic of Congo
ECA	Economic Commission for Africa
ECOWAS	Economic Community of West African States
ESC	Electoral Supervisory Commission (Zimbabwe)
EU	European Union
FDI	foreign direct investment
GDP	gross domestic product
GNP	gross national product
GSM	global system of mobile communication

HIPC	Heavily Indebted Poor Countries
HIV	Human Immunodeficiency Virus
HSIC	Nepad's Heads of State Implementation Committee
ICT	information and communications technology
IFIs	international financial institutions
IMF	International Monetary Fund
LPA	Lagos Plan of Action
MAP	Millennium Africa Recovery Plan
MCC	Medicine Control Council (South Africa)
MDC	Movement for Democratic Change (Zimbabwe)
MTN	Mobile Telephone Networks (South Africa)
NAI	New Africa Initiative
NBI	Nile Basin Initiative
NCA	National Constitutional Assembly (Zimbabwe)
NDI	National Democratic Institute for International Affairs
Nepad	New Partnership for Africa's Development
NGOs	nongovernmental organizations
NIEO	New International Economic Order
NNPC	Nigerian National Petroleum Corporation
OAU	Organization of African Unity
ODA	overseas development assistance
OECD	Organization for Economic Cooperation and Development
PRSP	Poverty Reduction Strategy papers
SADC	Southern African Development Community
SAOM	South African Observer Mission
SAPs	structural adjustment programs
SDIs	Spatial Development Initiatives
TB	tuberculosis
UN	United Nations
UNAIDS	Joint United Nations Programme on HIV/AIDS
UNCTAD	United Nations Conference on Trade and Development
UNDP	United Nations Development Programme
UNECA	United Nations Economic Commission for Africa
UNECOSOC	United Nations Economic and Social Council
UN-NADAF	United Nations New Agenda for the Development of Africa
UN-PAAERD	United Nations Program of Action for Africa's Economic Recovery and Development
WAPP	West Africa Power Pool
WHO	World Health Organization
WTO	World Trade Organization
ZANU-PF	Zimbabwe African National Union-Patriotic Front
ZCTU	Zimbabwe Congress of Trade Unions
ZESN	Zimbabwe Election Support Network
ZWVA	Zimbabwe War Veterans Association

Bibliography

Adedeji, A. (ed.) (1981) *Indigenization of African Economies*. New York: Africana Publishing Company.
———. (1989) *Towards a Dynamic African Economy, Selected Speeches and Lectures 1975–1986*. London: Frank Cass.
———. (2002) "Keynote Address: From the Lagos Plan of Action to the New Partnership for African Development and From the Final Act of Lagos to the Constitutive Act: Wither Africa?" Paper prepared for presentation at the African Forum for Envisioning Africa, Nairobi, Kenya, April 26–29.
Adeleke, T. (1998) "Black Americans and Africa: A Critique of the Pan-African and Identity Paradigms," *International Journal of African Historical Studies,* vol. 31, no. 3.
African Charter for Popular Participation in Development and Transformation. (1990) www.africaaction.org/african-initiatives/charter1.htm.
African Economic Community. (1991) *Treaty Establishing the African Economic Community.* Abuja, Nigeria: AEC.
Aguilar, M. (1998) *The Politics of Age and Gerontocracy in Africa.* Trenton, NJ: Africa World Press.
Ahonsi-Yakubu, A. (2001) "Political Institutions, Crime and Insecurity in Nigeria," *African Development,* vol. 26, nos. 1 and 2.
Ajayi, S., and Khan, M. (2000) *External Debt and Capital Flight in Sub-Saharan Africa.* Washington, DC: International Monetary Fund, IMF Institute.
Ake, C. (1987) *Democracy and Development in Africa.* Washington, DC: Brookings Institute.
Akeroyd, A. (2004) "Coercion, Constraints and 'Cultural Entrapments': A Further Look at Gendered and Occupational Factors Pertinent to the Transmission of HIV in Africa," in E. Kalipeni et al. (eds.) *HIV and AIDS in Africa: Beyond Epidemiology.* Oxford: Blackwell.
Akinrinade, S. (2002) "Nepad: The New Partnership for Africa's Development," *Bulletin of the Conflict, Security and Development Group,* no. 15.
Akukwe, C. (2002) "Africa and Nepad: What About HIV/AIDS?" *The Perspective* (Atlanta), April 23.
Alden, C. (2002) "A Blueprint for African Tiger Economies?" *Bulletin of the Conflict, Security and Development Group,* May-June.
Alden, C., and Schoeman, M. (2003) "The Hegemon that Wasn't: South Africa's Foreign Policy Towards Zimbabwe," *Strategic Review for Southern Africa,* vol. 25, no. 1, May.

Aluko, M. (2002) "The Institutionalisation of Corruption and Its Impact on Political Culture in Nigeria," *Nordic Journal of African Studies,* vol. 11, no. 3.

Amoako, K.Y. (2002) "Moving Nepad from Concept to Implementation." Opening statement by the Executive Secretary of the Economic Commission for Africa to the Conference of African Ministers of Finance, Planning and Economic Development, Johannesburg, South Africa, October 19.

———. (2003) "Nepad: Making Individual Bests a Continental Norm," *UN Chronicle,* no. 1.

ANC. (2002) "Zimbabwe Presidential Elections: Time for Healing!: Time for Reconstruction and Development," *ANC Today,* vol. 2, no. 11, March 15–21.

Andreski, S. (1968) *The African Predicament: A Study in the Pathology of Modernization.* London: Michael Joseph.

Anyang'Nyong'o, P., and Coughlin, P. (1991) *Industrialization at Bay: African Experiences.* Nairobi, Kenya: Academy Science Publishers.

Arrighi, G. (2002) "The African Crisis: World Systemic and Regional Aspects," *New Left Review* 15 (May–June): 5–35.

Asante, S. (1985) "Development and Regional Integration Since 1980,"in A. Adedeji and T. Shaw (eds.) *Economic Crisis in Africa: African Perspectives on Development Problems and Potentials.* Boulder, CO: Lynne Rienner.

———. (1991) *African Development: Adebayo Adedeji's Alternative Strategies.* Oxford, UK: Hans Zell.

Augelli, E., and Murphy, C. (1988) *America's Quest for Supremacy and the Third World: A Gramscian Analysis.* London: Pinter Publishers.

Auret, D. (1990) *A Decade of Development in Zimbabwe, 1980–1990.* Harare, Zimbabwe: Mambo Press.

Ayittey, G. (1995) "Nigeria: The High Cost of Erratic Financial Policies," *Economic Reform Today,* no. 1.

Bach, D. (1999) "Revisting a Paradigm," in D. Bach (ed.) *Regionalisation in Africa: Integration and Disintegration.* Oxford, UK: James Currey.

Bakare-Yusuf, B. (2002) "'Yoruba's Don't Do Gender': A Critical Review of Oyeronke Oyewumi's *The Invention of Women: Making an African Sense of Western Gender Discourses.*" Paper prepared for CODESRIA Conference on African Gender in the New Millennium: Perspectives, Directions and Challenges, Cairo, Egypt, April 7–10.

Baker, B. (2002) "When to Call Black White: Zimbabwe's Electoral Reports," *Third World Quarterly,* vol. 23, no. 6.

Barnes, J. (1992) *Gabon: Beyond the Colonial Legacy.* Boulder, CO: Westview.

Barnes, S. (1986) *Patrons and Power: Creating a Political Community in Metropolitan Lagos.* Manchester, UK: Manchester University Press.

Barnett, T., and Whiteside, A. (2002) *AIDS in the Twenty-First Century: Disease and Globalization.* London: Palgrave.

Barrell, H. (2000) "Back to the Future: Renaissance and South African Domestic Policy," *African Security Review,* vol. 9, no. 2.

Bartlett, D. (2001) "Human Rights, Democracy and the Donors: The First MMD Government in Zambia," *Review of African Political Economy,* vol. 28, no. 87.

Bassett, M., and Mhloyi, M. (1991) "Women and AIDS in Zimbabwe: The Making of an Epidemic," *International Journal of Health Services,* vol. 21, no. 1.

Bates, R. (1981) *Markets and States in Tropical Africa: The Political Basis of Agricultural Policies.* Berkeley: University of California Press.

———. (1989) *Beyond the Miracle of the Market.* Cambridge: Cambridge University Press.

Bathily, A. (1994) "The West African State in Historical Perspective," in E. Osaghae (ed.) *Between State and Civil Society in Africa.* Dakar, Senegal: Council for the Development of Social Science Research in Africa.

Bayart, J-F. (1986) "Civil Society in Africa," in P. Chabal (ed.) *Political Domination in Africa.* Cambridge: Cambridge University Press.

———. (1993) *The State in Africa: The Politics of the Belly.* London: Longman.

———. (2000) "Africa in the World: A History of Extraversion," *African Affairs,* 99.

Bayart, J-F., Ellis, S., and Hibou, B. (1999) *The Criminalization of the State in Africa.* Oxford, UK: James Currey.

Bekoe, D. (2002) "Nepad and Its Achilles Heel," *Alternatives: Turkish Journal of International Relations,* vol. 1, no. 4.

———. (2003) "Creating a Reliable African Peer Review Mechanism," *Chimera,* vol. 1, no. 4.

Berman, B. (1997) "The Perils of Bula Matari: Hegemony and the Colonial State in Africa," *Canadian Journal of African Studies,* vol. 31, no. 3.

Berry, S. (1992) "Hegemony on a Shoestring: Indirect Rule and Access to Agricultural Land," *Africa,* vol. 62, no. 3.

Biersteker, T. (1987) *Multinationals, the State and Control of the Nigerian Economy.* Princeton, NJ: Princeton University Press.

Blair, D. (2002) *Degrees in Violence: Robert Mugabe and the Struggle for Power in Zimbabwe.* London: Continuum.

Boahen, A. (1987) *African Perspectives on Colonialism.* Baltimore: Johns Hopkins Press.

Bond, P. (1999) "Global Economic Crisis: A View from South Africa," *Journal of World-Systems Research,* vol. 5, no. 2, Spring.

———. (2001) "The New Partnership for Africa's Development: An Annotated Critique," http://aidc.org.za/Nepad/Nepadannotatedcritique.pdf.

———. (ed.) (2002) *Fanon's Warning. A Civil Society Reader on the New Partnership for Africa's Development.* Trenton, NJ: Africa World Press.

———. (2003) "South Africa and Global Apartheid: Is the Reform Strategy Working?" Paper presented to the Transnational Seminar, University of Illinois/Champaign-Urbana, November 14.

Bond, P., and Manyanya, M. (2002) *Zimbabwe's Plunge: Exhausted Nationalism, Neoliberalism and the Search for Social Justice.* Pietermaritzburg, South Africa: University of Natal Press.

Boone, C. (1992) *Merchant Capital and the Roots of State Power in Senegal, 1930–1985.* Cambridge: Cambridge University Press.

———. (1998) "'Empirical Statehood' and Reconfiguration of Political Order," in L. Villalon and P. Huxtable (eds.) *The African State at a Critical Juncture.* Boulder, CO: Lynne Rienner.

———. (2003) *Political Topographies of the African State: Territorial Authority and Institutional Choice.* Cambridge: Cambridge University Press.

Boyce, J., and Ndikumana, L. (2002) *Africa's Debt: Who Owes Whom?* Working Paper no. 48, Political Economy Research Institute, University of Massachusetts at Amherst.

Bratton, M., and Van de Walle, N. (1994) "Neopatrimonial Regimes and Political Transitions in Africa," *World Politics,* vol. 46, no. 4.

———. (1997) *Democratic Experiments in Africa: Regime Transitions in Comparative Perspective.* Cambridge: Cambridge University Press.

Brautigam, D. (1997) "Substituting for the State: Institutions and Industrial Development in Eastern Nigeria," *World Development,* vol. 25, no. 7.

————. (2000) *Aid Dependence and Governance*. Stockholm: Alqvist and Wiksell.

Bretton, H. (1966) *The Rise and Fall of Kwame Nkrumah: A Study of Personal Rule in Africa*. London: Pall Mall.

Breytenbach, B. (2002) "Nepad and the New African Dawn," www.dse.de/ef/nepad/breytenbach.htm.

Browne, R., and Cummings, R. (1985) *Lagos Plan of Action vs. the Berg Report*. Lawrenceville, VA: Brunswick.

Butegwa, F. (2002) "Popularizing Nepad Among Women in Africa." Paper prepared for the Regional Conference on African Women and the New Partnership for Africa's Development, organized by the African Women's Forum, Ota, Nigeria.

Callaghy, T. (1984) *The State-Society Struggle: Zaire in Comparative Perspective*. New York: Columbia University Press.

————. (1986) "Politics and Vision in Africa: The Interplay of Domination, Equality and Liberty," in P. Chabal (ed.) *Political Domination in Africa: Reflections on the Limits of Power*. Cambridge: Cambridge University Press.

————. (1987) "The State as Lame Leviathan: The Patrimonial Administrative State in Africa" in Z. Ergas (ed.) *The African State in Transition*. London: Macmillan.

————. (1991) "Africa and the World Economy: Caught Between a Rock and a Hard Place," in J. Harbeson and D. Rothchild (eds.) *Africa in World Politics*. Boulder, CO: Westview.

Callaghy, T., and Ravenhill, J. (1993) *Hemmed In: Responses to Africa's Economic Decline*. New York: Columbia University Press.

Callaghy, T., Kassimir, R., and Latham, R. (2001) *Intervention and Transnationalism in Africa: Global-Local Networks of Power*. Cambridge: Cambridge University Press.

Campbell, H. (2003) *Reclaiming Zimbabwe: The Exhaustion of the Patriarchal Model of Liberation*. Cape Town, South Africa: David Philip.

Cardoso, F., and Faletto, E. (1979) *Dependency and Development in Latin America*. Berkeley: University of California Press.

Carter Center. (1999) *Observing the 1998–99 Nigeria Elections: Final Report*. Atlanta, GA: Carter Center.

CASS Newsletter. (2002) Nos. 3 and 4, November.

Catholic Commission for Justice and Peace in Zimbabwe. (1997) *Breaking the Silence: A Report on the Disturbances in Matabeleland and the Midlands, 1980 to 1988*. Harare, Zimbabwe: CCJPZ/Legal Resources Foundation.

Cerny, P. (1997) "Paradoxes of the Competition State: The Dynamics of Political Globalization," *Government and Opposition*, vol. 32, no. 2.

————. (1999) "Globalising the Political and Politicising the Global: Concluding Reflections on International Political Economy as a Vocation," *New Political Economy*, vol. 4, no. 1.

Chabal, P. (ed.) (1986) *Political Domination in Africa: Reflections on the Limits of Power*. Cambridge: Cambridge University Press.

————. (1994) *Power in Africa: An Essay in Political Interpretation*. New York: St. Martin's Press.

————. (2002) "The Quest for Good Governance and Development in Africa: Is Nepad the Answer?" *International Affairs*, vol. 78, no. 3.

Chabal, P., and Daloz, J.-P. (1999) *Africa Works: Disorder as Political Instrument*. Oxford, UK: James Currey.

Chan, S. (2001) "Commonwealth Residualism and the Machinations of Power in a Turbulent Zimbabwe," *Commonwealth and Comparative Politics*, vol. 39, no. 3.

Chattopadhyay, R. (2000) "Zimbabwe: Structural Adjustment, Destitution and Food Insecurity," *Review of African Political Economy*, 84.

Cheru, F. (1997) "Civil Society and Political Economy in South and Southern Africa," in S. Gill (ed.) *Globalization, Democratization and Multilateralism*. Basingstoke, UK: Macmillan.

Chikuhwa, J. (1998) *Zimbabwe: The Rise to Nationhood*. London: Minerva.

Chisala, C. (2002) "In Exchange for Morals: Nepad Joke," www.zambia.co.zm/capitalism/Nepadarticle.htm.

Chitiyo, T. (2000) "Land Violence and Compensation: Reconceptualising Zimbabwe's Land and War Veterans' Debate," *Track Two*, vol. 9, no. 1.

Christian Aid (2002) "Christian Aid Responds to Telegraph Article," May 15, www.christian-aid.org.uk/news/stories/020515s.htm.

Cilliers, J. (2002) *Nepad African Peer Review Mechanism: Prospects and Challenges*, Institute for Security Studies, Occasional Paper No. 64, November.

Clapham, C. (1969) *Haile Selassie's Government*. New York: Praeger.

———. (ed.) (1982) *Private Patronage and Public Power: Political Clientelism in Modern States*. London: Pinter.

———. (1985) *Third World Politics: An Introduction*. London: Croom Helm.

———. (1989) "Liberia," in D. Cruise O'Brien, J. Dunn, and R. Rathbone (eds.) *Contemporary West African States*. Cambridge: Cambridge University Press.

———. (1996a) *Africa and the International System*. Cambridge: Cambridge University Press.

———. (1996b) "Governmentality and Economic Policy in Sub-Saharan Africa," *Third World Quarterly*, vol. 17, no. 4.

Clark, J. (ed.) (2002) *The African Stakes of the Congo War*. New York: Palgrave.

Cohen, D., and Smith, S. (2002) "The New Partnership for Africa's Development: Integrating HIV/AIDS," www.atschool.eduweb.co.uk/cite/staff/philosopher/hivdev/nepad1.htm.

Cornia, G., and Helleiner, G. (eds.) (1994) *From Adjustment to Development in Africa: Conflict, Controversy, Convergence, Consensus?* London: Macmillan.

Cornwell, R. (2000) "A New Partnership for Africa's Development?" *African Security Review*, vol. 11, no. 1.

Craig, J. (2000) "Evaluating Privatization in Zambia: A Tale of Two Processes," *Review of African Political Economy*, 85.

Crisis in Zimbabwe Coalition. (2002) *Zimbabwe Report*. Harare, Zimbabwe: Crisis in Zimbabwe Coalition.

Crook, R. (1989) "Patrimonialism, Administrative Effectiveness and Economic Development in Cote d'Ivoire," *African Affairs*, no. 351, April.

Crowder, M. (1968) *West Africa Under Colonial Rule*. London: Hutchinson and Co.

Cruise O'Brien, D. (2003) *Symbolic Confrontations: Muslims Imagining the State in Africa*. London: Palgrave.

Cruise O'Brien, D., Dunn, J., and Rathbone, R. (eds.) (1989) *Contemporary West African States*. Cambridge: Cambridge University Press.

Dahl, J., and Shilimela, R. (2002) *Nepad and the African "Resource Gap": A Critical Examination*, NEPRU Working Paper No. 87, Windhoek: Namibian Economic Policy Research Unit.

Davidson, B. (1992) *The Black Man's Burden: Africa and the Curse of the Nation-State*. Oxford: James Currey.

Decalo, S. (1989) *Psychoses of Power: African Personal Dictatorships*. Boulder: Westview.

———. (1990) *Coups and Army Rule in Africa*. Newhaven, CT: Yale University Press.

Deng, F., and Zartman, I.W. (2001) *A Strategic Vision for Africa: The Kampala Movement*. Washington, DC: Brookings Institute.

Department of Foreign Affairs. (2001) "Millennium Partnership for the African Recovery Programme (MAP)," www.dfa.gov.za/events/map.htm.

———. (2003) *Nepad: Historical Overview*. Pretoria: DFA.

De Waal, A. (2002) "What's New in the 'New Partnership for Africa's Development'?" *International Affairs*, vol. 78, no. 3.

De Waal, A., and Raheem, T. (2004) "What Is the Value of Nepad?" *Africa Analysis*, no. 441, February 20.

Diamond, L. (1989) "Beyond Autocracy: Prospects for Democracy in Africa," in *Beyond Autocracy in Africa*. Atlanta: Carter Center for Emory University.

Downs, R., and Reyna, S. (eds.) (1988) *Land and Society in Contemporary Africa*. London: University Press of New England.

Doyal, L. (1994) "HIV and AIDS: Putting Women on the Global Agenda," in L. Doyal (ed.) *AIDS: Setting a Feminist Agenda*. London: Taylor and Francis.

Dunn, K., and Shaw, T. (eds.) (2001) *Africa's Challenge to International Relations Theory*. New York: Palgrave.

Ellis, S. (1999) *The Mask of Anarchy: The Destruction of Liberia and the Religious Dimension of an African Civil War*. London: Hurst and Co.

Ellis, S., and Ter Haar, G. (2004) *Worlds of Power: Religious Thought and Political Practice in Africa*. London: Hurst and Co.

Englebert, P. (2000) *State Legitimacy and Development in Africa*. Boulder, CO: Lynne Rienner.

Englebert, P., and Ron, J. (no date) "Primary Commodities and War: Congo-Brazzaville's Ambivalent Resource Curse," unpublished paper.

Enoki, Y. (2002) "Speech presented by Ambassador of Japan, Yasukuni Enoki, at the Africa Institute" (Pretoria), April 16, 2002, www.japan.org.za/speeches/speech_05.html.

Ergas, Z. (1987a) "Introduction," in Z. Ergas (ed.) *The African State in Transition*. London, Macmillan.

———. (1987b) "In Search of Development in Africa," in Z. Ergas (ed.) *The African State in Transition*. London, Macmillan.

European Union. (2000) "Presidency Conclusions," June 19–20. Brussels: European Union.

Fanon, F. (1961) *The Wretched of the Earth*. London: Penguin.

Fatton, R. (1999) "Civil Society Revisited: Africa in the New Millennium," *West Africa Review*, vol. 1, no. 1.

———. (2002) *Haiti's Predatory Republic: The Unending Transition to Democracy*. Boulder, CO: Lynne Rienner.

Food Security and Food Self Sufficiency in Africa. (no date), available at www.sas.upenn.edu/African_Studies/ECA/FoodSecure.html.

Frank, A. (1967) *Capitalism and Underdevelopment in Latin America: Historical Studies of Chile and Brazil*. New York: Monthly Review Press.

Frank, A. G. (1975) *On Capitalist Underdevelopment*. Bombay: Oxford University Press.

Frimpong-Ansah, J. (1991) *The Vampire State in Africa: The Political Economy of Decline in Ghana*. London: James Currey.

Games, D. (2003) *The Experience of SA Firms Doing Business in Africa: A Preliminary Survey and Analysis*. Braamfontein: South African Institute of International Affairs.

Gerhart, G. (2001) "Africa," (review of books) in *Foreign Affairs*, vol. 80, no. 6.

Gigaba, M. (2004) "Common Liberals Avoid the Roots of the Problem," *ANC Today*, vol. 4, no. 47.

Gills, B., Rocamora, J., and Wilson, R. (1993) *Low Intensity Democracy: Political Power in the New World Order.* London: Pluto Press.

Global AIDS Alliance. (2003) "Report Gives Nigerian President Obasanjo High Marks in Fight Against AIDS," September 22, www.globalAIDSalliance.org/press092203.html.

Global Policy. (2002) "Nepad Misunderstands the Politics of International Economics," *Global Policy*, June 14, www.globalpolicy.org/socecon/bwi-wto/wto/2002/0614fairtrade.htm.

Global Witness. (2002) *All the President's Men: The Devastating Story of Oil and Banking in Angola's Privatized War.* London: Global Witness.

Goetz, A. (1995) *The Politics of Integrating Gender to State Development Processes: Trends, Opportunities and Constraints in Bangladesh, Chile, Jamaica, Mali, Morocco and Uganda.* Geneva, UNRISD and UNDP Occasional Paper, Fourth World Conference on Women, Beijing.

Graham, Y. (2002) "Nepad's Slippery Milestones," *African Trade Agenda*, no. 5, December.

Guest, E. (2001) *Children of AIDS: Africa's Orphan Crisis.* London: Pluto Press.

Guest, R. (2004) *The Shackled Continent: Africa's Past, Present and Future.* London: Macmillan.

Gutkind, P., and Wallerstein, I. (eds.) (1976) *The Political Economy of Contemporary Africa.* London: Sage Publications.

Haggard, S., and Webb, S. (1994) *Voting for Reform: Democracy, Political Liberalization, and Economic Adjustment.* New York: Oxford University Press.

Hamill, J. (2002) "Despots or Aid?" *The World Today*, vol. 58, no. 6.

Hanlon, J. (2002) "Bank Corruption Becomes Site of Struggle in Mozambique," *Review of African Political Economy*, 91.

Harrison, G. (1999) "Clean-ups, Conditionality and Adjustment: Why Institutions Matter in Mozambique," *Review of African Political Economy*, 81.

———. (2002) *Issues in Contemporary Politics in Sub-Saharan Africa: The Dynamics of Struggle and Resistance.* London: Palgrave.

Harvey, C. (ed.) (1996) *Constraints on the Success of Structural Adjustment Programmes in Africa.* Basingstoke, UK: Macmillan.

Herbert, R. (2003) "Implementing Nepad: A Critical Assessment," in R. Culpeper (ed.) *Africa Report: Assessing the New Partnership.* Ottawa: North-South Institute.

Herbst, J. (1993) *The Politics of Reform in Ghana, 1982–1991.* Berkeley: University of California Press.

Hibou, B. (2004) "From Privatising the Economy to Privatising the State: An Analysis of the Continual Formation of the State," in B. Hibou (ed.) *Privatising the State.* London: Hurst and Company.

Hill, G. (2003) *The Battle for Zimbabwe: The Final Countdown.* Cape Town: Zebra Press.

Himbara, D. (1994) *Kenyan Capitalists, the State, and Development.* Boulder, CO: Lynne Rienner.

Hodges, T. (2001) *Angola: From Afro-Stalinism to Petro-Diamond Capitalism.* Oxford: James Currey.

Hope, K. (2002) "From Crisis to Renewal: Towards a Successful Implementation of the New Partnership for Africa's Development," *African Affairs*, vol. 101.

Human Rights Watch. (2001) "AIDS and Human Rights: A Call for Action," June 27. New York: Human Rights Watch.

Hunt, C. (1996) "Social vs. Biological: Theories on the Transmission of AIDS in Africa," *Journal of Health and Medicine,* vol. 42, no. 9.

Hyden, G. (1980) *Beyond Ujamaa in Tanzania: Underdevelopment and an Uncaptured Peasantry.* London: Heinemann.

———. (2000) "The Governance Challenge in Africa," in G. Hyden, D. Oluwu, and H. Okoth-Ogendo (eds.) *African Perspectives on Governance.* Trenton, NJ: Africa World Press.

Ikhariale, M. (2001) "Aluko and Obasanjo: Credibility and the Burden of Proof," http://www.nigerdeltacongress.com/articles/aluko_and_obasanjo.htm.

Ikpe, U. (2000) "Patrimonialism and Military Regimes in Nigeria," *African Journal of Political Science,* vol. 5, no. 1.

International Monetary Fund (IMF). (2002) *Balance of Payments Statistics Yearbook, 2002.* Washington, DC: International Monetary Fund.

Jackson, R. (1984) *Quasi-states: Sovereignty, International Relations and the Third World.* Cambridge: Cambridge University Press.

Jackson, R., and Rosberg, C. (1982) *Personal Rule in Black Africa: Prince, Autocrat, Prophet, Tyrant.* Los Angeles: University of California Press.

———. (1994) "The Political Economy of African Personal Rule," in D. Apter and C. Rosberg (eds.) *Political Development and the New Realism in Sub-Saharan Africa.* Charlottesville: University of Virginia Press.

Johnson, R. (2004) *South Africa: The First Man, the Last Nation.* Johannesburg: Jonathan Ball.

Joseph, R. (1987) *Democracy and Prebendal Politics in Nigeria: The Rise and Fall of the Second Republic.* Cambridge: Cambridge University Press.

———. (ed.) (1999) *State, Conflict and Democracy in Africa.* Boulder, CO: Lynne Rienner.

Kagoro, B. (2002) "Can Apples Be Reaped from a Thorn Tree? A Case Analysis of the Zimbabwean Crisis and Nepad's Peer Review Mechanism." Paper presented to the Southern Africa Research Poverty Network (SARPN) and Center for Civil Society workshop on "Engaging Nepad: Government and Civil Society Speak to One Another," University of Natal, Durban, July 4.

Kalipeni, E., Craddock, S., Oppong, J., and Ghosh, J. (eds.) (2004) *HIV and AIDS in Africa: Beyond Epidemiology.* Oxford: Blackwell.

Kanbur, R. (2001a) "Nepad Commentary: The First Wave," www.arts.cornell.edu/poverty/kanbur/neprev.

———. (2001b) "The New Partnership for Africa's Development (Nepad): An Initial Commentary," www.people.cornell.edu/pages/skl45.

King, S. (2003) *Liberalization Against Democracy: The Local Politics of Economic Reform in Tunisia.* Bloomington: Indiana University Press.

Kinsey, B. (1982) "Forever Gained: Resettlement and Land Policy in the Context of National Development in Zimbabwe," *Journal of International African Institute,* vol. 52, no. 3.

Kitunga, D., and Rusimbi, M. (2000) *Women Build Africa.* Quebec: Museum of Civilization.

Klein, M., Aaron, C., and Hadjimichael, B. (2002) "Foreign Direct Investment and Poverty Reduction," in Global Forum on International Investment, *New Horizons for Foreign Direct Investment.* Paris: OECD.

Kourouma, A. (2003) *Waiting for the Wild Beasts to Vote.* London: William Heinemann.

Krasner, S. (1999) *Sovereignty: Organised Hypocrisy.* Princeton: Princeton University Press.

Lancaster, C. (1999) *Aid to Africa: So Much to Do, So Little Done.* Chicago: University of Chicago Press.

Landsberg, C. (2004) *The Quiet Diplomacy of Liberation: International Politics and South Africa's Transition.* Johannesburg: Jacana.

Lemarchand, R., and Eisenstadt, S. (eds.) (1980) *Political Clientelism, Patronage and Development.* New York: Sage.

Leonard, D., and Straus, S. (2003) *Africa's Stalled Development: International Causes and Cures.* Boulder, CO: Lynne Rienner.

LeVine, V. (1980) "African Patrimonial Regimes in Comparative Perspective," *Journal of Modern African Studies,* vol. 18, no. 4.

Lewis, S. (2002a) "Nepad and HIV/AIDS," www.sarpn.org.za/Nepad/june2002/Nepad_hiv/index.php.

———. (2002b) "Text of the Speech to Opening Ceremonies of the G6B: Group of Six Billion, Peoples' Summit." Red and White Club, University of Calgary, June 21.

Leys, C. (1994) "Confronting the African Tragedy," *New Left Review,* no. 204.

———. (1996) *The Rise and Fall of Development Theory.* Oxford, UK: James Currey.

Liebenberg, I. (1998) "The African Renaissance: Myth, Vital Lie, or Mobilizing Tool?" *African Security Review,* vol. 7, no. 3.

Longwe, S. (1991) "Gender Awareness: The Missing Element in the Third World Development Project," in T. Wallace and C. March (eds.) *Changing Perceptions: Writings on Gender and Development.* Oxford, UK: Oxfam.

———. (2002a) "Assessment of the Gender Orientation of Nepad." Paper presented at the African Forum for Envisioning Africa: Focus on Nepad, Nairobi, April.

———. (2002b) "Nepad Reluctance to Address Gender Issues." Paper presented at NGO Forum, October 14–16, organized by the African Centre for Democracy and Human Rights Studies, that preceded the 32nd Session of the African Commission on Human and Peoples Rights, Banjul, The Gambia.

Lowe-Morna, C. (1999) *Redefining Politics: South African Women and Democracy: Experiences and Reflections of Women in the First Democratic Parliament of South Africa.* Johannesburg: Commission on Gender Equality.

Lyons, M. (2004) "Mobile Populations and HIV/AIDS in East Africa," in E. Kalipeni et al. (eds.) *HIV and AIDS in Africa: Beyond Epidemiology.* Oxford: Blackwell.

MacLean, S. (2002) "Mugabe at War: The Political Economy of Conflict in Zimbabwe," *Third World Quarterly* 25 (June).

———. (2003) "New Regionalism and Conflict in the Democratic Republic of Congo: Networks of Plunder and Networks of Peace," in A. Grant and F. Söderbaum (eds.) *The New Regionalism in Africa.* Aldershot, UK: Ashgate.

Maier, K. (2000) *This House Has Fallen: Nigeria in Crisis.* London: Penguin.

Makumbe, J. (1998) "Is There a Civil Society in Africa?" *International Affairs,* vol. 74, no. 2.

Maloka, E. (2002) "Nepad and Africa's Future," *Africa Insight,* vol. 32, no. 2.

Mandaza, I. (1986) *Zimbabwe: The Political Economy of Transition, 1980–1986.* Dakar, Senegal: CODESRIA.

Manyanya, M. (ed.) (2003) *The Zimbabwe Test: Why the New Partnership for Africa's Development Is Already Failing.* Harare, Zimbabwe: ZIMCODD.

Mathews, K. (1989) "The Organization of African Unity in World Politics," in R.

Onwuka and T. Shaw (eds.) *Africa in World Politics*. London: Macmillan.

Mayima-Mbemba, C. (2001) "La Logique des Puissants ou la Condition 'Humaine' Reservee aux 'Sous-Hommes,'" mimeograph, (Strasbourg).

Mbaku, J., and Takougang, J. (2004) "General Introduction: Biya and the Promise of a Better Society," in J. Mbaku and J. Takougang (eds.) *The Leadership Challenge in Africa: Cameroon Under Paul Biya*. Trenton, NJ: Africa World Press.

Mbeki, T. (1998a) "Statement by Deputy President Mbeki at the African Renaissance Conference," September 28, www.anc.org.za/ancdocs/history/mbeki/1998/tm0928.htm.

———. (1998b) "The African Renaissance, Statement made by Deputy President Thabo Mbeki, South African Broadcasting Corporation, Gallagher Estate, Midrand, South Africa, August 1998," in T. Mbeki, *Africa: The Time Has Come*. Cape Town: Tafelberg.

———. (1999) "Speech at the Launch of the African Renaissance Institute," Pretoria, October 11, www.anc.org.za/ancdocs/history/mbeki/1999/tm1011.html.

———. (2000) "Address at the Nigerian Institute of International Affairs," Abuja, October 3, www.anc.org.za/ancdocs/history/mbeki/2000/tm1003.html.

———. (2001) "Africa's People Central to Success of Recovery Programme," *ANC Today*, vol. 1, no. 2, February 2–8.

———. (2002a) *Africa—Define Yourself*. Cape Town: Tafelberg.

———. (2002b) "Sceptics Will Not Stop the Re-building of Africa," *ANC Today*, vol. 2, no. 38, September 20–26.

———. (2002c) "Letter from the President: Zimbabwe: 'Two Blacks and One White,'" *ANC Today*, vol. 2, no. 10, March 8–14.

———. (2002d) "Critics Ill-Informed About Nepad Peer Review," *ANC Today*, vol. 2, no. 45, November 8–14.

———. (2003a) "Nigeria Makes Progress in Tackling Challenges," *ANC Today*, vol. 3, no. 16, April 25–May 1.

———. (2003b) "Lecture at the Nigerian Institute of International Affairs," Lagos, December 4, www.anc.org.za/ancdocs/history/mbeki/2003/tm1204.html.

———. (2003c) "We Will Resist the Upside-down View of Africa," *ANC Today*, vol. 3, no. 49, December 12–18.

———. (2004) "When Is Good News Bad News?" *ANC Today*, vol. 4, no. 39, October 1–7.

Mbilinyi, M. (ed.) (2001) *Gender Patterns in Micro and Small Enterprises of Tanzania*. Dar-es-Salaam, Tanzania: MCDWAC Tanzania/Women's Research and Documentation Project.

McAdam, M. (2002) "A New Deal for Africa?" *Sustainable Times*, June, www.sustainabletimes.ca/articles/G-8nepad.htm.

MDC. (2001) "Why the African Union Will Fail," (mimeograph), Harare, Zimbabwe, July 23.

Medard, J. (1982) "The Underdeveloped State in Tropical Africa: Political Clientelism or Neo-patrimonialism," in C. Clapham (ed.) *Private Patronage and Public Power: Political Clientelism in Modern States*. London: Pinter.

Mehler, A. (1998) "Cameroon and the Politics of Patronage," in David Birmingham and Phyllis Martin (eds.) *History of Central Africa: The Contemporary Years Since 1960*. London: Longman.

Melber, H. (2002a) "South Africa and Nepad: Quo Vadis? The Policy Issues: Collective Responsibility Versus National Sovereignty?" Paper presented to the Swedish Development Forum, Stockholm, October 9.

————. (2002b) "The New Partnership for Africa's Development (Nepad)—Old Wine in New Bottles?" *Forum for Development Studies,* vol. 29, no. 1.

————. (2004) *The G8 and Nepad—More Than an Elite Pact?* Leipzig, Germany: University of Leipzig Papers on African Politics and Economics, no. 74.

Meldrum, A. (2004) *Where We Have Hope: A Memoir of Zimbabwe.* London: John Murray.

Mengisteab, K., and Logan, B. Ikubolajeh (eds.) (1995) *Beyond Economic Liberalization in Africa: Structural Adjustment and the Alternatives.* London: Zed.

Messiant, C. (2001) "The Eduardo Dos Santos Foundation: Or, How Angola's Regime is Taking Over Civil Society," *African Affairs,* 100.

Mills, G., and Sidiropoulos, E. (eds.) (2004) *New Tools for Reform and Stability: Sanctions, Conditionalities and Conflict Resolution.* Braamfontein: SAIIA.

Mitchell, T. (1999) "No Factories, No Problems: The Logic of Neo-Liberalism in Egypt," *Review of African Political Economy,* no. 82.

Mkhondo, R. (2004) "Nkuhlu Unpacks Nepad," *Leadership,* December/January.

Morisset, J. (2002) "Foreign Direct Investment in Africa: Policies Also Matter," in B. Ogutcu (ed.) *OECD Global Forum on International Investment.* Paris, France: OECD.

Moyana, H. (1984) *The Political Economy of Land in Zimbabwe.* Gweru, Zimbabwe: Mambo Press.

Moyo, J. (1998) "The African Renaissance: A Critical Assessment," *Southern African Political and Economic Monthly,* vol. 11, no. 7.

Moyo, S, (1986) "The Land Question in Zimbabwe," in I. Mandaza (ed.) *Zimbabwe: The Political Economy of Transition, 1980–1986.* Dakar: CODESRIA.

————. (1995) *The Land Question in Zimbabwe.* Harare, Zimbabwe: SAPES.

Mwakikagile, G. (2004) *Africa Is in a Mess: What Went Wrong and What Should Be Done.* Palo Alto: Fultus Books.

Nabudere, D. (2002) "Nepad: Historical Background and Its Prospects." Paper prepared for presentation at the "African Forum for Envisioning Africa," Nairobi, Kenya, April 26–29.

Naidu, S. (2003) "Unmasking South Africa's Corporate Expansion Under Nepad: Partnership or Economic Colonization of African Markets." Paper presented at "Africa: Partnership or Imperialism" conference, University of Birmingham, September 5–7.

Ndikumana, L., and Boyce, J. (2002) "Public Debts and Private Assets: Explaining Capital Flight from Sub-Saharan African Countries." Working Paper no. 32, Political Economy Research Institute, University of Massachusetts at Amherst.

Nepad Secretariat. (2001a) *New Partnership for Africa's Development (Nepad) (2001),* www.dfa.gov.za/events/Nepad.pdf.

————. (2001b) Communiqué Issued at the End of the Meeting of the Implementation Committee of Heads of State and Government on the New Partnership for Africa's Development, Abuja, Nigeria, October 23. Midrand, South Africa: Nepad Secretariat.

————. (2002) *Nepad Action Plans.* Midrand, South Africa: Nepad Secretariat.

————. (2003a) *Brief Report on the Work of Nepad Steering Committee and the Secretariat for the Last Five Months.* Midrand, South Africa: Nepad Secretariat.

————. (2003b) *Report on the Implementation of Nepad Process.* Midrand, South Africa: Nepad Secretariat.

————. (2004) *Regional Infrastructure and Nepad*. Midrand, South Africa: Nepad Secretariat.

Netshitenzhe, J. (1999) "Address on the African Renaissance," Government Communication and Information Service, at "Southern African Development Community: Towards a Common Future," local government conference, Johannesburg, July 28–30.

N'Galy, B., Ryder, R., Bila, K., et al. (1988) "Human Immunodeficiency Virus Infection Among Employees in an African Hospital," *New England Journal of Medicine,* 319.

Ngwenya, X., and Taylor, I. (2003) "Public-Private Partnerships and African Development: The Case of the N4 Toll Road," in F. Söderbaum and I. Taylor (eds.) *Regionalism and Uneven Development in Southern Africa: The Case of the Maputo Development Corridor.* Aldershot, UK: Ashgate.

Nordheim-Larsen, K. (1995) "Agenda Item 2: Development in Africa. Including the Implementation of the United Nations New Agenda for the Development of Africa in the 1990s," UNCTAD, Geneva, July.

Nwankwo, A. (2002) *Nigeria: The Stolen Billions.* Enugu, Nigeria: Fourth Dimension.

Nzioka, C. (1994) "AIDS Policies in Kenya: A Critical Perspective on Prevention," in P. Aggleton, P. Davies, and G. Hart (eds.) *AIDS: Foundations for the Future.* London: Taylor and Francis.

Odife, D. (no date) "Economic Policies, Democratisation and Investment Inflow in Nigeria," *Africa Economic Analysis,* http://www.afbis.com/analysis/investment.htm.

Okonta, I., and Douglas, O. (2003) *Where Vultures Feast: Shell, Human Rights and Oil.* London: Verso.

Omolo, K. (2002) "Political Ethnicity in the Democratization Process in Kenya," *African Studies,* vol. 61, no. 2.

Onimode, B. (1988) *A Political Economy of the African Crisis.* London: Institute for African Alternatives.

————. (ed.) (2004) *African Development and Governance Strategies in the 21st Century: Looking Back to Move Forwards: Essays in Honour of Adebayo Adedeji at Seventy.* London: Zed Books.

Onwuka, R., and Seasy, A. (1985) *The Future of Regionalism in Africa.* Basingstoke, UK: Macmillan.

Oppong, J., and Kalipeni, E. (2004) "Perceptions and Misperceptions of AIDS in Africa," in E. Kalipeni et al. (eds.) *HIV and AIDS in Africa: Beyond Epidemiology.* Oxford: Blackwell.

Organization of Africa Unity (OAU). (1980) *The Lagos Plan of Action for the Economic Development of Africa, 1980-2000.* Addis Ababa, Ethiopia: OAU.

————. (1986) *Africa's Economic Recovery and Development (UN-PAAERD).* Addis Ababa, Ethiopia: OAU.

————. (1989) *The African Alternative Framework to Structural Adjustment Programme for Socio-Economic Recovery and Transformation (AAF-SAP).* Addis Ababa, Ethiopia: OAU.

Osaghae, E. (1998) *Crippled Giant: Nigeria Since Independence.* London: Hurst and Company.

Othman, S. (1989) "Nigeria: Power for Profit: Class, Corporatism and Factionalism in the Military," in D. Cruise O'Brien, J. Dunn, and R. Rathbone (eds.) *Contemporary West African States.* Cambridge: Cambridge University Press.

Ottaway, M. (1999) *Africa's New Leaders: Democracy or State Reconstruction?*

Washington, DC: Carnegie Endowment for International Peace.

Owusu, F. (2003) "Pragmatism and the Gradual Shift from Dependency to Neoliberalism: The World Bank, African Leaders, and Development Policy in Africa," *World Development,* vol. 31, no. 10.

Oxfam. (2003) *Cultivating Poverty: The Impact of US Cotton Subsidies on Africa.* Oxfam Briefing Paper 30.

Palmer, R., and Parsons, N. (eds.) (1977) *The Roots of Rural Poverty in Central and Southern Africa.* London: Heinemann.

Parpart, J. (1988) "Women and the State in Africa," in D. Rothchild and N. Chazan (eds.) *The Precarious Balance: State and Society in Africa.* Boulder, CO: Westview Press.

Parpart, J. (1999) "Rethinking Participation, Empowerment and Development from a Gender Perspective," in J. Freedman (ed.) *Transforming Development.* Toronto: University of Toronto Press.

Patat, J.-P. (2002) "Nepad Isn't a New 'Marshall Plan,'" *African Geopolitics,* no. 6.

Pheko, M. (2003) "New or Old Partnership for African Women?" Cape Town: Alternative Information and Development Centre.

Rai S. (1998) "Class, Caste and Gender: Women in Parliament in India," in A. Karam (ed.) *Women in Parliament: Beyond Numbers.* Stockholm: IDEA.

Randriamaro, Z. (2002) "Nepad, Gender and the Poverty Trap: Nepad and the Challenges of Financing for Development in Africa from a Gender Perspective." Paper presented at the Conference on Africa and the Development Challenges of the New Millennium, La Palm Royal Beach Hotel, Accra, Ghana, April.

Reno, W. (1993) "Old Brigades, Money Bags, New Breeds, and the Ironies of Reform in Nigeria," *Canadian Journal of African Studies,* vol. 27, no. 1.

———. (1999) *Warlord Politics and African States.* Boulder, CO: Lynne Rienner.

———. (2000) "Clandestine Economies, Violence and States in Africa," *Journal of International Affairs,* vol. 53, no. 2.

———. (2000) "War, Debt and the Role of Pretending in Uganda's International Relations." Occasional Paper, Centre of African Studies, University of Copenhagen, July.

———. (2004) "The Privatisation of Sovereignty and the Survival of Weak States," in B. Hibou (ed.).

Riddell, R. (1980) *The Land Question: From Rhodesia to Zimbabwe.* London: Catholic Institute for International Relations.

Rimmer, D. (2003) "Learning About Economic Development from Africa," *African Affairs,* 102.

Robinson, W. (1996) *Promoting Polyarchy: Globalization, U.S. Intervention and Hegemony.* Cambridge: Cambridge University Press.

Rodney, W. (1972) *How Europe Underdeveloped Africa.* London: Bogle L'Ouverture Publications.

Rostow, W. (1960) *The Stages of Economic Growth: A Non-Communist Manifesto.* Cambridge: Cambridge University Press.

Rotberg, R. (2000) "Africa's Mess, Mugabe's Mayhem," *Foreign Affairs,* vol. 79, no. 5.

———. (ed.) (2004) *Crafting the New Nigeria: Confronting the Challenges.* Boulder, CO: Lynne Rienner.

Ruff, Y. (2004) "Is Your Business Still Waiting for the Nepad Infrastructure Investment Tour Bus?" *Traders: African Business Journal,* no. 17, February.

Russell, D. (2001) "AIDS as Mass Femicide: Focus on South Africa," *Off Our Backs,* vol. 31, no. 1.

Samatar, A. (1999) *An African Miracle: State, Class Leadership and Colonial Legacy in Botswana.* Portsmouth, NH: Heinemann.

Sandbrook, R. (1985) *The Politics of Africa's Economic Stagnation.* Cambridge: Cambridge University Press.

Santiso, C., and Loada, A. (2003) "Explaining the Unexpected: Electoral Reform and Democratic Governance in Burkina Faso," *Journal of Modern African Studies,* vol. 41, no. 3.

Sassou-Nguesso, D. (2002) "Overwhelming Majority Means Overwhelming Responsibility," *African Geopolitics,* no. 6, Spring.

Schatzberg, M. (2002) *Political Legitimacy in Middle Africa: Father, Family, Food.* Bloomington: Indiana University Press.

Schraeder, P. (1994) "Elites as Facilitators or Impediments to Political Development? Some Lessons from the 'Third Wave' of Democratisation in Africa," *Journal of Developing Areas,* vol. 29, no. 1.

Schlemmer, L. (2002) "Getting Real about Democracy in Africa: Nepad and the Challenge of Good Governance." Paper presented at an international colloquium on Cultures, Religions, and Conflicts, Mzaar, Lebanon, September 18–21.

Scott, G. (1998) "Who Has Failed Africa? IMF Measures or the African Leadership?" *Journal of Asian and African Studies,* vol. 33, no. 3.

Shiner, C. (1994) "The Silent Struggle," *Africa Report,* July/August 1994, vol. 39, no. 4.

Silver, B., and Arrighi, G. (2000) "Workers North and South," in L. Panitch and C. Leys (eds.) *Socialist Register 2001: Working Classes, Global Realities.* London: Merlin Press.

Singer, H. (1984) "Ideas and Policy: The Sources of UNCTAD," *IDS Bulletin* (July).

Siziya, S., and Hakim, J. (1996) "Differential Human Immunodeficiency Virus Risk Factors Among Female General Nurses, Nurse Midwives and Office Workers/Teachers in Zambia," *Central African Journal of Medicine,* vol. 42, no. 4.

Siziya, S., Hakim, J., Rusakaniko, S., Matchaba-Hove, R., and Chideme-Maradzika, J. (1996) "Non-Condom Use Among Female Nurses in Zambia," *Central African Journal of Medicine,* vol. 42, no. 7.

Söderbaum, F., and Taylor, I. (eds.) (2003) *Regionalism and Uneven Development in Southern Africa: The Case of The Maputo Development Corridor.* Aldershot, UK: Ashgate.

Soyinka, W. (1996) *The Open Sore of a Continent: A Personal Narrative of the Nigerian Crisis.* New York: Oxford University Press.

Stanecki, K. A. (2000) "The AIDS Pandemic in the 21st Century: The Demographic Impact in Developing Countries." Paper prepared for the XIIIth International AIDS Conference, Durban, South Africa.

Stationary Office. (2004) *House of Commons Foreign Affairs Committee Report on South Africa.* London: House of Commons.

Stein, H. (2000) *The Development of the Developmental State in Africa: A Theoretical Inquiry.* Occasional Paper, Centre of African Studies, University of Copenhagen.

Stichter, S., and Parpart, J. (eds.) (1988) *Patriarchy and Class: African Women in the Home and Workforce.* Boulder, CO: Westview Press.

Stiff, P. (2000) *Cry Zimbabwe Independence: Twenty Years On.* Johannesburg: Galago Press.

Stoneman, C. (ed.) (1988) *Zimbabwe's Prospects: Issues of Race, Class, State, and Capital in Southern Africa.* London: Macmillan.

Subramanian, A., and Tamirisa, N. (2001) *Africa's Trade Revisited.* IMF Working Paper, WP/01/33. Washington, DC: International Monetary Fund.

Szeftel, M. (1982) "Political Graft and the Spoils System in Zambia—The State as a Resource in Itself," *Review of African Political Economy,* no. 24.

Takougang, J., and Krieger, M. (1998) *African State and Society in the 1990s: Cameroon's Political Crossroads.* Boulder, CO: Westview.

Tandon, Y. (no date) *The Role of Foreign Direct Investments in Africa's Human Development,* http://attac.org/fra/list/doc/tandon.htm.

———. (2002) "Nepad and FDIs: Symmetries and Contradictions." Paper presented at the African Scholars' Forum on the New Partnership for Africa's Development (Nepad), Nairobi, April 26–29.

Tangri, R. (1985) *Politics in Sub-Saharan Africa.* London: James Currey.

———. (1999) *The Politics of Patronage in Africa: Parastatals, Privatization and Private Enterprise.* Trenton, NJ: Africa World Press.

Tangri, R., and Mwenda, A. (2001) "Corruption and Cronyism in Uganda's Privatization in the 1990s," *African Affairs,* 100.

———. (2003) "Military Corruption and Uganda Politics Since the Late 1990s," *Review of African Political Economy,* no. 98.

Taylor, I. (2001) *Stuck in Middle GEAR: South Africa's Post-Apartheid Foreign Relations.* Westport: Praeger.

———. (2002a) "The New Partnership for Africa's Development and the Zimbabwe Elections: Implications and Prospects for the Future," *African Affairs,* vol. 101, no. 404.

———. (2002b) "Good Governance or Good for Business? South Africa's Regionalist Project and the 'African Renaissance,'" in S. Breslin, C. Hughes, N. Phillips, and B. Rosamond (eds.) *New Regionalisms in the Global Political Economy: Theories and Cases.* London: Routledge.

———. (2003) "Conflict in Central Africa: Clandestine Networks and Regional/Global Configurations," *Review of African Political Economy,* vol. 30, no. 95, March.

———. (2004) "Political Legitimacy in Botswana's 'Developmental State.'" Paper presented for workshop on the "Potentiality of Developmental States in Africa: Botswana and Uganda Compared," Mbarara, Uganda, February 12–14.

Taylor, I., and Nel, P. (2002) "'New Africa,' Globalization and the Confines of Elite Reformism: 'Getting the Rhetoric Right,' Getting the Strategy Wrong," *Third World Quarterly,* vol. 23, no. 1.

Taylor, I., and Williams, P. (2002) "The Limits of Engagement: British Foreign Policy and the Crisis in Zimbabwe," *International Affairs,* vol. 78, no. 3, July.

———. (eds.) (2004) *Africa in International Politics: External Involvement on the Continent.* London: Routledge.

Tembo, K., and Phiri, T. (1993) "Sexually Based Cultural Practices Implicated in the Transmission of HIV/AIDS," *Society of Malawi Journal,* 46.

Thompson, G. (2003) *Governing Uganda: British Colonial Rule and Its Legacy.* Kampala: Fountain.

Thompson, L., and Leysens, A. (1996) "Comments: South African Foreign Policy Discussion Document," unpublished paper, August.

Tripp, A. (2001) "Women and Democracy: The New Political Activism in Africa," *Journal of Democracy,* vol. 12, no. 3.

———. (2003) "Forging Development Synergies Between States and Associations," in N. Van de Walle, N. Ball, and V. Ramachandran (eds.) *Beyond Structural Adjustment: The Institutional Context of African Development.* London: Palgrave.

Tsunga, A. (2003) "Does Nepad Promote Good Governance?" in M. Manyanya (ed.) *The Zimbabwe Test: Why the New Partnership for Africa's Development Is Already Failing.* Harare, Zimbabwe: ZIMCODD.

Turok, B. (1979) "The Penalties of Zambia's Mixed Economy," in B. Turok (ed.) *Development in Zambia: A Reader.* London: Zed Books.

UN. (2000) *The World's Women 2000: Trends and Statistics.* New York: United Nations.

UNAIDS. (no date) Fact Sheet 1, "HIV/AIDS and Human Security," www.unAIDS.org/security/Issues/human_security.html.

UNAIDS. (2000) *Report on the Global HIV/AIDS Epidemic.* Geneva: UNAIDS.

———. (2002) *AIDS Epidemic Update, December 2002.* Geneva: UNAIDS.

———. (2003a) *AIDS Epidemic Update: December 2003.* Geneva: UNAIDS.

———. (2003b) "Pre-Workshop Interviews: Dr. Gro Harlem Brundtland," April, http://aidsscenarios.unaids.org/scenarios/.

UNCTAD (2002) *Duty and Quota Free Market Access for LDCs: An Analysis of Quad Initiatives.* New York: UNCTAD.

———. (2003) *World Investment Report, 2003: FDI Policies for Development: National and International Perspectives.* New York and Geneva: UNCTAD.

———. (2004) *Economic Development in Africa: Trade Performance and Commodity Dependence.* New York and Geneva: UNCTAD.

———. (2004) *Global FDI Decline Bottoms Out in 2003 Press Release, TAD/1969.* New York and Geneva: UNCTAD.

UNDP. (2003) *Human Development Indicators, 2003,* www.undp.org/hdr2003/indicator/indic_149_1_1.html.

UNECA. (2002) *The African Peer Review (APR) Mechanism: Some Frequently Asked Questions.* Addis Ababa, Ethiopia: UN Economic Commission for Africa.

———. (2003) *Economic Report on Africa 2003.* Addis Ababa, Ethiopia: UN Economic Commission for Africa.

UNESCO. (1993) *Progress Report on the Appraisal and Assessment of the Implementation of the Abuja Declaration on Participatory Development: The Role of Women in Africa in the 1990's, A Regional Perspective.* New York: United Nations Economic and Social Council.

UN-NADF. (1991) *United Nations New Agenda for the Development of Africa in the 1990s.* New York: United Nations.

Vale, P., and Maseko, S. (1998) "South Africa and the African Renaissance," *International Affairs,* vol. 74, no. 2.

Van de Walle, N. (1994) "Neopatrimonialism and Democracy in Africa, with an Illustration from Cameroon," in J. Widner (ed.) *Economic Change and Political Liberalization in Africa.* Baltimore: Johns Hopkins University Press.

———. (2001) *African Economies and the Politics of Permanent Crisis, 1979–1999.* Cambridge: Cambridge University Press.

Van der Vliet, V. (2003) "Has Upcoming Poll Yielded Full Roll-out?" *Focus,* no. 32.

Van der Walt, L. (2003) "The Political Significance of Nepad," www.ainfos.ca/03/sep/ainfos00202.html.

Van der Westhuizen, J. (2003) "How (Not) to Sell Big Ideas: Argument, Identity and Nepad," *International Journal,* Summer.

Van Walraven, K. (1999) *Dreams of Power: The Role of the Organization of African Unity in the Politics of Africa, 1963–1993*. Aldershot, UK: Ashgate.

Wade, A. (2002) "Africa, An Outcast or a Partner?" *African Geopolitics*, no. 6, Spring.

Wallerstein, I. (1974) *The Modern World System: Capitalist Agriculture and the Origins of the European World-Economy in the Sixteenth Century*. New York: Academic Press.

———. (1979) *The Capitalist World Economy*. Cambridge: Cambridge University Press.

Wang, Z., and Winters, L. (1998) "Africa's Role in Multilateral Trade Negotiations: Past and Future," *Journal of African Economies*, 7, supplement 1.

Weber, M. (1974) *Economy and Society: An Outline of Interpretative Sociology*. Los Angeles: University of California Press.

Weinmann, J. (1996) *Zimbabwe's Land Crisis: A Reassessment*. Berkeley: University of California Press.

White, S. (1996) "Depoliticizing Development: The Uses and Abuses of Participation," *Development in Practice*, vol. 6.

Williams, G. (1987) "Primitive Accumulation: The Way to Progress," *Development and Change*, vol. 18, no. 4.

World Bank. (1981) *Accelerated Development in Sub-Saharan Africa: An Agenda for Action*. Washington, DC: World Bank.

———. (1989) *Sub-Saharan Africa: From Crisis to Sustainable Growth*. Washington, DC: World Bank.

———. (1999) *Intensifying Action Against HIV/AIDS in Africa: Responding to a Development Crisis*, www.worldbank.org/html/extpb/abshtml/14572.htm.

———. (2000) *Can Africa Claim the 21st Century?* Washington, DC: World Bank.

Wrigley, C. (1988) "Four Steps Towards Disaster," in H. Hansen and M. Twaddle (eds.) *Uganda Now: Between Decay and Development*. Nairobi: James Currey.

Yates, D. (1996) *The Rentier State in Africa: Oil, Rent Dependency and Neocolonialism in the Republic of Gabon*. Trenton, NJ: Africa World Press.

Young, C. (1994) "Zaire: The Shattered Illusion of the Integral State," *Journal of Modern African Studies*, vol. 32, no. 2.

———. (2004) "The End of the Post-Colonial State? Reflections on Changing African Political Dynamics," *African Affairs*, no. 103.

Zolberg, A. (1966) *Creating Political Order: The Party-States of West Africa*. Chicago: Rand McNally.

Zuckerman, E., and Garrett, A. (2003) "The Relative Success of PRSPs to Address Gender," www.sarpn.org.za/documents/d0000306/P306_PRSP_Gender.pdf.

Zulu, K. (2004) "Why We Are Failing African Girls," *BBC News Online*, November 30. Available at www.bbc.co.uk/1/hi/world/Africa/4052531.stm.

Index

About the Book

Enthusiastically embraced by African presidents, G7 leaders, and the UN General Assembly alike, the New Partnership for Africa's Development has been advanced as the vehicle that will vitalize the continent's economies. Ian Taylor critically explores just what Nepad is, and what potential it has—or lacks—for promoting African development.

Ian Taylor is senior lecturer in the School of International Relations at the University of St. Andrews and professor extraordinaire in political science at the University of Stellenbosch in South Africa. His recent publications include *Africa in International Politics: External Involvement on the Continent After the Cold War* and *Stuck in Middle Gear: South Africa's Post-Apartheid Foreign Relations.*